MARTIN LUTHER
THE MAN AND HIS WORK

LUTHER IN 1526

After a portrait by Lucas Cranach now
in the Kaufmann Gallery, Berlin

Martin Luther
The Man and His Work

by

Arthur Cushman Mc Giffert

New York
The Century Co.
1911

THE DE VINNE PRESS

TO MY WIFE

WHOSE INSIGHT AND HUMAN SYMPATHIES HAVE
HELPED ME TO INTERPRET ONE OF
THE MOST HUMAN OF THE
WORLD'S GREAT MEN

CONTENTS

CONTENTS

LIST OF ILLUSTRATIONS

LIST OF ILLUSTRATIONS

MARTIN LUTHER

MARTIN LUTHER

THE MAN AND HIS WORK

CHAPTER I

BOYHOOD AND YOUTH

GREAT men need not that we praise them; the need is ours that we know them. They are our common heritage. Whether we be of their faith or of another, whether our fathers fought with them or with their enemies, whether we stand where they stood or have traveled far on ways they dreamed not of, we are the richer that they lived.

This shall be a plain and literal tale. If its hero will but speak for himself and we may enter into some degree of intimacy and gain some measure of acquaintance with him as he was, this writing will not be vain.

He was very human, this hero of ours, fiery-tempered, passionate, imperious, lovable withal, warm-hearted, and generous to a fault. Full of contradictions, he had the frankness and carelessness of genius, and what he was he showed, and what he thought he said, without concealment or diplomacy. Like a Cromwell or a Napoleon in his masterful will, he was like our own Lincoln in his human sympathies, his simplicity of character, his transparent honesty. Like him he was too in his quickness of perception, his quaint humor, and his homeliness of speech.

He came, as so many of the world's great men come, of peasant stock. "I am a peasant's son; my father, my grandfather, and my great-grandfather were genuine peasants," he was accustomed to say, not without a touch of pride, and in spite of his opinion that "there is as little sense in boasting of one's ancestry as in the devil's priding himself on his angelic lineage." He was of the common people and was glad of it. It was one of the secrets of his power. "Rich folks' children," he once remarked, "seldom turn out well. They are complacent, arrogant, and conceited, and think they need to learn nothing because they have enough to live on, anyway. On the contrary, poor men's sons must labor to lift themselves out of the dust and must endure greatly. And because they have nothing to boast about or pride themselves upon, they trust God, control themselves, and keep still. The poor fear God, therefore He gives them good heads that they may study, become educated and intelligent, and be able to assist princes, kings, and emperors with their wisdom."

Luther's family was not of the lowest class. For generations his ancestors had owned their house and farm in the village of Möhra on the western side of the Thuringian hills. There are still Luthers in the same tiny hamlet, changed perhaps as little as the place itself. Common custom, admirably careful of those most needing care, made the youngest child heir of the ancestral home, and Hans Luther, an older son, after marrying Margarethe Ziegler, a maiden of good family from the neighboring town of Eisenach, went out to seek his fortune in the larger world. Sign of character that, and promise of more heroic venture in his first-born. It does not need the wilds of a new-

ANNO 1530 AM 29 TAG IVNII IST HANS LVTHER
D MARTINVS VATER INN GOTT
VERSCHIE DENN

From the painting by Lucas Cranach in the Wartburg, Eisenach

MARTIN LUTHER'S FATHER

found land and leagues of untracked forest to make the pioneer. From Möhra to Eisleben, the principal town in the county of Mansfeld, where Hans and Margarethe first tried their fate, was only a scant four-score miles, but it was the cast of the die. A new home and a new life were theirs at once. The Möhra boy became the founder of a new branch of his house in a new land, and the farmer's son became a miner. It was a rich and beautiful country. "Whom the Lord loves He gives a home in the county of Mansfeld," runs an old proverb, and what was more to the point in the eyes of Hans, mining was a prosperous industry in the copper-veined hills of the eastern Harz.

In Eisleben the first child was born on the night of the tenth of November, 1483. He was baptized the next day and named Martin in honor of the saint whose feast it was. Honor enough for any saint, and honor enough it might seem for any town. But where he first saw the light he came back to die, and Eisleben still shows with reverent pride both house of birth and house of death. Little she saw of him in the interval, for when he was only six months old the hope of better fortune led his parents to the neighboring town of Mansfeld. Here they lived to a good old age, a sturdy couple, "spare, small, and brown"; and here the boy grew up under the shadow of dark and wooded cliffs crowned by the castle of the counts of Mansfeld and pierced by the shafts of the mines. It was a thriving, busy place; a place of rude and arduous toil, with fortunes, as fortunes went in that day, often easily made and more easily lost.

For Hans and Margarethe worldly success came but slowly. The means of the growing family were scant enough. Often the mother was reduced to the un-wonted necessity of carrying home from the forest fuel for the hearth. But in time the days of narrow circumstance passed. Industry, frugality, and integrity ultimately triumphed. Hans became the proprietor of two furnaces of his own and the possessor of a comfortable house in the principal street, and at his death left a property by no means contemptible for the time and place. He was a substantial man, with the self-respect and pride of one who has bettered himself in life by his own exertions.

It is often easy, in looking back, to find even in humble parents traits that account more or less satisfactorily for the genius of a child far greater than themselves. But it is only the child's career that makes such traits conspicuous. No one, we may believe, would have selected Hans and Margarethe for the parents of one of history's greatest figures. And yet the honesty and sturdy common sense which made the father a trusted friend of the counts of Mansfeld, and a trusted counselor of the town, the vigor, courage, and self-reliance which enabled him to win and keep success, the sanity and independence which marked his attitude toward religion, as toward other things in life, gather significance in the light of what came after. It was a characteristic reply he made to a priest who was offering consolation as he lay critically ill, and was exhorting him to make his peace with God by giving money to the clergy: "I have many children. I will leave my property to them; they need it more." Pious he was, in his way, and a loyal member of the church, but he put the ordinary human obligations and responsibilities above all else and to them he was always faithful.

Significant also were the cheerful temper and wholesome humor of the mother. She looked always on the brighter side of life, and met even bitter expe-

Copied from the original portrait by E. A. Schmidt

MARTIN LUTHER'S MOTHER

From the painting by Lucas Cranach in the Wartburg, Eisenach

riences with a smile. It was a favorite saying of hers, which Martin loved to repeat, "If the world smiles not on you and me the fault is ours." She was imaginative and sensitive, the prey of all sorts of conflicting emotions, and she lived in devout and fearsome bondage to much that her husband must have laughed at. Mansfeld, with its somber woods and cavernous hills, was a congenial haunt of gnomes and fairies. Of the blacker sort they were apt to be. "In the mines," as Luther once said, "the devil teases and deceives people, makes a racket, and calls up specters before their eyes until they think they see a great heap of ore and pure silver where there is none at all. For if he can bewitch and fool men even above ground, by clear day, in the light of the sun, so that things look other than they are, he can do it still better in the mines." Margarethe felt the spell of the evil spirits, and their terror long lingered with the boy Martin. On one occasion she thought herself and her children bewitched by an unfriendly neighbor, and there was much ado to escape the curse.

Her oldest born was his mother's boy. When he reached maturity he looked remarkably like her in face and figure; and like her he was in temperament and disposition, with the stability and strength of his father's homely sense and obstinate will. In later years his mother used to say with pride that he was a dependable boy, the monitor of his brothers and sisters, to whom they all looked up, the inseparable companion and peculiar champion of his next younger brother, James.

Martin was not a pampered child. Hans and Margarethe took their parental responsibilities seriously and interpreted them rigorously. Both at home and in school discipline was harsh and sympathy scant for

childish fun and frolic. The rule was that of the rod.
Looking back upon his childhood, the grown man
could see little of joy or cheer in it. Public opinion,
when he was young, was much stricter, he tells us,
than in later days in the matter of games, card-playing,
dancing, theater-going, and sports of various kinds,
and his parents were of the strictest. They believed in
work, not play. On one occasion, for taking a trivial
nut, he was beaten by his mother until the blood came.
Reflecting upon it in later years, he was accustomed to
assert with emphasis that discrimination and moderation ought to be specially exercised in the government
of children. With them "the apple ought always to
lie beside the rod." And the serious effect upon the
character of an over-strenuous discipline he depicted
in the words, "Where such fear enters a man in childhood, it can hardly be rooted out again as long as he
lives. As he once trembled at every word of his father
and mother, to the end of his life he is afraid of a
rustling leaf."

It is difficult to associate such consequences with the
great reformer, whose courage was his most conspicuous trait, but he spoke out of his own experience, and
knew whereof he spoke. Though he recognized that his
parents loved him and meant well by him, their severity made so painful an impression on him that in later
life he held them responsible for his unhappy resolution
to become a monk, and in his treatment of his own
children he tried to make up to them for the sympathy
he had lacked and the harshness he had suffered. And
yet he is not the only boy by any means in that day, or
this, who has been angered by a beating, and has found
it hard to be reconciled again to his father. And if
fifteen whippings in a single morning at school are
rather more than most are called upon to endure, in

Martin's case there may well have been exceptional provocation. A merry, high-spirited boy he doubtless was, mischievous, perhaps, and fond of practical jokes, as in later years. Stupid and vicious he certainly was not, and kindlier handling, as he often said, would equally have met the need. Without doubt he was treated as well as other boys of his class. That he was to become a great man nobody then realized, and yet it is only because he was a great man that we know anything about his boyhood trials and grievances, and, as he himself appreciated, there are worse things, after all, than rough treatment.

The public school, where he started so young that he often had to be carried to and fro by an older companion, was poor enough. In such a town it is apt to be. The methods were crude and the instructors inefficient, and, as was too often the case, they tried to make up for their own shortcomings by domineering treatment of the pupils under their care. The schools in his boyhood were "hell and purgatory," Luther once said. But the grown man who later condemned both school and teachers unsparingly judged them from the vantage-ground of a larger world and an improved system; for in education, as in many other things, a new world was in the making while he lived. Whereas in his youth, he once declared, it took almost a lifetime to acquire enough Latin to say mass, now children studied it with pleasure and mastered the language easily and rapidly. "Is it not known to everybody," he wrote, with his customary vehemence, "that boys are now so well prepared that in their fifteenth or eighteenth year they have more knowledge than they could formerly get in all the high schools and cloisters put together? What did they learn in those days except to be donkeys, logs, and blocks? They studied twenty and even forty years, and then knew neither Latin nor German."

That Martin was sent away to school to the city of Magdeburg at thirteen, instead of being kept at home to aid in the support of the family, speaks volumes both for the boy and for his parents. It is true he once confessed that he was not a success at mining. Not altogether to his regret, Satan had begrudged him the gift of discovering the hidden metal. Evidently he had been obliged to try his hand at it while still a young lad. His want of skill may have had something to do with the decision to give him a schooling, but his mental gifts were the determining factor. Great things were expected of him, and his father at least looked forward to the time when he should hold the honorable and lucrative position of legal adviser to the counts of Mansfeld. His own advance in life gave him a natural desire to see his eldest son rise still higher in the social scale. Hans was no common miner, and Martin was no common boy. The son's promise and the father's hopes went hand in hand.

After the not uncommon fashion of the day, he carried little with him to Magdeburg beyond his parents' blessing. Both there and in Eisenach, where he was sent a year later, he begged and sang his way to food and schooling. In Eisenach he sang his way to more than both—the love and care of a woman's heart. His beautiful eyes and voice first won the attention of Frau Cotta, and she took him into her own home. Throughout his life both friends and foes always noticed his eyes—dark and deep, as if harboring wonderful and mysterious thoughts. And his voice in song and speech alike possessed a quality to magnetize and charm. It is little enough we know of the pretty idyl of his life in the well-to-do Cotta family. Here he had his first

HOUSE AT EISLEBEN SHOWN AS LUTHER'S BIRTHPLACE.   IT WAS
PARTLY DESTROYED BY FIRE AND REBUILT LATE
IN THE SEVENTEENTH CENTURY

taste of culture and refinement and of the gentler graces of life. From his foster-mother he learned the beautiful proverb, "On earth no dearer thing than woman's love to whom 't is given to possess," and he used often to repeat it in later years as a memento of his happy Eisenach days.

The influence of Martin's new environment was life-long. His intimate friendship with gentlefolk served to temper such roughness and uncouthness as he brought from the peasant's home and the mining town, and fitted him for association with the greater world. As a man he always showed extraordinary ease and freedom in dealing with men of all classes. This was certainly due at least in part to these formative years. In Eisenach, too, he found school and teachers to his liking. Trebonius, the principal, can have been no common pedagogue. Upon entering the presence of his classes he always removed his scholar's cap and insisted his teachers should do the same, because of the mayors, chancellors, doctors, and rulers of the future who occupied the benches. The teaching was of the best, and was in sharp contrast to the sort that Martin had hitherto enjoyed, or suffered. He here came in contact with the new humanistic spirit and methods for the first time, and he distinguished himself among his fellow-pupils for his aptitude in language and litera-ture. In the congenial atmosphere of home and school he developed rapidly and used his social advantages to so good effect and made such progress in his studies that at seventeen he entered the University of Erfurt, the greatest of the German universities of the day, attractive enough to win many friends, and well enough prepared to take his bachelor's degree at the end of a year.

Here he encountered new experiences. Erfurt was

a rich and populous city, in the heyday of its prosperity, "plagued," as one of its preachers said, "with plenty, as other places with want," proud of its wealth, its fame, its stately buildings, prouder still of its university whose occasions were gala-days for the whole town. Nothing else brings such joy in life, Luther thought, as comes to the new graduate when, examinations successfully passed, he is escorted through the streets in triumph by his fellow-students, with banners, torches, and music, and is hailed *Magister* by the citizens that line the route. Splendid days those, when the scholar was held in honor by all the world—stirring days they were, too, in university life. The new humanism, with its devotion to classical learning, was making rapid headway and was disputing the supremacy with the dominant scholasticism of the age. It was not a time of stagnation. Champions of the one and the other system were battling in friendly, sometimes hostile, rivalry.

Erfurt boasted the presence of some of the greatest representatives of both. Here one could study philosophy with Trutvetter, and the classics with Maternus, and hither, to study with one or both, or with others scarcely less famous, young men came from all parts of the country and even from abroad. It was a current saying, "Who would study rightly must go to Erfurt," and Luther himself, whose pride at being one of its graduates was lifelong, declared with pardonable exaggeration that the other universities were no more than primary schools beside it. Into its stimulating atmosphere he brought an eagerness and thirst for knowledge which set him rapidly forward. At the same time he threw himself with enthusiasm into the life of the place. He carried a sword according to common student custom, and dressed as his fellows

BRONZE STATUE OF MARTIN LUTHER IN EISLEBEN

By Siemering, unveiled in 1883 on the four-hundredth anniversary of Luther's birth

did. His father's circumstances had so improved that
he was able to keep him in comfort, and did not stint
him for money. Martin was no recluse. He was a
lovable, companionable fellow, witty and talkative. "I
say more in a day than the Emperor Charles in a
year," he once remarked in commenting upon the gravity and sobriety of the young monarch. Fond of joke
and jest he was too, and devoted to music, for which
he had a natural gift. When laid up for a short time
by an accident, he found an old lute in his chamber,
and before he was able to be out again learned to play
it well enough to make it a lifelong joy. Speaking of
music in later years, he called it one of the most beautiful and lordly gifts of God, ranking it next after theology in importance. And on one occasion he exclaimed
enthusiastically, "He who is musical is equal to anything."

Martin's intimates were not all scholars, by any
means. He tells an amusing tale of a room-mate he
had for a couple of years who never did any studying.
Repeatedly admonished for his indolence, he sat down
one day book in hand, and after glaring at it for half
an hour, threw it on the floor and stamped on it in
anger, with the exclamation, "You would make me a
fool, would you? From *studeo* [to study] comes
stultum [foolish]. Study always breeds the fool."
Evidently there was more than mere study in our
hero's college life. And yet there is no sign that he
indulged in wildness or dissipation. That kind of
thing was never particularly to his liking, and he had
better and more important business on hand.

He came into intimate relations with a little circle of
"poets," as they called themselves, who gave much of
their time to the cultivation of the art of fine writing
after classic models, and met regularly to hear and criti-

cize one another's effusions. But he found himself more attracted by philosophy than by literature. Fair progress was made in his humanistic studies, but he never cared as much for form as for substance, and grammar he always found irksome. The way he went about the learning of Hebrew some years later was characteristic of his general attitude, and, it may be added, of his good sense. He paid little attention to grammatical details, but read rapidly and copiously until he entered into the spirit of the language, and could read it with pleasure and sympathy.

Latin was the language of the class-room in Erfurt, as everywhere else, and it became a second mother tongue to him, as to all the scholars of the day; but classical elegance in composition he never attained. He often apologized for the rusticity and barbarity of his Latin style, comparing himself in his correspondence with scholarly friends to a goose among swans. Nor was this mere affectation of modesty, for he never hesitated to boast of his knowledge of philosophy in contrast with the ignorance of his contemporaries, friends and foes alike. His mastery of his mother tongue shows what he might have been as a Latin stylist had he cared to make the effort. Even as it was he wrote the language with fluency and with a vigor and raciness seldom equaled by the best writers of his day. He could use it well enough for all practical purposes; for more than this he cared little.

He did not learn Greek until later and then only for the Bible's sake. He was not singular in this. Few even yet were carrying their classical zeal so far, and the single teacher of Greek Erfurt boasted in his student days—great center of humanistic culture though it was—left the university during his first year. He loved the old Latin authors, both moralists and poets. He read

them extensively and stored his retentive memory with
apt quotations which in after years he used to good
effect.   One of the chief regrets of his days of controversy was his lack of leisure for such reading.   The
practical wisdom of the ancients interested him most.
He was always a student of life.   History and biography he was particularly fond of, and often lamented
the small attention given to both in the training of the
young.

The reigning philosophy of the day was that of the
schoolmen, and to this he chiefly gave himself.   Logic
absorbed a large part of the attention both of teachers
and pupils.   Continual disputation sharpened the students' wits and gave them skill in debate.   Martin
profited greatly by this exercise.   He became one of
the most powerful and resourceful disputants of the
day, and always recognized with gratitude the value
of the training he had enjoyed.   With the schoolmen,
theology and metaphysics went hand in hand, and if
form commonly meant more than substance, still their
study opened before the eager mind of the young
student all sorts of questions concerning the origin and
constitution of the universe, both spiritual and physical,
and with these questions he loved to busy himself.   He
was known among his companions as "The Philosopher," and his philosophical attainments were before
long the admiration of teachers and students alike.
The impression he made is illustrated by the remark
of the father of one of his intimates when Martin was
complaining of poor health and fearing an early
death: "Do not be afraid, my dear Baccalaureus.   You
will live to be a great man."   The words were casual
enough, no doubt, but they carry significance in the
light of their fulfilment, as they did to Luther himself,
who remembered and repeated them long after.

He did not particularly distinguish himself in his work for the bachelor's degree. When he took it in the summer of 1502, he was only thirtieth in a class of fifty-seven. But two and a half years later, when he got his M.A., he stood second in a class of seventeen. The pride of the father over his son's success was almost pathetic. He habitually addressed the young magister, home for a recess after the degree was won, with the ceremonious "you" of formal intercourse instead of the familiar "thou" of ordinary conversation.

His general education finished, Martin took up at once, in accordance with his father's long-cherished project, the study of law. But he had little liking for it. In later years he could not say enough in dispraise of the law and in contempt of the legal profession. The toilsome gathering of precedents particularly irked him, and he seemed to think it the lawyer's chief end to devise means of defeating justice. "Jurists," he declared, "commonly dispute and discuss about words. They alter the facts and fail to go to the bottom of them that the truth may be discovered. They say a great deal and use many words, but without understanding." "They take the money of the poor, and with the tongue thresh out both their pocket and their purse." They made bad Christians, he thought, and few of them would be saved. But in this he put them in no worse case than the speculative theologians. He once remarked boastingly that if he had studied law two years he would have known more about it than a certain famous lawyer of the day. Without doubt he would have distinguished himself, had he kept at it; but the whole thing was little to his liking, and he soon turned his back upon it. He did it in no ordinary way.

Luther's life was full of startling and unexpected crises, and the first and most startling of them all came

THE LILIE INN AT ERFURT, WHICH LUTHER IS
SAID TO HAVE FREQUENTED

in the summer of 1505, after he had been a law-student
for only a few weeks. He had just been home for
a brief visit. His progress in his work had been all
that could be desired, and his parents' pride and hope
were higher than ever, when suddenly, to the consternation of everybody and to the wrath of his father,
who was already thinking of an honorable marriage
for him which should still further improve his pros-
pects, he threw it all up and went into a monastery.
The immediate occasion of this extraordinary step was
a terrific thunder-storm which overtook him just outside the town when he was returning from his visit
home. In mortal dread of death, he threw himself
on the ground, crying to the patron saint of the miners,
to whom he had often turned in seasons of distress:
"Help, dear Saint Anna! I will become a monk."

The vow so rashly made he hastened to put into
execution. Fearing lest he might repent, he made his
preparations as rapidly as he could, sold his books,
including the costly "Corpus Juris" with which he had
been equipped for professional study by his proud
father, gave a farewell dinner to his friends, and, in
spite of their pleas and protestations, entered the
Augustinian monastery in Erfurt, on the morning of
the seventeenth of July, when he was only twenty-one
years old.

This was the most momentous event in Luther's
career. Upon it hinged all that followed. It cut his
life in twain. Nothing could be more extreme than the
contrast between university and convent; nothing more
unexpected than such a dénouement for the brilliant
young law-student. And yet his conduct was natural
enough. One of the commonest and most normal facts
in human history is the experience we call conversion,
a profound crisis which overturns everything and

2

brings to the surface what has hitherto lain dormant
or unnoticed; which changes the direction of one's life,
and reshapes one's career. In all ages and in all religions the experience has been familiar. Some forms
of faith make more of it than others, and sometimes
it occurs quite apart from all religious interest and
motive. But it is essentially the same even though its
outward fashion varies widely.

To such an experience the young Luther was pecu-
iarly susceptible. He was a serious-minded boy. He
had been piously trained, and religion was a very real
thing to him. His imagination was peopled with angels
and demons, and his life was lived in constant dependence upon the aid and protection of the saints. He
was emotional by temperament, subject to fits of depression, and exposed to attacks of anxiety and dread
as to his fate which at times almost drove him wild.
Even as a child he was frequently distressed by his
sins and terrified by the fear of eternal punishment.
The harsh treatment he was early subjected to had
given him a timorous conscience and made him abnormally apprehensive. His friends had little inkling of
his unquiet frame of mind, but a fellow-student reports
that once when he was washing his hands the future
reformer remarked, "The longer we wash, the un-
cleaner we are." The words sound apocryphal in this
connection, but in any case it is evident enough that
beneath the smooth surface of his daily life there were
troubled waters.

In the spring of 1505 the reaction after his hard
study for the master's degree, his growing distaste for
the legal profession, the death of a student friend,
all united to make him particularly sensitive and impressionable. The crisis came suddenly, as it often
comes, and secret forebodings and half-articulate impulses in a moment crystallized into a clearly formed

purpose, and the solemn vow was registered—a vow of
devotion to a new career which has taken countless
young Catholics into the priesthood or the monastery
and countless young Protestants into the ministry or
the mission field.

That, in Luther's case, it should have been the monastery was inevitable. There religion was taken most
seriously, and, to one like him, nothing less would
answer. For centuries it had appealed with subtle and
persuasive eloquence to the finest and most sensitive
spirits. If things went wrong, if the world seemed
empty, as empty enough it often seems to the most
gifted and eager young souls as they stand hesitating
on its threshold, the call of the solitary life, the life of
the spirit, invested as it was with a halo of sanctity,
came with almost irresistible fascination. Resisted it
might be, but all too often only at the expense of the
higher visions and the finer ideals of youth. The
realization of its spiritual purpose might be crude
enough in current monasticism and rude indeed the
awakening of many a trusting young neophyte. In
Luther's day its reputation was by no means unsullied.
By many a humanist the follies and stupidities and im-
moralities of the monks were castigated in rollicking
jest or in bitter satire. It was a current proverb,
"What the devil is ashamed to do, a monk does without
shame," and to a contemporary bishop was attributed
the saying, "Into the monastery with him! He is
worth nothing either to God or man!"

But of all this Luther was little aware. In Mansfeld
the clergy bore an excellent reputation and were held
in general respect. His father was their friend, and his
mother a reverent admirer. In Magdeburg he had been
under the instruction of members of a semi-monastic
order, the Brethren of the Common Life, and while
there was profoundly impressed by the spectacle of a

prince of Anhalt, emaciated by prolonged fasting, who went through the streets in monastic garb begging bread for the convent and staggering under the weight of the sack he carried. The sight of him, Luther says, aroused deep reverence in the onlookers and made them ashamed of their worldly way of living. In Eisenach there was a Franciscan monastery which had received large gifts from the family of Frau Cotta. Here Martin was kindly received, and among its inmates he found benefactors and lifelong friends. In Erfurt, with all its humanistic leanings, religious devotion was unbounded, and there were no fewer than eight monasteries in the city. To the young Luther, as to many of his friends, the monastic calling seemed the holiest of all, and the glamour of its sanctity was untarnished by suspicion or dislike.

He must frequently have thought of doing just what he now did. The vow that sprang to his lips in a moment of terror was only the utterance of a half-formed purpose, often entertained, perhaps as often struggled against. He spoke of it afterward as an unwilling vow, forced upon him by a sign from heaven, and his friends likened his experience to the miraculous conversion of the apostle Paul. But it was no mere precipitate resolution, made in haste and repented at leisure. Sudden as it seemed even to himself, it had been long preparing, and once in the monastery, he felt at home and took up the monastic life with profound relief as well as with unwavering devotion and exemplary zeal.

Of all the monasteries in Erfurt, the Augustinian bore the highest reputation for theological learning and for public service. Its rules were not as severe as some, and the young convert evidently did not choose it from mere blind zeal for his soul's salvation. Its inmates were the principal preachers of the town, and

THE UNIVERSITY AT ERFURT, WHERE LUTHER WAS A STUDENT

were noted for charity and good works. Here he believed he could put his talents to the best use, and the event proved that he was right.

Fired with enthusiasm, he passed within the convent doors and was buried to the world, as he believed, forever. His friends were stupefied. The happy, light-hearted companion, with his frank good-fellowship and his contagious merriment, how unfitted he seemed for the monastic career! But he was made for religion, little as they suspected it, and thenceforth, to the end of his days, his life was professionally and in reality a religious life. What had hitherto been not lacking, but secondary, now became primary and controlling and dominated all his thought and activity.

The surprising thing about Luther's entrance into the monastery was not the fact itself, but the lateness of the conversion leading to it. The experience he passed through is apt to come earlier in life, if it comes at all. But Luther was later than most men in some of the other experiences of his life as well as this, and it was a happy thing for him that it was so. That the coming reformer spent his most impressionable years not within the walls of a cloister, but in the bracing and expanding atmosphere of a great university, mingling intimately with some of the brightest and most eager minds of his age, sharing in their ambitions, their labors, and their pleasures, was of incalculable benefit to him and to the Protestant Church, whose founder he became. Not in the monastery merely did he get his training, and not out of its retired sanctity alone did the great movement come. The larger world had a hand in making it and him. Though set apart by his monastic vow for more than fifteen years, he never lost his touch with human interests. Devout and zealous monk as he was, he was always more a man than a monk.

CHAPTER II

LIFE AS A MONK

TO a young man of twenty-one who for four years had breathed the free air of a great university, and gone his own independent way, the monastic life must have been peculiarly irksome. Hedged about it was by the most minute and exacting rules. The convent was a training-school for manners as well as for virtue and piety, and its regulations concerned the pettiest details of conduct. How to walk, to stand, to speak, to dress, to eat, as well as how to pray—all was carefully prescribed, and not a moment of the day was left unprovided for. From the time of rising, long before dawn, until the hour when lights must be out and all in bed, nothing was left to individual choice, and the novitiate at least was never alone, for all his duties and devotions were performed under the constant supervision of others.

Humility and obedience were the virtues chiefly aimed at. That the neophyte should be divested of all pride and self-confidence, and should learn to have no will of his own, was an indispensable preparation for the true monastic life. "The monks," Luther says, "sought to try one's obedience by requiring that unreasonable, burdensome, childish, and foolish things be done with willing and joyful hearts." Partly with this in view, partly as a result of the natural desire of the older monks to see their younger brethren undergo as much as they had endured, the most menial employments were laid upon them. They were compelled to sweep, scrub, and do kitchen and chamber work, and if they showed disinclination to their tasks, only the more was exacted of them.

The Augustinian was a mendicant order, and begging was a part of its creed. It was doubtless something of a trial to the young and brilliant master of arts to go through the familiar streets clad in monastic garb, with a sack on his back, begging bread from house to house. At any rate, whatever he thought of it, according to his friend and biographer Mathesius, it seemed to the university authorities too great an indignity to be put on one of their graduates, and at their solicitation he was allowed to confine his begging to the outlying villages. From his own lips, so far as we can learn, were heard no complaints of the duties laid upon him and of the humiliations to which he was subjected. He performed his tasks without murmuring, and submitted without protest to the chastening experiences of his new surroundings.

It may well be believed that his reputation and attainments did not make his association with the other inmates of the convent any easier. "My cloister brothers," he once remarked, "were annoyed at me because I was a student. They said, 'As with me, so with thee; put the sack on his neck.'" His enemies at a later date accused him of overweening pride and self-conceit, and he was apparently never very popular with the Erfurt monks. Perhaps he was not so amiable and companionable as he might have been, for the contrast between the ambitious, eager, and talented friends he had left and most of those with whom he was now thrown was very marked. Earnest as he was in his desire to give himself to religion, and willingly

as he assumed the burdens and endured the discipline
of his self-chosen calling, he could hardly find it easy
to recognize his new brethren as his equals and to
reconcile himself to lifelong association with them;
and if he held more or less aloof, it was only natural
in the circumstances. But, despite all, his resolution
did not waver. He was given plenty of time and opportunity to change his mind and return to the world.
He was not allowed to become a novitiate until autumn,
and more than a year elapsed before he took the irrevocable vow and was enrolled as a full member of the
order. Until then he might at any time have withdrawn. Thereafter to do so was a crime in the eyes
both of church and state.

The solemn ceremony attending the taking of the
threefold vow of poverty, chastity, and obedience produced upon him an impression never effaced. Before
the assembled monks he was obliged to swear: "I,
Brother Martin, make profession and promise obedience to Almighty God, to the Holy Virgin Mary, to
the Holy Father Augustine, and to thee the prior of
this convent, who standest in the place of the General
of the Order, to live until death in poverty and chastity, according to the rule of the said Father Augustine."

In later years he repeatedly recalled this oath with
trembling, and the ease and light-heartedness with
which many of his friends and followers severed their
monastic ties, when the great break with Catholicism
came, shocked him exceedingly even after he himself,
with much searching of heart, had turned his back
upon the convent life.

The Erfurt cloister was one of the principal theological schools of the Augustinian order, and thither
young monks came from far and near to pursue their

studies. To his superiors Luther seemed fitted for the career of a theologian both by his natural ability and by his university training, and accordingly as soon as he had taken the vow he began to prepare himself for the priesthood. He was ordained in the spring of 1509, and on the second of May conducted mass for the first time. According to common custom, the event was celebrated with much pomp. "The first mass," Luther says, "was regarded as a great affair. It brought in much money, until it fairly rained gold. It was a regular net to catch offerings and presents. The canonical hours were celebrated with torches. The young priest danced with his mother, if she was still alive, while the onlookers fairly wept for joy. If she was dead, he said a mass for her and freed her from purgatory."

In Luther's case a banquet was given in the monastery, to which his family and friends were invited, and he and his father met for the first time since his last visit home on the eve of his withdrawal from the world. Wishing to honor the occasion duly, and perhaps to impress the monks with his importance, Hans Luther appeared upon the scene with a cavalcade of twenty horses, a number of friends from Mansfeld, and a substantial present for the monastery. It had taken him a long time to forgive his son and receive him again into favor. His disappointment and anger were too deep to be easily assuaged. His friends had done everything they could to bring about a reconciliation, reminding him that the best one has is none too good to offer to the Lord and that he ought to be proud to give his oldest and most promising son; but Hans was obdurate and refused to be mollified or comforted. Finally the death of two of his younger boys and the unfounded report that Martin, too, had succumbed to the plague softened the stern old miner's heart. Even now, however, he was only partly resigned to the situation, and he did not hesitate to let it be known. At the banquet his feelings found expression in the impatient exclamation, "I must sit here and eat and drink when I should much rather be anywhere else." When Martin tried to justify himself, he remarked dryly, "Have you not heard a child should honor his father and mother?" While to the protest that he had been driven into the monastery by a sign from heaven, his only reply was, "God grant it was not a lying and devilish specter."

These words of his father Luther never forgot. They caused him much anguish of spirit. Doubts of the wisdom and righteousness of his course began to trouble him, and he gave himself with increasing ardor and devotion to the duties of his new calling, trying to still his conscience and win the approval of God. If up to this time the novelty of the monastic life, the multitudinous tasks it involved, and the constant association with others by night and by day, had kept him from thinking much about himself, he now began to suffer a return of his old anxiety and depression. The rules required the monk, after his novitiate was past, to be much alone, engaged in prayer and self-examination. Luther was given a cell of his own, a seven-by-nine room quite bare of ornaments and comforts, with a single small window looking out upon the graveyard of the convent. Daily confession was a part of his duty, and the introspection thus promoted, good as it might be for many a man, was the worst possible thing for one of his disposition. Periods of despondency and despair a youthful genius such as he would have had to suffer anywhere: in the solitude of the cloister they were doubly frequent and severe. His need was to be doing things. Inaction always chafed and fretted him, and for one of his heroic mold, who was built for large and strenuous deeds, the petty employments of the monastery, when the halo of the place had somewhat paled, were only mockery. Not content with them, he gave himself to hard study and particularly to ascetic practices of the most extreme kind. Like many another monk denied the legitimate exercise of his powers in a larger field, he sought satisfaction in heroic deeds of self-mortification. He once said: "If ever a monk gained heaven by his monkery, I must have done so. All the brethren who knew me will bear me witness. For I should have martyred myself, if I had kept it up longer, with watching, praying, reading, and other labors."

It was characteristic of him that he did not leave it to others to prescribe how he should live. He had chosen the monastic career despite his father's very different plans for him, and in the convent, faithful as he was in discharging the required duties, he was not content therewith, but must go his own independent way, marking out the path of holiness for himself. He fasted for days at a time, and spent night after night without sleep, until wakefulness became a confirmed habit and at times fears were entertained for his reason. If he had had anything but an iron constitution, he could not have stood what he did. As it was, he permanently injured his health, and laid up much physical suffering for his later years.

His ascetic practices gained him a reputation for piety far beyond the walls of the monastery. He was held up as a model of holiness to monks and nuns of other and distant convents, and the odor of his sanctity penetrated even to the outer world. With it all his anxiety and distress only increased. He had en-

tered the monastery not, like many another, because he
coveted the solitary life or craved holiness and longed
to give himself to religious exercises, but from fear of
the divine wrath. This made him abnormally apprehensive and prevented him from finding joy and satisfaction in his self-imposed tasks. He was beset always
with anxiety lest he was not doing enough to propitiate
an angry Deity, and he knew nothing of the delight of
quiet meditation upon spiritual things and intimate
fellowship with a gracious God. The harder he tried
to take the divine favor by storm, the greater became
his despair. Instead of winning the righteousness he
was feverishly pursuing, he found his offenses multiplying day by day. Not that he was really growing worse,
but in the monastery many things were considered
wicked with which the ordinary man had no concern.
At the time he said his first mass he was so overcome
with dread lest he make a mistake in word or gesture,
and thus commit a mortal sin, that he almost fled from
the altar. The experience is a common one with those
who have some public duty to perform for the first
time, but mistakes in such a case are not usually interpreted as sins. It was Luther's religious reading of
the situation that made it particularly harrowing.

And not simply was the sacred ceremony of the
mass beset with danger to his sensitive conscience, the
minute monastic code of manners and morals offered
him abundant opportunity for sin. Nothing could well
be ethically more unwholesome than to interpret any
violation of its thousand and one precepts as an offense
against God, and it is not surprising that the young
monk who was thus interpreting them grew more and
more morbid. Above all, he was troubled because he
could not control his thoughts and feelings. Not external acts alone seemed evil, but wandering mind and

IOANNES STAVPITVS D. THEOLOGIÆ ORDIN. S. AVGVSTINI EREMITAR
EX DISPENSAT: IONE APLICA ABBAS S. PETRI PRÆFVIT ANN III M ES V & ANNO M DXXIII

JOHANN VON STAUPITZ

Portrait in possession of the Benedictine Convent of St. Peter
at Salzburg

unruly emotions and especially the all too frequent
lack of real joy and exultation in his devotions.

His unhappiness, to be sure, was not constant.
Speaking of his own experiences at a later time he
once said: "I know a man who has often, though only
for brief periods, suffered the pains of hell such as no
tongue or pen could describe and no one could believe,
if he had not himself felt them. If they had lasted for
a half or even a tenth part of an hour, he would have
perished altogether and his bones would have crumbled
to ashes." In the very nature of the case such agony
could not continue indefinitely. There were periods
when he was well satisfied with himself and enjoyed
peace with God and his own conscience; seasons, too,
when he was thinking of other things and sharing in
the every-day interests of convent life. We get many
hints in his writings that the Erfurt monastery was the
scene, as we should expect it to be, of much good-
fellowship and pleasant recreation. In the common
room there was plenty of mirth and jollity. Stories
and jokes enlivened the conversation, and relieved even
for him the tension of monastic discipline. It was a
motto of the shrewd and urbane nobleman Von Staupitz, Vicar-General of the Augustinian order, who was
a welcome guest at many a princely board, "Reverent
in worship, merry at table," and though the cloister
rules enjoined silence at meals, the spirit of the motto
was doubtless observed by his monks. Luther himself
had too keen a sense of fun not to enjoy this side of
life. He has preserved for us many amusing monastic
tales, often grotesque, sometimes coarse, which he
heard in his convent days. The devil figures largely in
them. Without his satanic highness we cannot imagine
how the brothers could have got along. He filled the
place sometimes assigned to the monks themselves in

similar tales which passed current outside the monastery walls.

But in spite of all the good-fellowship and common human pleasures, Luther's distress was continually recurring. Very likely his periods of mental suffering loomed unduly large in his memory as he looked back upon them in later years. Unconsciously he may easily have exaggerated their frequency and intensity. But the experiences he recounts are just what might have been expected in one of his temperament and disposition, and there can be no doubt they were severe and excruciating enough. His reading of Paul and Augustine, in the course of his theological study, gave rise to the fear that he was one of the reprobate and his sufferings the agony of the damned—a fear which has frequently brought torment to morbid and overwrought souls. Instead of loving God, he turned away from Him in horror and wished there were no God. Even Christ was read in the same somber terms, and the sight of a crucifix frightened him, he says, like a thunderbolt.

His state of mind gave his superiors much concern. Few were able to understand him. Some thought him unbalanced in mind; others suspected he was under the control of evil spirits. In later days his enemies pointed to his unhappy experiences in the convent as proof of demoniacal possession, and he himself interpreted them as assaults of his lifelong antagonist, the devil.

Now and then he found help from one or another brother. Having complained to his preceptor of the troubles he was enduring, he was comforted by the reply, "Son, what are you doing? Do you not know that the Lord Himself has commanded us to hope?" On another occasion an old confessor, when he found

him tormenting himself with all sorts of sins that were
no sins, brought him up sharply with the admonition:
"You are a fool. God is not angry with you; it is you
who are angry with God." But it was from Staupitz
permanent relief came. He was greatly interested
in Luther's case, and conceived a strong admiration and affection for the passionate and perturbed
young spirit. He once remarked that he had never felt
any such troubles, but so far as he could see, they were
more necessary to Brother Martin than food and drink.
When Luther wrote him, "Oh, my sin, my sin, my
sin!" he replied: "You wish to be without sin, and you
have no real sin. Christ is the forgiveness of genuine
sins like parricide, blasphemy, sacrilege, adultery, and
so on. Those are true sins. You must have a catalogue with real sins written in it if Christ is to help
you. You must not go about with such trifles and
trumpery and make a sin out of every inadvertence."
He told Luther frankly he did not know what to do for
him, but his influence was very helpful, nevertheless.
He succeeded in delivering him from the fear that he
was reprobate by convincing him that his distresses
were sent him for his own good, in order to train him
for an important career; and what was still more, he
led him to believe that God was merciful and forgave
freely the one who threw himself on Christ in faith and
ceased to trust in his own merits. This was no new
idea. On the contrary, it had been the comfort of
multitudes of pious souls in every age, but, driven by
the harsh discipline of his early life to see God only
in the aspect of a stern judge, Luther had hitherto been
altogether blind to it. Gradually, under Staupitz's
tutelage, his eyes were opened, and a new gospel
dawned upon his gaze.

His liberation from despair was not immediate, nor

was it accomplished by a mere word. Long afterward, when faith in God's forgiving love had completely displaced his early notions, he still suffered at times from religious depression, and had to contend, as he thought, with the assaults of Satan, in the shape of bitter doubts and fears. It was more than a new gospel he needed—engrossing occupation, release from constant thought of self, opportunity for work and service fitted to his powers. This, too, Staupitz understood, and soon summoned him to a new field and to the absorbing tasks of a busy and useful life.

THE University of Wittenberg was founded in 1502 by the Saxon Elector Frederick the Wise. In the division of Saxony in 1485 between the two brothers Ernest and Albert,—when Ernest fixed the shares, and Albert took his choice between them,—the electoral dignity fell to the older son, but Leipsic, with its university, to the younger. Electoral Saxony was thus left without a university, and to repair the loss Frederick established his in 1502. The new institution owed its charter to the emperor, not to the pope, and enjoyed a greater degree of academic freedom than would otherwise have been the case; but there was no thought of making it a harbor of radical ideas, and its professors were obliged to take the common oath that they would teach nothing contrary to the established doctrines of the church. The elector was fortunate in securing some of the celebrated teachers of the day, among them the learned physician and humanist Pollich of Leipsic and the scholastic philosopher Trutvetter of Erfurt. In fact, both the old and the new learning were fairly represented, and the infant university bore good promise of prosperity and usefulness. The prospectus of 1507 shows that the noble art of

CLOISTER OF THE AUGUSTINIAN MONASTERY IN ERFURT,
APPROXIMATELY AS IT WAS IN LUTHER'S TIME

CHAPEL OF THE AUGUSTINIAN MONASTERY IN ERFURT

advertising is not a monopoly of modern times. "Those who are eager for knowledge should come to Wittenberg. The air is excellent, the plague is entirely past, and living is cheap, costing only eight gold gulden a year. There one can learn not only science, but also the best manners. The university, moreover, has received from pope and emperor all the privileges and advantages enjoyed by the most ancient schools, and one may be assured that not even Padua or Bologna, the mother of them all, possesses a greater number of learned men."

Wittenberg, which shared with Torgau the honor of being an electoral residence, was selected as the site of the university partly because the funds of the wealthy castle church could be used for its support, partly because there was an Augustinian monastery there which could be relied upon for teachers of philosophy and theology. Its ecclesiastical connections were therefore very close. Staupitz was one of Frederick's chief advisers in the matter, and he assumed a professorship and became the first dean of the theological faculty. In furtherance of the elector's plan, he called to Wittenberg competent monks from other places to aid in the work of instruction. He also made the convent a school for advanced theological training such as the Erfurt monastery had long been, and, as a result, young Augustinians came in large numbers to complete their studies and to enjoy at the same time the advantages of the new university.

Among those drafted for the work of instruction was the young Luther, who was brought thither in the autumn of 1508 to teach Aristotelian logic and ethics. A few months afterward he wrote his friend Braun of Eisenach that philosophy was distasteful to him and he much preferred theology—"that theology, namely, which explores the kernel of the nut, the heart of the wheat, and the marrow of the bone." The contrast between this and his early love of philosophy is worthy of notice, and shows the influence of his years in the monastery. His wish to teach theology was already in the way of being gratified, for a few days before he wrote he took the bachelor's degree, giving him the right to lecture on certain biblical books assigned by the faculty. There is an entry in the university records to the effect that he failed to pay the required fee. Later he himself appended the explanation that he had no money to pay it with. He was still bound by his oath of perpetual poverty; he lived in the monastery and received nothing for his teaching. His inability to meet the requirements in this matter is therefore not surprising, and was probably not counted to his discredit.

It cannot be doubted that, in summoning him to Wittenberg, Staupitz was moved by the desire to take him out of himself and give him an engrossing occupation in the midst of new scenes; but of course the appointment would have been impossible had he not already given promise of fitness for the place. He had been a faithful and zealous student, and the reputation brought with him from the university had been enhanced by his growing attainments both in philosophy and theology. He was very diligent in the study of William of Occam and other schoolmen and, according to his friend Melanchthon, almost knew by heart the writings of Peter D'Ailly and Gabriel Biel. The latter, but recently deceased, was the pride of the University of Erfurt and the favorite schoolman of the age in Germany.

Luther's studies also embraced the writings of the church fathers and particularly the Bible, to which he was becoming more and more attached. It was in his twentieth year, he tells us, that he first saw a complete copy of the Scriptures in the university library at Erfurt. He had hitherto supposed they embraced only the lessons read in the public services, and was delighted to find much that was quite unfamiliar to him. His ignorance, it may be remarked, though not exceptional, was his own fault. The notion that Bible reading was frowned upon by the ecclesiastical authorities of that age is quite unfounded. To be sure, it was not considered part of a Christian's duty, as it is in many Protestant churches, and few homes possessed a copy of the Scriptures; but they were read regularly in church, and their study was no more prohibited to university students of that day than of this, and was probably as little practised by most of them then as now.

The theological professors of Erfurt differed widely in their estimate of Bible-study. Some favored it, ascribing to the biblical writers an authority superior to the fathers and schoolmen; others advised against it, because everything of value in the Bible could be found in the writings of the theologians, and its study was apt to foster pride and promote a seditious and revolutionary spirit. Staupitz heartily believed in it, and made it an important part of the requirement in the theological course of the Erfurt monastery. A red-leather copy of the Vulgate was put into Luther's hands soon after he entered the convent, and he studied it with such diligence that he knew it, so he says, from cover to cover and could tell exactly where every passage was to be found.

At the time he took up his work in Wittenberg it was a small and mean town of some three thousand inhabitants. It was walled and somewhat strongly fortified, and the elector, who was an indefatigable builder, had beautified it with a number of imposing structures; but it still resembled a poor village rather than a city, and the contrast with Erfurt was extreme. The country, moreover, was flat and sandy, very unlike the beautiful Thuringian hills, from which Luther had come. His first impressions were distinctly unfavorable. He wondered why a university should have been established in so unpromising a place, and was sure it was due to the sins of the early settlers that they were cursed with such a land. He found the people cold and inhospitable as well as ignorant and boorish. The place lay, he thought, on the very edge of civilization, and a few miles to the north and east would have meant pure barbarism. But it was here he made his home for the greater part of his life, and it was here the Reformation had its birth.

CHAPTER III

VISIT TO ROME

IN the autumn of 1511, after his return from a stay
of nearly two years in Erfurt, whither he had gone
apparently to teach theology in his old monastery,
Luther was suddenly despatched to Rome by Staupitz.
The Vicar-General's plans for effecting certain changes
in the administration of the Augustinian order in Germany were opposed by some of the convents, and he
consequently wished to lay the matter before the curia.
The monastic rules required the brethren to travel two
by two, and Luther went as the companion of an older
monk, who was intrusted with the chief responsibility
for the business in hand. That Luther was selected
to accompany him was another mark of his superior's
favor, for a journey to Rome was one of the rarest
and most highly coveted privileges that could fall to
the lot of any monk. Not merely the natural interest
attaching to foreign travel, but the opportunity to visit
scenes made sacred by apostles and martyrs, and to
gain the boundless merit awaiting the believing pilgrim
to the many illustrious shrines of the Eternal City,
made a journey to Rome an event in the life of the
pious equaled only by a pilgrimage to the Holy Land.

The fortunate young monk set out with eager enthusiasm, and traveled with open ears and eyes. The
fascination of the goal did not prevent his seeing and
hearing many things on the way. The journey was

made on foot, the two companions walking one behind the other, with bowed heads, murmuring their prayers as they went, and food and lodging were found in the monasteries that everywhere lined the principal routes of travel. It was a tramp of twelve or thirteen weeks, as a rule, going and coming. The two monks traveled leisurely, and took five months for the trip, including four full weeks in Rome. We have no connected account of the journey, but Luther referred to it frequently in later years, and it is interesting to notice the things he particularly saw and heard.

He found the Southern Germans obliging and hospitable and contrasted them with the unfriendly Saxons, who, when a traveler appeared, would greet him with the words: "My dear sir, I don't know what I can give you to eat. My wife is away from home, and I cannot put you up." The scenery of Switzerland apparently moved him little,—the age had not awakened to its beauty and grandeur,—but he noticed the countless herds of cattle, the industry and frugality of the people, and the good roads making travel easy. "In Switzerland," he once remarked, "they have the shortest miles."

In Italy he had many of the sensations of one visiting for the first time a country of an older and more mellow civilization than his own. In comparison with the Italian peninsula, the Germany of that age was rude and uncouth enough. He was astounded at the wealth and luxury of the people, who had more delicious things to eat on fast days than the Germans on feast days, and he was particularly envious because of the elegance of their clothing. It pained his eyes, he remarked years afterward, to see his own countrymen in trousers like a ruffled pigeon, hopping about in a short coat like a magpie.

POPE ALEXANDER VI

Detail from a painting in Rome by Pinturicchio

He was much struck with the fruitfulness of the
land and could not say enough of its high state of
cultivation and the superior methods of agriculture
employed. The size of the grapes, peaches, and other
fruits excited his admiration, and the olives and
lemons which grew in the most unpromising places
became the text for many a sermon of later years. The
Po, whose like he had never seen, he called a prince
among rivers—"A merry water, with the Alps and
the Apennines on either side." For all the beauty and
fertility of the country, the air, he discovered, was
very treacherous. One night he and his companion
slept with open windows and awoke in the morning
with fever and a raging thirst, and found themselves
obliged to drink water, "deadly as it was," because
they could not endure even the smell of wine. They
were finally cured, he avers, by eating a couple of
pomegranates.

The sweetness of the Italian language delighted him,
and he picked up many expressions which he remembered as long as he lived. He was a natural linguist,
but admits he could not vie with the Flemish, of whom
it was said, "If they were carried through Italy or
France in a sack, they would learn the language on
the way." Like many another traveler in a foreign
land, he thought the Italians knew their own tongue
very imperfectly, and was outraged by the bad Latin
of the monks, whom he condemned as a set of igno-
ramuses because, it may be supposed, they spoke it
otherwise than he!

He was greatly impressed with the hospitals and
other charitable institutions. "In Italy," he said, "the
hospitals are very well fitted out and excellently built.
The food and drink are good, the servants diligent, the
physicians learned, the beds and clothing beautifully

clean, and the rooms finely painted. As soon as a patient is brought in, his garments are removed and an accurate record of them made by a notary, and they are carefully kept for him until he has recovered. He is clothed in a white frock and laid in a beautiful, well-made bed with clean sheets. Soon two physicians are called, and attendants appear with food and drink in clean dishes and glasses which they do not touch even with the tips of their fingers. Women of good birth are also on hand, carefully veiled that they may not be recognized, who spend several days in turn caring for the sick, and then return home. All this I saw in Florence, so well kept were the hospitals there. The foundling asylums are also similarly managed. Children are nourished, trained, and educated in the best possible fashion, and are well clothed and most carefully watched over." A fine tribute, this, to the Italians, and an illuminating commentary on the conditions that must have existed by contrast in Germany.

The characters and manners of the people also interested him. He found them much more temperate than the Germans, but tricky, cunning, and suspicious, not open and trustful like his own countrymen. Their more formal and conventional social customs seemed unpleasant to him in comparison with the greater freedom and familiarity of the Germans, and pointed, he thought, to a corruption of morals unknown in the North. One seems almost to hear a New England Puritan speaking of the impressions of his first trip to Europe. The pride of the people and their contempt for the Germans, whom they laughed at for their stolidity, simplicity, and lack of culture, greatly annoyed him. In revenge he speaks with the utmost scorn of the nervousness and excitability of the Italians, and the noise they made over the smallest trifles.

It was like him to take the brothers sharply to task, as he is reported to have done in one of the convents where he stopped overnight, for their lax observance of the prescribed rules of fasting. As a result of his well-meant efforts, he almost lost his life, escaping only by the aid of a friendly porter. The incident did not increase his confidence either in the piety or the virtue of the Italians. He brought back, indeed, a very poor opinion of the religious and moral condition of the country. Vice was shamefully prevalent, the churches were almost deserted, and the use of the phrase "a good Christian" to denote a harmless but weak-minded person seemed typical of the general attitude.

Approaching Rome from the north, the traveler by the highroad catches his first glimpse of the city some half-dozen miles away, where the road slopes gradually toward the Tiber. Here Luther, overcome with emotion, threw himself on his knees and cried: "Hail, Holy Rome! Thrice holy thou in whom the blood of the martyrs has been poured out!" Over the Milvian bridge the two companions made their way and entered the city by the Porta Flaminia. Just inside it stood the Augustinian monastery, where they were to stay, and the church of Maria del Popolo, where, according to tradition, Brother Martin said his first mass within the city walls. A contemporary guide-book intended for the use of pilgrims, a copy of which was very likely in his hands as he went about the city, gives a very characteristic account of the origin of the church:

Where the church is, there once stood a great walnut-tree in which devils made their home. Whoever happened to pass by they vilified and slandered, and no one knew who did it. It was revealed to St. Pascal the pope that he should cut down the tree and build a church in its place to the honor of our dear Lady. The pope therefore

went to the Porta Flaminia with a great procession of
clergy and laity and rooted the tree out of the earth.
Under it there was found a coffin containing the body of
the wicked Nero, who put St. Peter and St. Paul to death
with many other Christians. The same Nero set fire to
Rome in twelve places that he might see how great a
conflagration it would make. The Romans consequently
wished to put him in prison, but he stabbed himself, and
was buried in the above-mentioned place. Afterward
Pope Pascal burned to ashes the body of the wicked Nero
and the walnut-tree, and exorcised all the devils that were
in the tree, and built a church, which was called Maria
del Popolo because of the multitude of people there.

The business which brought the two monks to Rome
seems not to have taken much of Luther's time. He
praises the admirable methods of the curia and its
celerity and skill in despatching business, but he was
interested chiefly in other things, and during his four
weeks in the city he was an eager and indefatigable
sight-seer.

For Italian art, then at the zenith of its glory, he
had little appreciation. It could hardly be expected that
he would, and he never pretended an interest he did not
feel. For ancient Rome he had more of an eye. Then, as
now, only broken fragments of it remained. Rome, he
said, "is like a dead carcass compared with its former
state, for houses now stand where were roofs in other
days, so deep is the debris. This can be clearly seen by the
banks of the Tiber, which are piled two spear-lengths
high with rubbish." He spent two weeks visiting all
the ruins, at the peril of his life, for they were a
favorite haunt of brigands, who levied heavy toll of
purse and limb upon pious and worldly alike. The
Pantheon, the Colosseum, the baths of Diocletian, and
the aqueducts spanning the Campagna with their

From a photograph by Anderson

POPE JULIUS II, AFTER THE PAINTING BY RAPHAEL IN THE
UFFIZI GALLERY, FLORENCE

gaunt arches, interested him most. He wondered that
the ancients were able to accomplish so much, and to
attain so high a degree of civilization, without a knowledge of the true God, and the transformation of the
heathen Pantheon into a Christian church gave him
congenial food for moralizing. And yet he was alive
to the greatness of the old world, and his admiration
for it speaks through all he says. If he did not bring
to Rome the enthusiastic devotion to the classical an-
tique that marked the humanists of the day, he at least
had a knowledge of human history and a fondness for
it which made its dead monuments alive with interest.

But he was more devotee than sight-seer, and the
greater part of his stay in Rome was spent in visiting
churches and other sacred places and in performing
acts of religious devotion. The city's chief interest
for him lay not in its art treasures or antiquities, but in
the "hundreds of thousands" of martyrs who had con-
secrated it with their blood. Their relics he sought
diligently in church and catacomb, and from the sight
of them he hoped to gain rich spiritual blessings. He
climbed on his knees the Scala Santa, reputed to have
been brought from Pilate's palace in Jerusalem, where
it was trodden by Christ at the time of his trial, and
the ascent of which insured years of indulgence to the
pious and believing pilgrim. He made a general confession of all the sins of his past life, an act already
performed twice, but promising in Rome far greater
rewards of grace, and he said mass ten times during
his stay in the city. He even wished his father and
mother were dead that he might be able to release
them from purgatory by his penitential exercises. He
was troubled with no doubts, but ran, as he said, from
holy place to holy place, greedily swallowing all that
was told him, however improbable or absurd. "O

dear God," he cried, "what did I not believe! Everything seemed true, and nothing was so preposterous or false that I did not accept it gladly." His pious heart was torn with emotion or kindled with ecstasy as he visited the scenes hallowed by apostles and martyrs and gazed upon their sacred relics. Never more credulous and simple-minded believer set foot in the holy city and reveled in its wealth of pious memories.

He saw much, it is true, to trouble and distress him. The city was perhaps no worse than other great capitals, but it was the first he had visited and its corruption pained and amazed him. Then, too, the monks he met were much less reverent than the simple-hearted German, and made light of many things he held dear. It was not unnatural that they should take delight in shocking the unsophisticated young pilgrim, and doubtless they painted Roman life in lurid colors before his astonished eyes. He was told extraordinary tales about the debauchery and vice of great church dignitaries, including the late Pope Alexander VI of notorious memory—tales which lost nothing in the telling. But he was too devout a soul, too absorbed in the sacred treasures of the holy city, and too engrossed in the task of securing divine favor by works of penance, to think much about such tales. If others were not all they should be, he would do his duty the more faithfully. Distrust of the church or questions as to the sanctity and authority of the papacy did not enter his mind. In later years he not infrequently spoke sharply of the worldly and warlike character of the great soldier and statesman Julius II, who was pope at the time of his Roman visit, but when in the holy city, we may be sure, he thought of him only with devout reverence. It was of this period of his life he said long afterward, "I was so filled, yes, so intoxicated with the pope's teaching that I should have been ready with great eagerness to murder, or at least to approve and assist in the murder of all that did not obey and submit to him in every last syllable."

The significance of his visit to Rome has been greatly exaggerated by most historians. The presence of the founder of Protestantism in the very stronghold of the papacy which he afterward so earnestly opposed seems full of dramatic possibilities, and it is easy, especially for those who paint contemporary Catholicism only in the darkest colors, to think it must have aroused his reforming spirit and started him upon his great work. But the truth is the Roman journey was no more than an interesting episode in his life, and though it doubtless enriched his mind and broadened his outlook, as all travel does, it had nothing whatever to do with his career as a reformer. That career had other and altogether different roots. To be sure, when the break with Rome came, it was easier to attack the pope because of what he had seen and heard in the papal capital, for things then took on a new aspect, and idle tales to which he had hardly given heed were made to justify an enmity all the more bitter because of the devotion it succeeded. In this mood he once declared he would not take a hundred thousand gulden for the experiences of his Roman visit; but when he said it he was thinking of the incidents which meant least to him when he was actually there and made scarcely any impression at the time upon his reverent soul.

He gained, indeed, all he had hoped from his pilgrimage, and returned as devout as ever and with a new enthusiasm for Holy Mother Church, which the sight of the countless mementos of a long and glorious past could not but kindle in his sensitive and passionate heart.

CHAPTER IV

PREACHER, PROFESSOR, AND DISTRICT-VICAR

IN the spring of 1512, Luther was back again in Wittenberg, enriched by the experiences of his Italian journey and prepared to give himself with new enthusiasm to his university work. He was already a marked man. That he had seen the sacred city greatly enhanced his reputation with his brother monks, and the signal favor of Staupitz naturally attracted attention to him. He was evidently proving his ability, for new duties and responsibilities were laid upon him by his patron, and he was advanced rapidly to one position of influence after another.

In October, having completed the requirements and engaged in the customary disputations, he was given the doctorate of theology by the University of Wittenberg. During his recent stay in Erfurt he had taken the degree of Sententiarius, a necessary step in the line of promotion to the doctorate. As Sententiarius he was expected to lecture upon the "Sentences" of Lombard, the great theological text-book of the Middle Ages, and he did so for a year and a half before setting out upon his Italian journey. There still exists a copy of Lombard's work with marginal notes made at this time by Luther himself. These as well as similar notes in certain volumes of Augustine's works show how independent he already was in his way of looking at things and how confident of the correctness of his opinions. Of deviation from catholic orthodoxy there is no sign, but there are many severe words about theologians whom he disagreed with, giving a foretaste of the vivid imagination and picturesque language characterizing all his polemic. He already had the reputation of being unduly critical and contentious, and the Erfurt monks, we are told, were not altogether sorry when he left them permanently.

The doctorate to which he was promoted in Wittenberg gave him the right to teach the whole subject of theology without limitations of any kind except those imposed by loyalty to university and church. The doctor's oath ran as follows:

I swear obedience and due reverence to the dean and masters of the theological faculty, and promise to do all I can to promote the welfare of the university and particularly of the theological faculty; not to take the degree elsewhere; not to teach vain and foreign doctrines which are condemned by the church and hurt pious ears, but to inform the dean within eight days if I know of their being taught by any one; to maintain the customs, liberties, and privileges of the theological faculty to the best of my ability, God helping me, and the holy evangelists.

The degree was a costly affair, and, at the solicitation of Staupitz, the elector defrayed the expense. One of the earliest autographs of Luther we possess is his receipt for the sum of fifty gulden, which he had to walk all the way to Leipsic to fetch for himself, almost returning home without it, in his impatience at the redtape involved. Unnecessary formalities always annoyed him, and if he had had his way, he would have made short shrift of the elaborate bureaucratic methods of the day.

That he took the doctor's degree in Wittenberg in-

stead of Erfurt brought down upon him the wrath of
the authorities of the latter university, who felt they
had a claim on him as their own Magister and Sententiarius, and resented his going elsewhere for the highest degree. As a matter of fact, he ought to have obtained a dispensation from them before taking it in
Wittenberg. His failure to do so, probably due to
mere carelessness, was thoroughly characteristic, for
he often showed a disregard of the conventionalities
and proprieties that made him many enemies. In this
particular case, the bad feeling in Erfurt was overcome
only after years, and as a result of humble apologies
on his part and of the good offices of common friends.

Although it was the natural and obvious thing for
a Sententiarius to take the doctor's degree, Luther did
it very unwillingly, and only in obedience to the imperative command of Staupitz, who wished to retire
from his professorship and make his protégé his
successor. This fact explains the young scholar's
reluctance. For the duties and responsibilities of his
superior's chair he felt, as was not unnatural, scarcely
qualified. At the age of twenty-nine to succeed his
famous teacher and patron, whom he held in unbounded reverence, might well seem to almost any one
too large a task.

Despite his hesitancy to take the degree, he was always proud of it. As a doctor of theology, he claimed it
gave him not only the right, but the duty, to teach the
truth as he found it, and in later years he continually
appealed to it in justification of his innovations. That
he had not sought the degree, but had taken it against
his will, called thereto, as he later believed, by God,
gave him all the more confidence in his course. "Who
compelled the Lord to make me a doctor? Since He
did it of His own will, let come what may!"

In addition to his duties as professor, he also had regular preaching to do. Practice in preaching was a necessary part of his preparation for the doctor's degree, but greatly as he loved it afterward, when he was accustomed to find the hour spent in the pulpit the most beautiful of all the day, he dreaded to begin, and Staupitz was obliged to use pressure to compel him to do so, dragging him into it by the hair, as Luther once remarked. Years afterward, talking to a young theologian who found preaching a great burden, he said: "Yes, my dear fellow, it was the same with me. I shrank from it just as you do; but I had to undertake it. I was forced to it, and I began in the refectory, before the brothers. Oh, how frightened I was! I had fifteen arguments with which I tried to persuade Dr. Staupitz, under this very pear-tree, to let me off, but they did no good. Finally when I said, 'You are trying to kill me; I cannot live three months,' he replied: 'Very well, in God's name. The Lord has large affairs on hand, and needs wise men up yonder.' "

Despite his trepidation at seeing so many heads before him, as he once put it, the preacher's gift was his. Vivid imagination, picturesqueness of style, fluency of speech, personal magnetism, passionate earnestness, and an uncommon knowledge of the religious emotions born of his own heart-searching experiences—all these he had. He knew, too, the great secret of effective preaching, simplicity. "I preach as simply as I can," he once remarked, "that common men, children, and servants may understand; for the learned already know it all, and I do not preach for them." No wonder he made an impression upon those who heard him and his reputation grew apace. He was soon in demand as a supply in the city church, and in 1514 became the regular incumbent of its pulpit. The little

4

town of Wittenberg had never heard his like before.
Few towns indeed had, for he was one of the great
preachers of history. Beginning modestly, his power
steadily increased until he held his congregations in the
hollow of his hand. We have hundreds of sermons
from his pen, after the first few years unconventional
and unsystematic for the most part, often conversa-
tional and almost casual in style, and sometimes commonplace enough, but again rich in matter, glowing
with genius, and inimitable in their appeal to the heart
of the common man. He did not hesitate to repeat
himself, and upon certain great themes he loved to
preach over and over again. "The time and the occasion," as he said, "make a preacher. I cannot allow
myself to be bound to particular words. I often say
the same things in different words."

During this period his influence in the Augustinian
order was also steadily advancing. In the summer of
1512, he was made subprior of the Wittenberg convent, and not long afterward was placed in full charge
of theological instruction within its walls. His success
as a teacher was very great, and young monks came in
increasing numbers to put themselves under his tutelage, until he had to protest that the convent was over-
taxed and could not accommodate all that were sent
to him.

In 1515, when only thirty-one years old, he was
appointed district-vicar of the order for a term of
three years, and had to look after the interests and
superintend the affairs of eleven monasteries. The
knowledge and experience thus gained were of incalculable benefit to him. The administrative duties of
the position were very onerous, and required him to be
much away from Wittenberg and to give his attention
to all sorts of matters, from the appointment and re-

PRESENT APPEARANCE OF THE MARKET-PLACE AT WITTENBERG

At the left is the city hall, dating from the sixteenth century; in the background rise the towers of the city church; and at the right is College Street, leading to the Luther House. The nearest statue in the market-place is that of Melanchthon, that of Luther being in the middle ground

moval of priors to the repair of buildings and the auditing of accounts. He was at once business manager of the convents under his charge and spiritual adviser to their inmates.

He was a strict disciplinarian, as is shown, for instance, by the following passage from a letter to the provost of a monastery of another order concerning a brother who had committed some serious offense.

It is difficult for me to advise you what to do with him, for I am ignorant of your statutes. If they do not provide life imprisonment or capital punishment for such a crime, it seems to me he should receive as severe a penalty as they allow, for it is not you who punish, but justice and law, whose minister, not lord, you are. Do not be dissuaded by the fact that you are as great a sinner or a greater. It is enough to confess this to God. But here for the sake of edification we must nearly always punish those better than we, teach those more learned, rule those more worthy, that the Lord's words may be fulfilled, "The princes of the Gentiles rule over them as over inferiors, but the princes of believers minister to them as to superiors," for He says, "He who is the greater among you let him be your servant," etc. Therefore preserve humility and gentleness of heart toward him, but treat him rigorously, for power is not thine, but God's, while humility ought to be not God's, but thine.

At the same time he had a warm regard for his monks, and showed uncommon sympathy and kindness toward offenders. Witness this letter to the Augustinian prior in Mayence:

I am sorry to hear that a certain brother, George Baumgartner, from our cloister in Dresden, who fled, alas! because guilty of shameful conduct, has taken refuge with you. I thank you for your faithfulness and kindness in receiving him, that the scandal might be stopped. He is my lost sheep and belongs to me; mine it is to seek him and to restore the erring one, if it please the Lord Jesus. So I beg you by our common faith in Christ and by the order of St. Augustine that, if you can, you will send him to me to Dresden or Wittenberg, or will lovingly persuade him to return of his own free will. I shall receive him with open arms if he comes. He need have no fear of my displeasure. I know, I know, that offenses must come, and it is no marvel when a man falls, but it is a miracle when he recovers himself and remains steadfast. Peter fell that he might know he was human. To-day even the cedars of Lebanon fall, though while they stand they reach the heavens. Yes, even an angel in heaven fell,—a wonder it was indeed,—and Adam fell in paradise. So is it surprising the reed should bend before the storm and the smoking flax be extinguished?

The amount of work entailed by his various responsibilities is indicated clearly enough in a letter to Lang, written in 1516.

I almost need two secretaries, for I do hardly anything the whole day long but write letters. It may be I continually repeat myself in consequence; if so, you will understand why. I am lecturer in the cloister and reader at meals; I am daily asked to preach in the parish church; I am director of studies; I am vicar, which means being prior eleven times over; inspector of fish-ponds at Leitzkau; advocate of the Herzbergers' cause at Torgau; I am lecturing on Paul, and gathering material on the Psalms —all this besides my letter-writing, which, as I have said, takes the greater part of my time. Rarely do I have time to observe the hours of prayer, or to say mass, and I am plagued besides by temptations of the world, the flesh, and the devil. Behold what a man of leisure I am!. . .

You write that you began to lecture on the Sentences yesterday. I shall begin to expound the Epistle to the Galatians to-morrow, although I fear, with the plague here, I shall not be able to continue. Already it has robbed us of two or three, but not in one day. The smith opposite has just buried a son who was in good health yesterday, and another is infected. Yes, it is here, and is beginning to rage with violence, especially among the young. You counsel me to flee to you for refuge in company with Brother Bartholomew. But why? I hope the world will not come to an end, though Brother Martin perish. If the plague spread, I shall send the brothers away. As for me, seeing I have been placed here, my vows of obedience demand that I remain until ordered elsewhere. Not that I do not fear death, for I am not the apostle Paul, but only a reader of the apostle; but I hope the Lord will deliver me from my fear.

Despite all the occupations to which he refers, he still had to discharge his religious duties as a monk. Seven times a day he was required to engage in his devotions, and they consumed much time. He once remarked that when it proved quite impossible, as it often did, to observe the canonical hours day by day, he would shut himself in his cell on Saturday and make up in a single day for all the omissions of the week. This kind of thing, of course, tended to weaken the hold of his monastic ties upon him. Evidently conscientious as he still was, his life was no longer primarily that of a monk. He was a teacher, a preacher, and an administrator, and his various functions took him out into the world and brought him into as intimate contact with men and affairs as if he had never seen the inside of a monastery. He often lamented it, and longed for the quiet and seclusion of the Erfurt days; but there can be no doubt he was much happier and his life far more wholesome as it was.

With all his labors, he was not without social recreation. His vivacity and enthusiasm, his contagious hu-

mor, his fascinating conversation, his novel way of
looking at men and things, and his personal charm, all
combined to give him warm admirers wherever he
went, and in Wittenberg the circle of his friends was
large and apparently included everybody worth knowing in the little city. An amusing note of invitation
to his old and intimate friend George Spalatin, the
elector's chaplain, gives us an interesting glimpse of
the social side of his life.

Greeting. Come with the father confessor and his
friend about nine o'clock. If the Lord Christopher, the
ambassador, is with you, bring him, too. The duty of
inviting him has been intrusted to my Otto. Farewell,
but see that you also procure wine for us; for you know
you are coming from the castle to the monastery, not
from the monastery to the castle.

It is this same Spalatin whose praise of Luther is
the earliest explicit testimony we have to his character
and ability. Writing in 1514 to their common friend
Lang, he spoke of Luther's rare combination of the
keenest judgment with great learning and purity of
character. For many years he was an important figure
in Luther's life. He had belonged to the literary
circle in Erfurt, where the two first met, and for a
long time was freer in his views than his friend, though
he was cooler and more cautious, a man of the world
rather than a religious zealot, and would never have
thought of devoting himself to the work of reform.
When the great controversy came, he stood with
Luther, but he did what he could to restrain his im-
petuosity and to keep him from going too far. A tact-
ful courtier and a wise counselor, he held an important
place at court, and his influence with the elector was
great. He did much to promote Luther's credit with

From an old print

GEORGE SPALATIN

the prince, and was commonly the medium of communication between the two. In fact, he was an invaluable as well as a dearly loved friend, and Luther's correspondence with him, covering many of the most critical years of his life, is one of our most important and interesting sources of information.

The famous painter, Lucas Cranach, who stood very high in the community and was for a time burgomaster of the town, though considerably older than Luther, was also one of his intimates. He was not merely an artist, but a prosperous business man, whose printing establishment and apothecary shop materially added to the financial returns from his studio. He had come to Wittenberg originally on Frederick's invitation to fill the position of court painter, and was ultimately raised to the nobility. From his brush we have many faithful, if not inspired, portraits of some of the leading notables of the day, including the reformer himself, whom he painted frequently. With him and his family Luther enjoyed the closest friendship as long as he lived, and the stately home of the prosperous artist was one of his favorite resorts.

He was on terms of affectionate intimacy, too, with many of his colleagues, among others the brilliant and impetuous theologian Carlstadt, the more sober and solid Nicholas von Amsdorf, the punctilious and cautious ecclesiastical lawyer Jerome Schurf, and the liberal and cultivated jurist Christopher Scheurl. To the latter, who early left Wittenberg to become city councilor of Nuremberg, Luther once wrote in a playful mood: "The money I realized by the sale of the books you sent I have given, in accordance with your directions, to the poor—that is, to myself and the brethren, for I have never known anybody poorer than I."

In his relations with all his friends, Luther's commanding personality asserted itself unmistakably. He dominated every circle he belonged to, and his intimates, as time passed, recognizing more and more his superior genius and capacity for leadership, fell naturally, whether older or younger, into the position of followers. To be sure, many were offended by him, and thought him arrogant and overbearing, but in most of those who knew him there was steadily growing affection and loyalty.

Curiously enough, Luther never met the Elector Frederick, near as were the palace and the monastery, and intimate as were his relations with some of the members of the court. It was like him not to seek the acquaintance of his prince, for he was the last man to curry favor with the great. Frederick thought highly of him, and showed him many marks of favor. Soon after Luther's arrival in Wittenberg, he had been assured by Staupitz that the young scholar would yet be an honor to his darling university, and as early as 1512 he had heard him preach and been much impressed. But at first there was no reason for summoning him to court, and after Luther had gained worldwide prominence, the elector's native prudence kept him from identifying himself too intimately with the reformer's affairs.

On Luther's part, natural loyalty was enhanced by genuine respect for his sovereign. Writing to Spalatin in 1518, he expressed his thanks "to the most illustrious prince for the fine and truly princely gift of venison which he sent our new graduates, and which I told them came from him. The mind of the most kindly and generous prince, as you justly call him, has pleased me especially, for man, too, loves a cheerful giver."

The following are a few of his many references to him in later days:

The Elector Frederick was a wise, judicious, capable, and skilful ruler, who hated all display, hypocrisy, and sham. He led a pure life and never married. . . . Such a pious, God-fearing, prudent prince is a great gift from God. He was a real father to the fatherland, he ruled well, and kept both cellar and garret full. He held his officials and servants to a strict account. When he visited one of his own castles, he paid for his food and lodging, like any other guest, that the stewards might not afterward put in exorbitant bills for his entertainment. Thus it came about that he left his land large treasures and supplies. . . . He gathered in with shovels and gave out with spoons. . . . He had the custom of allowing his counselors to express their opinions and then doing the exact opposite, yet with such reason that they could say nothing. This he did not learn, nor was he trained to it, but he had the gift naturally, and although many tried to influence and control him, he put out his horns and would have none of it. Often when his counselors gave him advice which seemed good, he yet obstinately refused to take it. Why he did so, only himself knew; but it was surely at God's suggestion, for he was born one of God's miracles.

Despite Luther's admiration for his prince, he did not hesitate to express himself frankly about him or to him. In the year 1516, in a letter to Spalatin, he remarked:

Many things please your prince and glitter in his eyes which displease God and are held of no account by Him. I do not deny he is exceedingly wise in secular affairs, but in those pertaining to God and the soul's salvation I consider him, as well as Pfeffinger, sevenfold blind. I do not say this in a corner to malign them, nor do I wish you to keep it quiet. I am prepared whenever opportunity occurs to say it to their faces.

The following letter to Frederick himself, written something over a year later, is characteristically direct and outspoken:

My most gracious and dear lord, Duke Frederick, Elector of Saxony; most gracious lord and prince. As your grace promised me some time ago, through Hirsfelder, a new gown, I now wish to remind your grace of it. But I beg, gracious lord, as before, that if Pfeffinger is to arrange the matter, he will do it in reality and not with fine speeches merely, for he can spin good words, but they do not make good cloth.

It has also been told me, gracious lord, by the prior at Erfurt, who had it from your grace's confessor, that your grace is displeased with Dr. Staupitz, our dear and worthy father, because of something he has written. When he was here and visited your grace at Torgau, I spoke about it to him and expressed my regret at your displeasure, and although we talked at length about your grace I could not discover that he thought of your grace in any but the most affectionate fashion. He remarked finally, "I do not believe I have ever done anything to displease my most gracious lord except to love him too much." Therefore I beg you, gracious lord, in his behalf and partly at his suggestion, that you will count on his good will and faithfulness as in the past.

Also, gracious prince, that I may show my loyalty to your grace and earn my court dress, I have heard that your grace, after the collection of the present tax, intends to levy another and perhaps heavier one. If your grace will not despise a poor beggar's prayer, I entreat that this, for God's sake, may not be done; for I and many who love your grace are deeply distressed because the present tax has robbed your grace's last days of so much good fame and affection. God has endowed your grace with large wisdom, so that you see further in these matters than I, and perhaps any of your grace's subjects, but it may well be—so indeed God wills it—that great

CHRISTOPHORUS SCHEURL
Consil. Cæs. Saxon. et Reipub. Norib.

From an old print

CHRISTOPHER SCHEURL, THE
JURIST

wisdom sometimes learns from less in order that no one
may depend on himself, but on God our Lord alone.
May He preserve your grace in health for our good, and
afterward give your grace eternal salvation.   Amen.
Your grace's obedient chaplain, Dr. Martin Luther of
Wittenberg.

During all these years, despite multiplying duties
and distractions, Luther's chief work, and most absorbing interest, was his university teaching.   The
chair he was appointed to in succession to Staupitz
was a biblical chair.   There were three regular foundations in the theological faculty, devoted to instruction respectively in Thomas Aquinas, in Gabriel Biel,
and in the Bible.   The last was undoubtedly due to
Staupitz himself, and its establishment was very
timely, in view of the growing interest of the age in
biblical study.   It was thus not on his own initiative
that Luther took the Bible instead of the theology of
the schoolmen as the subject of his teaching, though
his taste and training made the work peculiarly congenial.   As a rule, professors of theology preferred to
give themselves to dogmatics and considered the teaching of the Bible rather the work of beginners.   But
Luther's interest was identical with that of his eminent predecessor, as Staupitz well knew when he decided upon him as his successor.

The new incumbent interpreted the duties of his
chair strictly, and to the end of his life lectured upon
the Bible alone.   At first he contented himself with
expounding the text of the Vulgate, the traditional
Latin version of the Catholic church, but he soon felt
the need of going back to the original tongues, realizing, as he said, that "the farther from the spring, the
more water loses taste and strength," and he therefore

took up the study of both Hebrew and Greek with his friend Lang, who had long been an enthusiastic humanist and an accomplished linguist. Though Luther never became a great expert in either language, he read both easily, and made large use of them in his biblical work. The energy of the man in thus acquiring two new languages while in the midst of the active work of teaching and preaching was genuinely characteristic.

Erasmus's famous edition of the Greek New Testament appeared in 1516. Luther was lecturing at the time upon Paul's Epistle to the Romans and he showed his conscientiousness and his desire to be fully up to date in his work by immediately making the new Greek text the basis of his comments in the class-room. He was always alive, indeed, to the progress of scholarship in his chosen field.

In his methods of teaching he was original and unconventional in the extreme. He was continually referring to the events of the day and viewing them in the light of the particular writer he was interpreting. He drew largely upon the every-day experiences of his students for illustrative material, and even made considerable use of their vernacular speech. Latin was the regular language of the class-room, but he did not hesitate, unacademic as it was, to introduce German words and phrases whenever he could thus make the Bible text more vivid and expressive, much as one might indulge in colloquialisms or slang to-day. Of course he was criticized. At the same time, his work took on a reality and an interest elsewhere quite unknown, and his reputation as a teacher grew apace.

His instruction was by no means scientific in character. The Bible was a practical book to him, and in his interpretation it was always its practical value upon which he laid chief stress. Often he was as much interested in making it religiously valuable to his students as in getting at its original meaning. He treated the Old Testament in the most unhistorical fashion, finding types and prophecies of Christ in every part of it; and into the most unlikely passages both of Old Testament and New he read his gospel of the forgiving love of God revealed in Christ. But the very fact that he interpreted the whole Bible from a single point of view, together with his enthusiasm, his skill in rendering the text into the vernacular, and the novelty of his methods, made a tremendous impression. He soon became the most popular teacher in the university, and gained an ever larger following among the students. Here, they felt, was a real man, who insisted on going to the heart of things, and was bound by no narrow conventions and traditional sophistries. Even his colleagues came frequently to hear him, and the famous scholar, Dr. Martin Pollich, predicted he would yet completely revolutionize the teaching of theology.

To do this, indeed, soon became his chief ambition. More and more as time passed he grew impatient with the prevailing scholastic methods and with the schoolmen themselves, to whom they were due. Theology, he believed, ought to be vital and practical instead of philosophical and speculative, as they had made it. He had no quarrel as yet with their doctrines,—he was orthodox, as they, too, were,—but their spirit was not his. His exclusively practical interest in theology was typical of his general attitude. Speculation as such, science as an end in itself, truth for truth's sake, never appealed to him; only matters immediately bearing on life and character he felt to be worthy the attention of a serious man.

His knowledge of the greatest schoolmen, Thomas

Aquinas, Bonaventura, and the like, was very limited
and he was never altogether just to them. He viewed
scholasticism too exclusively in the light of its later
exponents, such as William of Occam and Gabriel Biel.
For Aquinas, had he known him well, he would have
felt less antipathy than for the latter. The "Angelic
Doctor" was much more of an Augustinian than they,
while at the same time, with all his formalism and interest in speculation, he was a good deal of a mystic
and made communion with God the supreme end of
theology. But Luther read him only through the eyes
of his later interpreters and so included him in the
common condemnation. As a matter of fact, even had
he known him better he could not have found him
permanently congenial, for Thomas was a philosophical theologian, and read Christianity principally in
intellectual terms, while Luther was exclusively practical. Moreover, the careful balancing of opinions, and
the drawing of fine distinctions, in which Thomas as
well as the other schoolmen chiefly delighted, were altogether foreign to his impetuous genius. He was always
more preacher than scholar. As a rule, he saw only one
side of a question, and he instinctively put things in
extreme and paradoxical fashion.

The presiding genius of medieval scholasticism was
Aristotle, and Luther's growing distaste for the scholastic spirit and method resulted not unnaturally in a
growing dislike for the great Stagirite. His formal
logic he found empty and barren, and the matters
of chief interest to the inquiring mind of the Greek
sage he cared little about, while for the questions he
thought really important no satisfactory answers were
to be found in the peripatetic philosophy. "Wilt thou
know what Aristotle teaches?" he once exclaimed. "I
will tell thee frankly. A potter can make a pot out

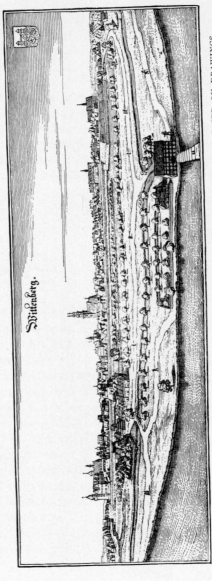

Wittenberg.

WITTENBERG ON THE ELBE, SAXONY (AFTER A SEVENTEENTH-CENTURY ENGRAVING BASED ON DRAWINGS
MADE IN THE SIXTEENTH CENTURY)

At the left is seen the castle, and adjoining it the small tower of the castle church. In the middle of the picture rise the towers of the city church near the market-place. At the extreme right of the picture is the Augustinian monastery where Luther lived. A little to the left, now used as infantry barracks, is the old university. As a fortress, Wittenberg was subjected to the rigors of war, and was not dismantled until 1875.

of clay; this a smith cannot do unless he has learned how. If there is anything higher in Aristotle, do not believe a word I say." "In the universities," he remarked on another occasion, "the Bible and Christian faith are little taught, and only the blind heathen Aristotle reigns. It pains me greatly that the damnable, proud, cunning heathen has led astray and fooled so many of the best Christians with his false words. God has plagued us with him because of our sins."

It is significant of his controlling interest that he ranked Cicero much higher than Aristotle.

Cicero handled the finest and best questions in philosophy: Whether there be a God? What God is? Whether He takes an interest in human affairs? And he holds that there must be an eternal Spirit. Aristotle was a skilful and cunning dialectician, who followed the right method in his teaching; but the facts and their meaning he did not elucidate, as Cicero did. He who would learn the true philosophy should read Cicero.

He was particularly pleased with Cicero's arguments for the existence of God, while Aristotle's disbelief in divine creation and providence, and in the immortality of the soul, made him, as he thought, quite unfit to be a teacher of Christians. At this time Luther measured every writer by the standard of Christian orthodoxy, and, estimated thus, Aristotle could hardly seem other than a blasphemer. The detached and scientific attitude of the schoolmen, enabling them to use the Aristotelian philosophy without being troubled with the religious beliefs of its author, was not his. His practical interest made such a frame of mind quite impossible.

He was by no means the first to attack Aristotle and the schoolmen. The revolt against traditional methods had begun long before his day and was steadily gaining strength, particularly where the influence of the new humanism was felt. But his opposition was exclusively religious and very unlike that of most of his contemporaries. The difference is seen in his complaint that the schoolmen, following their master Aristotle, made too much of human reason, while one of their chief faults in the eyes of the humanists was the irrationality and antiquated nature of their teaching. The difference is seen also in his condemnation of the naturalism of the pagan philosopher. Because Aristotle emphasized human ability and free will instead of man's impotence and constant need of divine grace, his moral teaching, Luther thought, was peculiarly dangerous and was the worst of his many sins. That the reformer thus reached by his own independent path a position very common in his day was characteristic of him. Over and over again the same thing happened, and in it lies one of the secrets of the tremendous influence he wielded.

In February, 1517, he sent his friend Lang a paper full, as he said, of blasphemies and curses against Aristotle, Porphyry, and the dogmatic theologians, asking him to show it to his old teacher Trutvetter and others. He realized the radical character of his attitude. That it would excite criticism he was well aware, and both now and later, as his letters show, he was almost boyishly eager to know what his friends would say. In May he wrote Lang, "Our theology and that of St. Augustine, by the grace of God, are making excellent progress and gaining control in our university. Aristotle is gradually declining, and his permanent extinction is not far off." This was no idle boast. He was actually winning over to his own point of view one colleague after another, and his influence

From the original painting in the Uffizi Gallery, Florence

LUCAS CRANACH, PAINTED BY HIMSELF

in the Wittenberg faculty was da...
beyond Wittenberg, too, his ideas
ground. Under his direction, in Septembe...
number of theses denouncing Aristotle's influenc...
theology were defended by one of his pupils in a disputation for the master's degree. Upon reading them Christopher Scheurl, then residing in Nuremberg, wrote that a great change in theological studies was in prospect, and soon it would be possible to become a theologian without either Aristotle or Plato. In this he was only giving voice to an opinion shared by many of his acquaintances, whose admiration for the young Wittenberg professor was steadily growing.

In some places, on the other hand, Luther was acquiring a bad name for himself, and especially with his old teachers at Erfurt his reputation was not improving. They not unnaturally thought him over-proud, self-conceited, and presumptuous, and were incensed to see him emancipating himself more and more from the traditions in which he had been trained and from the authorities whom he had been taught to reverence.

t in the reformation of theolog-
not prevent him from concerning
ny other matters needing betterment.
, his eyes were increasingly opened to
s in one and another sphere, and wherever
he   hem, he was quick to attack them. He had
the tr   reformer's conscience—the sense of responsibility for others as well as for himself, and the true
reformer's vision of the better things that ought to be.
He was never a mere faultfinder, but he was endowed
with the gifts of imagination and sympathy, leading
him to feel himself a part of every situation he was
placed in, and with the irrepressible impulse to action
driving him to take upon himself the burden of it.
In any crowd of bystanders he would have been first
to go to the rescue where need was, and quickest to see
the need not obvious to all. The aloofness of the mere
observer was not his; he was too completely one with
all he saw to stand apart and let it go its way alone.
Fearful and distrustful of himself he long was, but
his timidity was only the natural shrinking before new
and untried duties of a soul that saw more clearly and
felt more keenly than most. The imperative demands
inevitably made upon him by every situation led him
instinctively to dread putting himself where he could
not help responding to the call of unfamiliar tasks;

but once there, the summons was irresistible, and he threw himself into the new responsibilities with a forgetfulness of self possible only to him who has denied its claims, and with a fearlessness possible only to him who has conquered fear. He might interpret his confidence as trust in God, won by the path of a complete contempt of his own powers; but however understood, it gave him an independence and a disregard of consequences which made his conscience and his vision effective for reform.

As a preacher in the Wittenberg church he soon abandoned the all-too-common custom of delivering mere essays on speculative theology, and turned his attention to questions of immediate practical concern. The moral conditions of university life, and particularly the relations between the students and the young women of the town, left much to be desired. The citizens had not yet adjusted themselves to the new situation arising from the presence of hundreds of young and often unruly fellows in the quiet little city, and they found themselves helpless before the growing demoralization. Luther soon became familiar with existing conditions, and began to speak his mind about them in no uncertain terms. He denounced parents for the laxity of their discipline, and called upon the university and city authorities to take the matter actively in hand. He brought down upon himself the enmity of many, both for his plain speaking and his fancied invasion of the sacred liberties of university life; but he succeeded in bringing about a great improvement and won the lasting gratitude and confidence of the better citizens. Before long he was the most powerful influence for righteousness in town and university, as he continued to be to the end of his life.

But he did not confine himself to conditions in Wittenberg. In the spring of 1515 he was appointed to preach at the triennial convention of his order, meeting in Gotha, and instead of choosing some theological or philosophical theme appropriate to the occasion, which might give him opportunity to display his ability and learning, as most young men would have done, he preached a simple but effective sermon on the vice of slander, sadly prevalent in monasticism, as he knew from his own experience. His wealth of imagery, his command of epigram, and his power of invective, appear very strikingly in this discourse, as also his penchant for homely and coarse figures, but the most notable thing about it is the practical interest dictating both selection of subject and mode of treatment, and his fearlessness in handling the conditions attacked. The sermon attracted wide attention and gained the favorable notice of one of the leading humanists of the day, the celebrated Rufus Mutianus of Gotha. It evidently made a strong impression also on many of the assembled monks, for it was at this convention Luther was appointed district-vicar.

It was characteristic of his type of mind that he was not only alive to the shortcomings of his own class, but was glad to have them exposed by anybody. Erasmus's frequent attacks upon the vices and follies of monks and priests struck a responsive chord in his heart, and were read with no little pleasure. He was not of those who see only good in the party to which they belong, and defend it against all comers. On the contrary, he welcomed the freest criticism both from within and from without as salutary and helpful, and did not hesitate to publish to the whole world his own strictures upon conditions prevailing within the circles he knew best. Such a man was bound to find fresh food for criticism with every passing year, and was sure ultimately to become a thorn in the side of all thick-and-thin supporters of the existing order.

Meanwhile his thought was beginning to dwell upon the condition of the church at large and upon evils everywhere all too common. In an interesting letter written in reply to an inquiry from Spalatin as to his opinion of the merits of the famous Reuchlin controversy, which had been started by the Dominicans of Cologne, the great heresy-hunters of the day, he wrote:

My brother John Lang has asked in your name what I think of the cause of the innocent and most learned John Reuchlin against his Cologne rivals, and whether he is guilty of heresy. You know I have a great esteem and affection for the man, and my judgment is liable to suspicion because, as we say, I am not free and neutral. Nevertheless, as you ask me, I will say what I think, that there is nothing dangerous in what he has written. I wonder greatly at his opponents, because they involve so plain an affair in difficulties worse than a Gordian knot, when he protests solemnly and repeatedly that he is not setting up articles of faith, but simply expressing his judgment. These two things absolve him in my opinion so completely from suspicion that even if he had made a collection of all heresies in his report, I should hold him sound and pure in the faith. For if such expressions of opinion are not free from danger, it is to be feared these inquisitors will begin to swallow camels and strain out gnats, and will pronounce the orthodox heretics, whatever they say. What is it they are doing but trying to cast out Beelzebub without the finger of God? It is this I often mourn and lament, that we Christians are wise abroad and foolish at home. There are a hundred worse evils in all the streets of Jerusalem, and every place is full of spiritual idols. These intestine foes ought to be opposed with all our might, but we leave them alone and concern ourselves with foreign matters. It is certainly the devil who persuades us to neglect our own affairs for others which we cannot mend. I protest, is it possible to think of anything more foolish? Are there not enough terrible evils on which these unhappy men of Cologne may exercise their wisdom, zeal, and charity, that they find it necessary to start an inquiry about matters so remote?

The letter is instructive both for its outspoken defense of the famous humanist and Hebraist at a time when many liberals, for fear of consequences, hesitated to express an opinion, and also for the concern it shows for the moral and religious condition of Christendom. In 1515 there appeared the first instalment of the famous "Letters of Obscure Men," one of the cleverest and most amusing satires of the age. They were published anonymously, but the principal author is now known to have been an Erfurt humanist and former student friend of Luther's, Crotus Rubianus. They exposed the ignorance and obscurantism of Reuchlin's enemies in most merciless and telling fashion and brought upon them wide-spread contempt. While Luther deprecated the flippant tone of the work, he sympathized with the author's purpose, for he felt as impatient as any liberal with the reactionary attitude of Reuchlin's scholastic opponents and was as eager to see them overthrown.

His lectures on the Epistle to the Romans, delivered in 1515–1516 and only recently recovered, abound in dark pictures of the state of the church at large. Priests and laymen, higher and lower ecclesiastics, secular and monastic clergy, the extortions of the Roman curia and the morals of the capital of Christendom, all come in for severe denunciation in phraseology typically vigorous and paradoxical.

In 1516, learning that the elector was thinking of

having Staupitz made a bishop, he wrote Spalatin urging him to use his influence against the plan, on the ground that the vicar-general was much too good for the position:

Those happy times are gone by when it was a fortunate thing to be a bishop. Now there is no more miserable place, with its reveling and carousing after the manner of Sodom and Rome. You see this well enough when you compare the life and work of the old bishops with those of our day. The best of them are immersed in public wars, while their homes have become a very hell of insatiable greed.

The language is characteristically exaggerated, though it could be matched over and over again in the writings of the day. Such a judgment of contemporary prelates was altogether too sweeping and severe; but, like his lectures on the Epistle to the Romans, it shows the awakening spirit of the reformer, and contrasts most strikingly with the simple and devout faith of the Roman pilgrim. The traveling he was doing as district-vicar, and the responsibility the position laid upon him for the spiritual welfare of others, were opening his eyes as the Italian journey had not done, and he was becoming aware of evils to which he had hitherto been quite blind.

The same year he preached in the Wittenberg church a series of sermons on the Decalogue, taking occasion to attack in no uncertain terms many prevalent superstitions. Astrology, witchcraft, saint-worship, religious pilgrimages, and the popular beliefs current in every age concerning lucky and unlucky days, omens, signs, and charms, were considered in great detail and with an extraordinary wealth of illustration, furnishing us much interesting information about the popular beliefs of the time. Astrology he makes merry sport over, his lack of faith in it contrasting favorably with the credulity of many of the leading men of his day. "My dear Astrology," he calls it, "which would gladly be an art if its inborn folly did not prevent it." The existence of witches he could not doubt,—nobody did then,—and he was in favor of punishing them without mercy and even burning them at the stake; but he spoke disapprovingly of the excesses to which the belief in witchcraft was carried, and tried to distinguish between genuine and spurious manifestations.

His attitude toward saint-worship is especially instructive. He did not condemn the practice,—he was a loyal son of the church and recognized its legitimacy and value,—but he complained that it had degenerated into a mere selfish scramble after temporal goods, while the true adoration of the saints, consisting in imitating their perfections and praising God for His gifts to them, was almost wholly forgotten. "We honor them," he exclaimed, "and call upon them only when we have a pain in our legs or our head, or when our pockets are empty." One saint, he went on to say, was invoked for protection against fire, another against pestilence, another against thunder-storms, another against this or that illness—blindness, toothache, and the like. Each trade and occupation had its patron saint, and in looking to them for wealth or fortune all thought of higher things had been abandoned.

He was obliged to recognize that the church approved the practice of appealing to the saints for help in bodily distresses and temporal need, but she preserved the proper order, he declared, for she prayed first for grace and forgiveness of sins, and what he condemned was not the desire for earthly goods, but the putting them before everything else. The common abuse had gone so far, he believed, that it would be better if the festivals of the saints were altogether abandoned and their very names forgotten.

The custom of making religious pilgrimages he also criticized sharply. Its rapid growth during recent years, one of the characteristic phenomena of the age, he attributed to the devil. It had resulted, he complained, in the wide-spread neglect of household duties and of the ordinary means of grace, and had brought demoralization into many homes and communities. "If you have a wife or servants," he remarked, "who claim they are driven by the Spirit to go upon a pilgrimage, hear my advice: take a good oaken cross and sanctify them with a few lusty strokes on the back, and you will see how the devil is exorcised by this finger of God." To be sure, he did not wish to oppose a time-honored practice approved by the church. "Let any one go on a pilgrimage who feels compelled to, but let him learn that God can be served at home a thousand times better by giving the money the journey would cost to the poor, or to wife and children, and bearing one's cross with patience."

Luther was not the first to attack these and similar practices. Within a few years many voices had been raised in like criticism or condemnation, and some of the things he said were only reflections of their writings. But his utterances were none the less significant of his own development. He was not simply imitating others—this he never did. He was being taught by his own experience and observation, as well as by his reading, and that he was coming to conclusions already reached by others meant all the more for his future influence.

For the abuses and excesses he was denouncing he held the clergy responsible. He had begun by criticizing his fellow-monks. Under the influence of a growing recognition of the evils of the world outside the monasteries he soon went on to condemn the clergy at large. Because they had not done their duty in preaching the true Gospel of Christ superstition had spread widely, and true faith in God and dependence upon Him were all too little known. Evidently while the reforming spirit was growing in him he was gaining increasing clearness as to the remedy needed, and the restraint imposed by his inborn respect for existing authorities was proving less and less of a hindrance.

Though he was not yet as widely known in the learned world as Carlstadt and some other colleagues, his official position as district-vicar of the Augustinian order, and his local fame as the most popular professor in the university, gave his opinions considerable weight, and many were listening with interest to what he had to say. In Wittenberg itself his standing was so high he could say and do what he pleased without forfeiting the respect and affection of town and university; but there were some even there who thought him too censorious, and others who shook their heads over his utterances and feared he was becoming heretical, while in places less devoted to him he was beginning to be looked upon with suspicion and dislike as a dangerous radical.

At the same time, in all he was doing he was in no way transgressing the limits of orthodoxy or putting himself out of harmony with the church. He was only attacking practical abuses, as any earnest preacher might have done, and as many were doing. Anything like heresy or schism he was still wholly opposed to. It seemed to him as to most others to argue only pride and self-confidence. The following passage from a sermon preached in the summer of 1516 throws an interesting light upon his attitude at the time and reveals his loyal devotion to the pope:

Unless Christ had given all his power to a man there would have been no perfect church, because no order, since whoever wished could say he was ordained by the Holy Spirit. Thus the heretics did, each one setting up his own principle, until there were as many churches as persons. Christ wishes to exercise no power except through the man to whom he has committed it, that he may gather all into one. This power he has so strengthened as to excite against it all the forces of earth and hell; as he says, "The gates of hell shall not prevail against it," by which he means, they will fight and be stirred up but will not conquer, that it may be known the power is of God and not of man. They therefore who renounce this unity and order have no reason to pride themselves on great illuminations and wonderful works as do our Picards and other schismatics. For obedience is better than the sacrifices of fools who know not what evil they do.

There is no sign that he was passing in these days through a mental struggle or consciously breaking with his past. He was developing steadily and naturally, assuming each task as it was laid upon him and addressing himself to one evil after another as he became aware of them. It was a happy, busy time, and he was growing daily in power and in the consciousness of power. He had immured himself in a convent, expecting to spend his whole life apart from the world, but he had become instead a public figure who was counting for something far beyond his cloister and the boundaries of his order, while day by day his interests were multiplying and his horizon was widening.

CHAPTER VI

THE ATTACK ON INDULGENCES

THE pious Elector Frederick the Wise was an indefatigable relic-hunter, and his castle church of All Saints contained more than five thousand sacred objects gathered from all parts of Christendom. There still exists a catalogue of them, illustrated with drawings by the famous Wittenberg painter Lucas Cranach. A gruesome collection it was, for the most part,—a lock of St. Elizabeth's hair, a portion of St. Euphemia's head, two fingers and a hand of the Holy Innocents, a tooth of St. Beatrice, a piece of St. Juliana's leg, and the like,—but it had cost a large amount of time and money, and Frederick was as proud of it as any modern art-collector of his pictures and statuary. The church was a favorite place of pilgrimage, for large indulgence was to be gained from the sight of its holy treasures and from contributions to its support. On October 13, 1516, the eve of the anniversary of its dedication, Luther preached from its pulpit on the subject of indulgences, attacking their abuse in sharp terms, to the great annoyance of the elector. It was a characteristic thing to do. To criticize indulgences, even in the most guarded fashion, in the castle church, on the day of all days when its stores of grace were dispensed in largest measure, was an act whose boldness was equaled only by its tactlessness. It is not strange the elector was offended. The only cause of wonder

76

is that he seems not to have laid it up against the preacher, for we hear of his annoyance only through a casual remark of Luther's made long afterward, and we find the critic preaching again upon the same subject from the same pulpit on another festival in February, 1517.

He had already referred to the matter in connection with his strictures upon pilgrimages, complaining, with the exaggeration all too characteristic of him: "When it is evening the pilgrims to this or that shrine, or to the celebration of this or that saint's day, return home with full indulgence; that is, full of beer and wine, full of unchastity, and other horrid vices." Even now he did not question the legitimacy of indulgences, but he attacked the abuses to which they almost inevitably led on the part of the ecclesiastical authorities as well as of the people. Thus he said:

Concerning indulgences, although they are the very merits of Christ and his saints, and are therefore by all means to be received with reverence, they are nevertheless made the most shameful agents of avarice. For who seeks through them the salvation of souls and not rather the contents of the purse? . . . Indulgences promote a servile righteousness, for they do nothing but teach the people to fear, to flee, to shudder at the punishment of sin instead of the sin itself, when they ought rather to be exhorted to love punishment and to embrace the cross. Would that I lied when I say indulgences are rightly named, because to indulge is to permit, and indulgence is impunity and permission to sin, and license to avoid the cross of Christ.

Liable to such abuses as they were, in that age they served too important a purpose to be lightly dispensed with, for upon them religion depended in no small measure for support. Without them the erection of many a church, monastery, and hospital would have been impossible, and the permanent endowments of such institutions often consisted of the indulgence they were privileged to grant the pilgrims to their shrines or the contributors to their support.

Severely as the doctrine has been denounced by Protestant theologians, it was in reality only the recognition of one of the commonest of human instincts— the attempt to make amends for questionable conduct by religious practices. This is not confined to any one communion, but in the Catholic Church it is most encouraged. One of the striking things about Catholicism, it may be remarked in passing, and one of the secrets of its age-long hold upon a large portion of the race, is its extraordinary humanness, the way it recognizes and makes a place for common human impulses, putting even the least worthy of them to some use. Inevitably pernicious results will sometimes follow, and follow they did in the wake of the indulgence traffic as carried on in the later Middle Ages.

That traffic was based ultimately upon the Catholic penitential system which is as old as the second century. According to ancient and modern Catholic belief forgiveness for sins committed after baptism can be secured only through the sacrament of penance. This requires repentance, confession to a priest, and the performance of acts involving some labor or sacrifice on the part of the penitent, such as fasting, almsgiving, or going upon a pilgrimage. The absolution pronounced by the priest in the confessional insures release from guilt and eternal punishment, but satisfaction must still be rendered in the form of works of penance. If not enough of these are done before death they must be continued in purgatory until the debt is fully discharged. Only then is the penitent believer prepared to enter heaven. In the early Middle Ages the custom grew up of permitting the substitution of some other form of penance for that regularly prescribed by the church. This permission constituted what later came to be called an indulgence. Large use was made of it in connection with the crusades, when in order to encourage enlistment in the crusading armies pope after pope assured the soldiers of the cross that their service would be accepted in full discharge of the penance otherwise required of them. This was later extended to those who equipped and sent substitutes in their place, or in other ways contributed to the support of the crusading forces.

After the crusades had ceased, granting indulgences in return for the payment of money was continued and the funds raised were employed to promote all sorts of sacred ends. In the thirteenth century a doctrinal basis for the practice was found by one of the great schoolmen. The church, he taught, was in possession of a treasury of merits composed of the good deeds of Christ and His saints, upon which the pope could draw for the advantage of penitents meeting any conditions he might fix. Later the benefit of indulgences was extended to souls in purgatory, and the privilege of securing their release from its pains was granted to their surviving friends and relatives upon the payment of a certain sum.

Theoretically indulgences affected only the temporal satisfaction required of the penitent either here or in purgatory, but this was not always kept clearly in mind, and often they were supposed to release the purchaser from all the consequences of his misdeeds, a popular misconception sometimes connived at by the authorities.

The whole indulgence traffic, particularly as it existed in the fifteenth and sixteenth centuries, was harmful in the extreme. There was the constant temptation, on the one hand, to employ it to raise funds for selfish ends, and, on the other hand, to substitute the mere payment of money for true penitence and amendment of life. Both temptations were frequently yielded to, and the result was wide-spread and growing demoralization.

Looking back upon that period, Catholics of to-day are as severe as Protestants in their condemnation of the situation, and while indulgences are still given under certain conditions, granting them for money was long ago prohibited, and has since been unknown in the Catholic Church.

It was the money abuse that chiefly aroused the indignation of Luther and many other good Catholics; for he was by no means the only one in his own or earlier days to criticize indulgences. Among others, his own superior, Staupitz, had spoken very sharply about them, a fact to which Luther later appealed in support of his own conduct. But all these criticisms left unmolested the penitential system out of which indulgences had grown. That system was rooted in the very heart of traditional Catholicism; to attack it was to put oneself outside the pale of the historic faith. This was the last thing Luther thought of doing. As yet he was playing only upon the surface, all unaware of the volcanic depths beneath.

Meanwhile, in order to raise funds for the rebuilding of St. Peter's Church at Rome, Pope Leo X, following the example of his predecessor, Julius II, proclaimed a so-called "plenary indulgence," phrased in very sweeping terms and offering to believing purchasers all sorts of benefits, including remission of

From a carbon print by Braun & Co. of the painting in the Pitti Palace, Florence

POPE LEO X, BY RAPHAEL

sins, freedom from the necessity of penance, and the release of their deceased friends from purgatory.

The young Archbishop and Elector of Mayence, Albert of Brandenburg, a Hohenzollern prince, being in need of a large amount of money to pay Rome for the privilege of assuming the archbishopric, when he already held two other sees, made an arrangement with the pope whereby he was to superintend the traffic in a part of Germany, receiving half the proceeds in reward for his services. He engaged for his chief agent a Dominican prior, John Tetzel by name, a man of learning and reputation and a preacher of great popular power, who had already abundantly proved his ability to raise money for sacred ends. Such a passage as the following from one of his sermons shows how he appealed to the emotions of his audience:

Do you not hear your dead parents crying out "Have mercy upon us? We are in sore pain and you can set us free for a mere pittance. We have borne you, we have trained and educated you, we have left you all our property, and you are so hard-hearted and cruel, that you leave us to roast in the flames when you could so easily release us."

Tetzel took general charge of affairs and appointed many other preachers to aid him in the work. Elaborate arrangements were made for the campaign, and everything possible was done to attract and impress the people. According to an eye-witness, when the agent appeared in a town he was met by priests, monks, city councilors, teachers, scholars, men, women, maidens, and children, who escorted him in procession with banners, candles, and singing, the papal bull being carried in state upon a velvet or golden cushion, and a red cross being set up in the church, with the pope's arms

6

above it. "In short, God Himself could not have been more magnanimously received."

The parish clergy were directed to prepare their flocks for the approaching visit of Tetzel or his assistants, and they were carefully instructed both how to preach and how to deal with their parishioners in the confessional, that eagerness for the grace of Christ dispensed through the indulgences might be enhanced. We are inevitably reminded of the way modern revivalists have often planned their campaigns and had the ground made ready in advance. Indeed, the effects aimed at by Tetzel, and the methods employed to produce them, were not unlike those seen in great revival seasons to-day. To arouse the conscience and deepen the conviction of sin, and then to lead the awakened and anxious soul to look for help to a supernatural power—this was what he undertook to do, and he knew well how to do it.

It is true, the comparison between the indulgence traffic and the modern revival should not be carried too far, for the former was poisoned by the greed for gain almost inevitably attaching to it. But it must not be forgotten that, despite the evils shared with many such religious campaigns, and the greater evils peculiar to itself, it was still approved, as it had been for centuries, by multitudes of pious and God-fearing men.

In Luther's day, however, disapproval of it was steadily growing. As frequently happens, particularly in periods of social upheaval, when the public conscience is apt to be peculiarly sensitive, the excessive abuse of a time-honored practice, whose legitimacy had hitherto been taken for granted, was leading men to question the practice itself, and many complaints of the harm it was doing both religiously and morally were heard even from devout churchmen and prominent ecclesiastics.

On economic grounds, too, hostility was spreading. The traffic, it was felt, was taking large sums of money from the pockets of the people without giving them any tangible returns. As a rule, every new papal indulgence was hailed with gratitude by the masses, and the pope only met the popular wish in proclaiming them; but this was the fifth witnessed by that generation, and many were beginning to realize that the thing had been overdone, and were growing heartily tired of it. There were still those glad enough to buy, especially women and children; but most heads of families were waxing impatient at having their hard-earned savings frequently drawn upon, and particularly hated to see their money, as in the present case, go to swell the coffers of the Fuggers, the great money-lenders of the day, who had advanced a large sum to the archbishop, and to whose reimbursement his share of the proceeds, as everybody knew, was to be devoted. It is noticeable that Tetzel had frequently to complain of bad coins given for the letters of pardon, with the evident intention of satisfying importunate wives and neighbors without incurring unnecessary expense.

The Elector of Saxony, unwilling to have his subjects pay the debts of the Elector of Mayence, and desiring to protect his own ecclesiastical foundations, refused to allow Albert's agents to enter his dominions; but in the spring of 1517, Tetzel appeared at Jüterbog, a small town lying just across the border, twenty miles northeast of Wittenberg. Many of Luther's flock found their way thither, and returned with letters of indulgence and with very exaggerated and demoralizing notions as to their efficacy. When he refused to accept them in the confessional in lieu of repentance and penance, he was complained of to Tetzel and threatened with prosecution for heresy and

contumacy. Writing about the matter to Staupitz a
few months later, he said:

I remember, Reverend Father, having learned from
you, as by a voice from heaven, that penance is not genuine unless it spring from a love of righteousness and
God. Just when my heart was full of this thought,
behold, new indulgences began to be proclaimed through
the country in the most noisy fashion, while no effort
was made to incite the soul to war against sin. The
preachers neglected altogether the need of true penance,
and emphasized in ways never before heard not so much
as its least valuable part, which is known as satisfaction,
but the complete remission even of that. Finally, they
taught impious and false and heretical doctrines in so
authoritative, not to say foolhardy, a manner, that if
any one even whispered a contrary opinion, he was immediately denounced as a heretic, condemned to the
flames, and declared worthy of eternal damnation.

Many years afterward, in one of his typical polemic
works, he gave the following account of the affair:

It happened in the year 1517 that a Dominican monk,
John Tetzel by name, a great ranter, went up and down
selling grace for gold as dear or as cheap as he could.
The Elector Frederick had once saved his life in Inns-
bruck, for he had been condemned by the emperor Maximilian to be drowned in the river Inn, for his virtue's
sake, you may well believe. This the man confessed
frankly, being reminded of it by the elector long afterward when he began to slander us Wittenbergers.
I was at the time a preacher in the cloister and a young
doctor fresh from the forge, ardent and merry in the
holy Scriptures. When many people from Wittenberg
ran after indulgences to Jüterbog and Zerbst, and I, so
truly as my Christ has redeemed me, did not know what
indulgences were,—as, for that matter, nobody did,—I

From the painting by Lucas Cranach, in St. Petersburg

ALBERT, PRINCE OF BRANDENBURG, ELECTOR AND ARCHBISHOP OF MAYENCE

began to preach gently that it was certain there were better things to do than buy indulgences. I had already preached against them to the same effect here in the castle, and incurred the Elector Frederick's ill will, for he was very fond of his castle church. But to come to the true cause of the Lutheran uproar, I let the matter go on as it would until news reached me of the shocking and horrible things Tetzel was preaching—as, for instance, that he had received such grace and power from the pope that he could even forgive a person who had violated the Mother of God, if the proper amount were put in the box; that the red cross of indulgence, with the pope's arms, when set up in church, was as powerful as the cross of Christ; that in heaven he would not change places with St. Peter himself, for he had saved more souls with indulgences than the apostle with his preaching; that there was no need of sorrow or repentance or confession of sins, if indulgences were bought. He sold indulgences also for future sins, and all was done in the most shameful fashion, for money's sake alone.

Where Luther got the grotesque tale about Tetzel related at the beginning of this passage we do not know. At any rate it may be dismissed as quite devoid of truth. Tetzel seems to have been a man without particularly high ideals or sensitive conscience, but there is no adequate ground for the accusations of dishonesty and immorality so frequently brought against him. He gained an unenviable notoriety from the controversy precipitated by Luther, and all sorts of slanderous stories were naturally told about him.

That he preached the many abominable things currently reported and repeated here in part by Luther may also be denied. We still have some of his sermons and other writings and they furnish no justification for such charges. At the same time, though the specific counts in Luther's indictment are without support,

the impression made upon the common people by
Tetzel and his agents was quite bad enough. The benefits of indulgences were magnified beyond all warrant,
and in the effort to attract purchasers, assurances were
given which could not fail to work mischief and promote moral callousness and indifference.

That Luther should feel profoundly outraged by
the whole sorry business was inevitable. He was,
above everything, downright and sincere, instinctively
hostile to all duplicity and pretense, while the indulgence traffic, as appeared more clearly than ever in
Tetzel's campaign, was through and through a sham;
on the one side, greed for gain consciously masquerading under the form of regard for the people's good;
on the other, the insidious and subtle self-deception
of imagining that anything but reality counts in the
moral realm—the effort to salve one's conscience by
hollow acts of devotion and to escape by the payment
of money the inevitable consequences of one's deeds.
Clear-eyed and intolerant of all sophistry, Luther
hated it with a growing hatred; and the pretended
piety of the whole transaction incensed him only the
more.

Religion was the most sacred of all affairs to him.
For its sake he had long ago broken with his father
and abandoned a career of great worldly promise, and
in his religious life he had passed through the most
agonizing and exalted experiences possible to a human
soul. To make it a matter of buying and selling, to
offer divine grace for gold, and to attempt to purchase
the forgiveness and favor of God—all this was to
befoul the holiest of all relationships; and, like the
prophets of old, his pious soul waxed hot within him.

It would seem, in view of it all, that he must at
once attack Tetzel with his wonted energy and disre-

gard of consequences; but strangely enough, he held his peace. Quick as he had hitherto been to denounce any evil confronting him, now, in the face of the worst and most crying abuse yet encountered, he took careful counsel with himself. Tetzel soon left the neighborhood and passed on to other places, but Luther continued to deliberate in silence. For more than six months, though plied with questions from far and near as to his opinion of the traffic, he made no sign, but set himself to study quietly the whole subject of indulgences. The present campaign, he saw clearly enough, was far more demoralizing than anything he had preached against in the castle church; but it was carried on under the auspices of the primate of Germany and of the pope himself, and it would not do to attack it recklessly and indiscriminately. He must discover, if he could, the right and wrong of the whole matter.

His character and training made the situation peculiarly difficult. Had he been a humanist, he would have laughed the whole thing to scorn as an exploded superstition beneath the contempt of an intelligent man; had he been a scholastic theologian, he would have sat in his study and drawn fine distinctions to justify the traffic without bothering himself about its influence upon the lives of the vulgar populace. But he was neither humanist nor schoolman. He had a conscience which made indifference impossible, and a simplicity and directness of vision which compelled him to brush aside all equivocation and go straight to the heart of things. With it all he was at once a devout and believing son of the church, and a practical preacher profoundly concerned for the spiritual and moral welfare of the common people.

Here was a case where the ecclesiastical authorities

he had always reverenced were sanctioning a practice the demoralizing consequences of which were becoming ever clearer to him. He could not wash his hands of the matter, and yet he could not grapple with it without involving the highest dignitaries of the church he loved and honored. He must have suffered agonies during that critical summer of 1517, striving to reconcile positions essentially irreconcilable, struggling to keep his faith and yet be true to his conscience which threatened it with shipwreck, torn by a conflict of loyalties whose inconsistency he was just beginning to realize. His distress can hardly have been less severe than in his convent days at Erfurt. But there was only one possible outcome for a man who had fought himself through the earlier crisis as he had done, and had since been standing for what he deemed right, maugre neighbors, students, colleagues, princes, and prelates. Wait as he might, he must ultimately enter upon the conflict, whatever the consequences to himself or others.

But even when his mind was made up and the die cast, he proceeded in a way that seems at first sight as strange as his long delay. Instead of thundering against Tetzel from the pulpit or publishing a polemic pamphlet such as no one but he could write, or issuing an open letter to the archbishop calling him sharply to account, as he was quite capable of doing, he invited the theologians of Wittenberg and the neighborhood to a disputation. It was a common custom to celebrate important anniversaries of the castle church by theological debates, and on October 31, just a year after he had first preached upon indulgences from its pulpit, adopting the usual method of announcing such a debate, he posted a placard on the church door giving notice of the proposed disputation, and stating the theses he intended to defend. There were ninety-five of them, written in Latin in his own hand, and they were preceded by this announcement:

In the desire, and with the purpose, of elucidating the truth, a disputation will be held on the subjoined propositions at Wittenberg, under the presidency of the Reverend Father Martin Luther, Augustinian monk, master of arts and of sacred theology, and ordinary lecturer upon the same in that place. He therefore asks those who cannot be present and discuss the subject orally to do so by letter in their absence.

The theses themselves reveal at once the professor and the preacher. The Latin language and the method of argumentation proclaim the professor, but the vivid, direct, and often picturesque style betrays the preacher. He might elect to throw his criticisms into scholastic form, but he felt it to be no scholastic question he was discussing, and the earnestness of a practical appeal crept into the document in spite of him.

That he chose to bring the indulgence traffic to public debate does not mean that he was afraid to speak his mind categorically or was still in doubt about the right or wrong of the matter. On the contrary, he was quite clear upon all but a few minor and unimportant details. He desired a debate simply because he wished to give the demand for reform, already fully determined upon, the support of a formal university decision. Reinforcement, rather than enlightenment, was what he sought.

The subject of indulgences was very difficult and complicated. Upon many of the matters connected with it the church had never pronounced itself officially, and the opinions of theologians were greatly divided. Had he been troubled only by the flagrant abuses of venders and buyers, a debate would have been superfluous; but he had become convinced that both the practice and the principles underlying it were wrong, and the evils could not be mended without laying the ax at the root of the tree. Upon such a question theologians alone were regarded as competent to express an opinion, and hence he appealed to them. He declared himself willing to yield completely if his theses should meet with defeat, but he was confident of his ground and sure they must prevail. He was therefore in earnest in his wish for a debate, and resolved to use as a weapon of reform the victory he was convinced would follow.

The theses themselves are abundant proof of this. There is no sign of doubt or uncertainty, no beating about the bush, no confusion of the main issue by irrelevant questions, but a direct assault both upon the theory and practice of indulgences. If hitherto he had criticized only their abuse, now he attacked indulgences themselves in the most outspoken fashion. He complained that they were nets wherewith to catch money, and hindered the proclamation of the true gospel. Christians should be taught, he went on to say, that he who neglects any one in need in order to save money for their purchase brings down upon himself the anger of God; and unless he has superfluous wealth, is bound to keep what he has for the use of his own household instead of lavishing it upon pardons. Moreover, he so minimized their effects and limited their scope as virtually to deprive them of all value.

The final blow was struck in the thirty-sixth and thirty-seventh theses, in the sweeping assertions: "Every Christian who feels true compunction has of right plenary remission of punishment and guilt without letters of indulgence"; and "Every true Christian, whether living or dead, has a share in all the benefits of Christ and the church, given him by God, even without such letters." Certainly where this was believed, little hope could remain of finding a market for the spiritual wares Tetzel had to offer.

But the theses were not simply an attack upon indulgences. They went much further and cut much deeper, for they repudiated the principles upon which the whole practice rested. In the very first thesis it is declared, "Christ wished the entire life of believers to be repentance." And the conclusion is drawn that the outward acts of penance, everywhere regarded as satisfactions for sin, were only the natural expression of inner penitence, suggesting that the divine forgiveness is not conditioned in any way upon satisfaction, but upon repentance alone. This meant the implicit rejection not only of indulgences, but of the whole penitential system accepted in the Catholic Church both east and west since the second century. The matter was not carried further in the theses, but it is clear enough where Luther stood and how far he had traveled from the Catholicism he had been born and bred in.

He did not realize the irreconcilable difference between himself and the church, nor did he appreciate his complete lack of harmony with the pope, though he may have suspected it, for he was no longer a mere naïve and inexperienced young monk. But, however that may be, he expressed the conviction, "If pardons were preached according to the spirit and mind of the pope, all the questions raised about them would be resolved with ease, nay, would not exist"; and though he had emptied them of all value, he yet declared, "Bishops and curates are bound to receive the commissaries of apostolic indulgences with all reverence," and, "He who speaks against their truth, let him be anathema." He felt himself driven to oppose those who preached "their own dreams in place of the pope's commission," and to exert himself "against the wantonness and license of the preachers," but in this he believed he was only showing himself loyal both to church and pope. His divided attitude was entirely natural, and simply shows how sincere he was and how seriously he took the situation.

He sent a copy of his theses to the Archbishop of Mayence with a letter of explanation, in which he said:

Pardon me, most reverend Father in Christ, most illustrious Prince, that I, the dregs of humanity, have the temerity to address a letter to your Sublimity. The Lord Jesus is my witness that, conscious of my insignificance and wickedness, I have long put off what I now do with a bold face, moved by a sense of the duty I owe you, most reverend Father in Christ. May your Highness deign to look upon one who is but dust, and understand my wish for your pontifical forbearance. In your most illustrious name there are carried about papal indulgences for the building of St. Peter's. I do not so much complain of the utterances of the preachers, which I have not heard, as of the false opinions everywhere entertained by the common people; for the poor creatures believe that if they buy indulgences, they are sure of salvation, that souls fly out of purgatory as soon as they throw their money into the box, and that the grace is so great that there is no sin which cannot be absolved thereby. . . .

In addition, most reverend Father in the Lord, in the instructions for the use of the agents published in your name it is said, doubtless without your Reverence's knowledge and consent, that one of the principal benefits to be had from indulgences is the inestimable gift of God whereby man is reconciled to Him and all the punishments of purgatory blotted out, and that to those who buy pardons contrition is unnecessary. What can I do,

PRESENT APPEARANCE OF THE CASTLE CHURCH
IN WITTENBERG

most excellent Patron and most illustrious Prince, but pray your Reverence, through the Lord Jesus Christ, to look into the matter and do away wholly with those instructions and command the preachers to adopt another style of discourse, lest perchance some one may finally arise and refute them in print, to the confusion of your most illustrious Highness. This I should greatly deplore; but I fear it may be done unless matters be speedily mended.

The mingled respect and menace of this extraordinary letter are very interesting. Evidently Luther realized that he had to deal not merely with Tetzel and his agents but with the Primate of Germany himself. His views on penance and indulgences, he doubtless knew well enough, were out of harmony with those prevailing in high quarters, but he apparently still hoped, even if not very confidently, that his attack might not mean a break with the rulers of the church, that rather than have the whole subject of indulgences thrown open to public debate they would be glad to disavow responsibility and lay the blame for all the abuses upon their subordinates. At any rate, he left this way of escape open to the Archbishop, and assumed as long as he could his own essential harmony with the constituted authorities in his struggle for reform. Whatever their attitude might ultimately prove to be, he was at least sure he held the true Christian faith and was a loyal son of the church. Commenting upon the theses shortly afterward, he declared: "Although friends have been saying for some time that I am a heretic and blasphemer because I do not interpret the teaching of church and Scriptures in a Catholic sense, nevertheless, relying upon my own conscience, I believe they are mistaken and I truly love the church of Christ and desire to honor it."

He had been for some time engaged in opposing the schoolmen. In the theory of indulgences and even in the penitential system itself—though, as a matter of fact, the latter was much older than they—he saw only another evidence of their nefarious influence; and it is not surprising that he could think himself an orthodox Catholic even while taking the radical positions he did. His own bishop, Scultetus of Brandenburg, to whom he sent a copy of the theses, declared he found nothing heterodox in them. To be sure, he was a man of humanistic leanings and more or less out of sympathy with scholasticism; but he was a strict disciplinarian, and would not for a moment have tolerated an attack upon church or pope.

Luther also sent the theses to his friend Lang, requesting him to communicate them to the Erfurt professors, as he had already done with his attack upon Aristotle. He wrote as follows:

Behold, I am sending you some more paradoxes, my most reverend Father in Christ. If your theologians are offended at them and say, as all are saying concerning me, that I express my judgment and condemn the opinions of others too rashly and proudly, I reply through you that I should be greatly pleased at their ripe and sober modesty if they really exhibited it in fact instead of simply finding fault with my levity and precipitancy. For it is easy, as I see, to censure this vice in me. . . . So far as my boldness or modesty is concerned I know for certain, that if I am modest the truth will not be made more worthy by my modesty, or if I am bold, more unworthy by my boldness. This alone I ask of you and your theologians, that without troubling themselves about my character, they express their opinion of my statements and conclusions, and, if they find any errors in them, tell me what they are. For who does not know that without pride, or at least the appearance of pride and the suspicion of contentiousness, nothing new can be done? However great your humility in attempting the unusual, you are always accused of pride by those who think otherwise. Why were Christ and all the martyrs put to death, and learned doctors visited with hatred, but because they were thought arrogant and contemptuous of ancient things, or proposed novel ways without taking the advice of those who were expert in the old? I do not wish them to expect me to be so humble—that is, so hypocritical—as to submit whatever I say to their advice and decision. What I do, I wish to do not by man's will or counsel, but by God's. If it be of God, who shall stop it? If it be not of God, who can forward it? Not my will, nor theirs, nor ours, but Thine be done, Holy Father who art in Heaven. Amen.

In this letter, written but a few days after the posting of the theses, he first signed himself, with a play upon his name such as the humanists loved to indulge in, Martinus Eleutherius (Martin the Free), for some time a favorite form of subscription in letters to intimate friends. It throws an interesting light upon his state of mind. He had been troubled and perplexed for many months; when finally a decision was reached and the decisive step taken, he felt a sense of exhilaration all the greater because of the preceding struggle. He had not rushed precipitately into the conflict; he had weighed the matter carefully and held back as long as he could; but once committed to the attack, the joy of battle was upon him, and there was no yielding until victory was won.

The reception accorded his theses was very diverse. Tetzel was naturally angered by them, and many others not financially interested in the traffic, as he was, were shocked and distressed. Most of Luther's own friends were greatly alarmed, and, even though sym-

pathizing with his attitude, felt he had gone altogether
too far. Referring to the matter long afterward, he
said:

God brought me forward wonderfully, and led me into
the game quite without my knowledge more than twenty
years ago. Things went very poorly at first. The day
after the festival of All Saints in the year 1517, when I
had ventured to oppose the grave and public error of indulgences, Dr. Jerome Schurf, while we were walking
together to Kemberg, took me sharply to task, exclaiming: "You would write against the pope? What do you
hope to accomplish by it? They will not suffer it." And
I replied, "What if they must suffer it?"

He had evidently expected the disapproval of his
friends, for he kept his own counsel and told nobody
of his intentions. "In the beginning of my career,"
he once remarked, "when I wrote against indulgences
and their abuse, I received from Heaven the gift of
depending upon myself instead of others." His colleagues, as is apt to be the case, found fault with him
because they feared he would bring the university into
disrepute and decrease the attendance, and his brother
monks were distressed at the scandal they foresaw he
was preparing for the Augustinian order. "When I
first attacked indulgences, and all the world opened
their eyes and thought I had attempted too much, my
prior and subprior, troubled by the cry of heresy, came
and begged me not to bring disgrace upon the order.
But when I replied, 'Dear fathers, if it be not begun
in God's name, it will soon come to naught, but if it
be, let Him look after it,' they had nothing more to
say."

On the other hand, in many circles the theses met
with warm approval. Duke George of Saxony, pos-

sessing, like his cousin Frederick, ecclesiastical foundations supported by indulgences, was greatly annoyed at the papal competition, and, though later one of Luther's bitterest enemies, expressed himself at the time as delighted with the theses. The Elector Frederick, while guarded in his utterances, as was his wont, was evidently pleased with the daring young monk and glad to have a check put upon Tetzel's traffic. The theses, it is true, were fitted to discredit indulgences altogether, and so interfere also with some of his own institutions; but he took no exception to Luther's action, and public opinion in some quarters even credited him with being himself the instigator of the attack, his willingness to see a neighboring elector, with whom he was not on the best of terms, inconvenienced being assumed as a matter of course. At any rate, though this assumption was unwarranted, he stood by his monk and professor even when the attack grew bitterest, and refused to deliver him over to his foes.

But most surprising to Luther himself, and historically of greater importance than anything else, was the tremendous chorus of approval that arose from the nation at large. To his great astonishment, the theses were at once translated into German and read by all classes of people in all parts of the country. In the polemic work quoted on page 84 he observed:

In fourteen days the theses ran through all Germany; for the whole world was complaining of indulgences, especially as preached by Tetzel. When all the bishops and doctors were silent and nobody ventured to bell the cat,—for the Dominican heresy-hunters had frightened every one with the threat of the stake, and Tetzel himself had persecuted certain priests who had criticized his shameless methods,—then I became famous, because at last some one had appeared who dared to take hold of the

7

business. But the glory of it was not agreeable to me, for I myself did not know what indulgences were, and the song threatened to become too high for my voice.

Writing in the spring of 1518 to Christopher Scheurl, who had sent him from Nuremberg a copy of the theses with a German translation, he said:

You wonder I did not send them to you, but it was not my plan or my wish to have them get into general circulation. I intended first to discuss them with a few in this neighborhood, that, if condemned by the judgment of others, they might be suppressed, or, if approved, might be published. But now, contrary to my expectation, they are being repeatedly translated, so that I repent having given birth to them. Not that I am averse to having the truth made known to the people, for there is nothing I desire more; but this is not the best way to instruct them. For there are certain points I am in doubt about, and I should have said some things in a very different way and with greater assurance, or should have omitted them altogether, if I had seen what was to happen.

He had no idea that the impatience and discontent of the people were as wide-spread as they proved to be. He had not looked to them, nor had he counted on their support. He had indeed the scholar's inbred contempt for the opinions of the uneducated. But their enthusiastic response to an appeal not meant for them, when those to whom it was addressed showed themselves indifferent or hostile, changed the whole situation. He gained a following, and the people gained a leader. Hitherto he had been monk, professor, preacher, district-vicar; now he sprang in a moment into national prominence. The hearts of men in all parts of the land turned toward him, and his heart turned toward them. For the religious principles underlying the theses they cared little, for the arguments sustaining them still less. They saw only that here was a man, muzzled by none of the prudential considerations closing the mouths of many in high places, who dared to speak his mind plainly and emphatically, and was able to speak it intelligently and with effect upon a great and growing evil deplored by multitudes. It is such a man the people love and such a man they trust.

He might regard his theses only as propositions for debate, but they were widely interpreted as a direct and uncompromising attack. And they were applauded not merely because of dislike for the indulgence traffic, but also because of discontent with the encroachments of the papacy in many lines and hostility to the overmastering influence of a foreign power in national affairs. Restlessness over the situation was becoming steadily more and more wide-spread. The promise for the future involved in Luther's stand appealed to the nation and aroused its enthusiasm. "Ho, ho, he is come who will do what is needed!" some one is reported to have cried when he read the theses, and his exclamation well voiced the feeling of multitudes as they looked with admiration on the daring monk and thrilled with sympathy for his act. Just what was to happen nobody knew; a break with papacy and church few anticipated; but that a man had appeared who could be counted on to grapple with existing evils and to lead the way toward a better state of things multitudes felt even if but dimly. From this time on Luther always had the people in mind, appealed to them, and regarded himself as their spokesman, while they listened eagerly to all he had to say and were quick to follow where he led.

It is the fashion nowadays to belittle the importance of his act in posting the theses,—the modern historian looks with suspicion upon all dramatic incidents,—but it made him a popular leader and for such a leader as he was yet to be Germany had long been waiting.

CHAPTER VII

THE GATHERING STORM

"I HOPED the pope would protect me, for I had so fortified my theses with proofs from the Bible and papal decretals that I was sure he would condemn Tetzel and bless me. But when I expected a benediction from Rome, there came thunder and lightning instead, and I was treated like the sheep who had roiled the wolf's water. Tetzel went scot-free, and I must submit to be devoured."

Thus Luther describes the treatment received from Rome, and the description is in no way overdrawn. At first the cultivated and liberal humanist who enjoyed the papacy under the name of Leo X thought the affair of no importance, and dismissed it as a mere monk's quarrel. Luther was told that he remarked sarcastically upon hearing of the theses: "A drunken German wrote them. When he is sober he will think differently." Whether the report is true or not, the words are entirely in keeping with what we know of Leo's character. After a time, however, it became clear that the theses were having their effect, and the sale of indulgences was rapidly falling off. From the beginning the campaign had not gone as well as had been hoped, and the sums obtained in Germany, usually the best market for such wares, fell far short of the wishes of archbishop and pope. Little as they might care about the right or wrong of Luther's criticism, they were

both deeply interested in the financial side of the traffic, and anything affecting it unfavorably, they agreed,
must be suppressed.   In a monarchy like the papacy,
constitutional safeguards availed little.   Theoretically
the question of indulgences was at least in part an open
one, and in the absence of conciliar decisions, wide
differences of opinion were legitimate; but whether
legitimate or not, any opinion was bound to be
frowned upon if it seriously curtailed the papal income.

The matter was first taken up by the Archbishop of
Mayence, who threatened the Wittenberg monk with
condemnation for heresy, evidently expecting he would
be frightened and immediately recant.   But Luther was
made of other stuff, and though such a response to his
theses was not what he had looked for, he was above
being terrified even by so august an ecclesiastic.   Seeing that his threat availed nothing, and apparently
loath to involve himself in a possible quarrel with
Staupitz and the Augustinian order, the easy-going
archbishop finally washed his hands of the whole matter and referred the case to Rome.   There the situation did not seem at first to call for ecclesiastical action,
and the pope contented himself with requesting the
general of the Augustinian order, resident in Rome,
to silence his troublesome monk.

Meanwhile Tetzel, who had the best opportunity of
observing the effects of the theses, felt it necessary to
take active measures to counteract them.   Early in
1518, the new university of Frankfort-on-the-Oder,
where the rivalry with Wittenberg was keen, conferred
upon him the degree of doctor of theology, and his
promotion was made the occasion for a great demonstration by the Dominicans, who assembled to do him
honor three hundred strong.   Tetzel employed the

From an old print

DR. PFEFFINGER

opportunity thus offered to publish a series of counter-theses, dealing with indulgences, and subsequently another dealing with the power of the pope. The second set out in clear and emphatic fashion the doctrine of papal infallibility, held by a party in the church ever since the later Middle Ages, but given dogmatic definition only at the Vatican Council of 1870. Christians should be taught, it is said, that "The authority of the pope is superior to that of the universal church and council, and his statutes must be humbly obeyed"; that "The pope cannot err in those things which are of faith and necessary to salvation"; and that "They who speak slightingly of the honor and authority of the pope are guilty of blasphemy." Nothing could well be more extreme than this. Where such a notion prevailed, of course the criticism of indulgences or of any other practice approved by the pope must be regarded as illegitimate, and Luther's protestations of devotion to the welfare of the church could avail him little.

While hostility was steadily growing in many quarters, the Wittenberg students showed their sympathy with their favorite professor by publicly burning Tetzel's theses on indulgences in the market-place. Writing to his friend Lang in March, 1518, Luther said:

The indulgence-sellers are thundering mightily against me from the pulpit, and as they have not bad enough names to call me by, they add threats, assuring the people that I shall most certainly be burned within a fortnight, or a month at most. They are also publishing counter-theses until I fear they may burst with the immensity of their wrath. If by chance you have heard about the burning of Tetzel's theses, I will give you the facts, that you may not be misled by exaggerated reports such as are wont to get abroad in a case like this. When the students learned that a man had come from Halle, sent by Tetzel, the author of the theses, being deeply disgusted as they are at the old sophistical studies and exceedingly devoted to the Holy Scriptures, perhaps also desiring to show their partiality to me, they immediately got hold of him and threatened him for daring to bring such a document here. Buying some copies and seizing others, they burned all he had, to the number of eight hundred, having previously announced that those who wished to attend the conflagration and funeral of Tetzel's theses should gather in the market-place at two o'clock. All this they did without the knowledge of the prince, senate, rector, or any of us. The grave injury done the man by our supporters displeases me as well as every one else. I am without blame, but I fear the whole affair will be laid at my door. It has caused much talk, especially among Tetzel's adherents, and no little righteous indignation. What will come of it I do not know, except that my position is made still more dangerous.

A little later he wrote his old teacher, Trutvetter of Erfurt:

I wonder you can believe I had anything to do with the burning of Tetzel's theses. Do you think that I, a monk and theologian, have so lost all common sense as to inflict such a grave injury on a man of his position in a place not belonging to me? But what can I do when everybody believes all sorts of things about me? Can I stop the mouths of all the world? Let anybody say, hear, and believe anything he pleases. I will do whatever the Lord gives me to do, and, God willing, never will I be afraid, or venture beyond what He commands.

Despite the storm gathering about his head, Luther went on as usual with his regular work, paying no attention to his enemies' attacks and interesting himself in university affairs as if nothing uncommon had happened. One of the extraordinary things about the man was the way he could detach himself from the conflict even when it had grown hottest, and could teach and preach and write as if all were serene. Often when in the thick of the fight he would produce a scriptural commentary or a devotional work such as might be expected to come only from the pen of one whose whole life was spent in quiet study or in the calm of religious meditation; and this even after he had developed into one of the most active, vigorous, and unresting combatants the world has ever seen.

During the months succeeding the posting of the theses, he said little in public about the matter on everybody's lips. In the spring he published a German tract on indulgences which annoyed the Roman authorities even more than the theses because addressed directly to the populace. At the request of his bishop, he promptly stopped its sale, and also withheld an elaborate commentary he had been preparing on the theses, preferring, as he said in dutiful monastic phrase, to obey rather than to work miracles, even if he could. The bishop saw, however, that the hope of putting an end to the agitation by keeping Luther quiet was vain, and soon withdrew his request and left the Wittenberg professor his freedom of action.

In May the triennial convention of the Augustinian order in Germany met at Heidelberg, and Luther went to report upon his administration as district-vicar and turn over his office to a successor. Friends advised him not to go for fear he would meet with trouble, and the elector only reluctantly gave him permission to make the journey, writing Staupitz: "Doctor Martin Luther having been summoned by you and other officials of the Augustinian order to a convention at Heidelberg is ready to obey and attend the meeting, though we do not willingly grant him leave to be absent from the university. As you once informed us you would make of the man a doctor of our own with whom we should yet be very much pleased, we do not like to have him long away from his lectures, and we hope you will see to it that he returns to us without delay."

Luther himself had no other thought than to attend, as his office required him to do, and he left Wittenberg the middle of April, traveling on foot by way of Coburg and Würzburg. Writing to Spalatin en route, he said:

I think you have heard from our Pfeffinger all we talked about when I met him in the village of Judenbach. It was a comfort to me, among other things, to have the chance of making the rich man poorer by a few coins. For you know how I like to incommode the rich, if in any way I conveniently can, especially if they are friends. He took pains to pay for the dinner even of two unknown companions, at the cost for all of us of ten groschen. Even now, if I can, I shall get the treasurer of our illustrious prince here in Coburg to pay our expenses; but if he is unwilling, we live nevertheless at the prince's cost. . . . All is going well, thanks be to God! though I must confess that I sinned in traveling on foot. The sin, to be sure, needs no letters of indulgence, for my contrition is perfect, and fullest satisfaction has already been imposed upon me. I am exceedingly fatigued, and empty wagons are never to be found; so I am crushed, I repent, I render satisfaction enough and to spare.

Although he traveled at his own expense, the frugal elector provided an escort who went most of the way with him. Luther wished to reward the man for his faithfulness, but being too poor to do so adequately, took pains to write Spalatin from Würzburg, request-

From a copy painted by E. A. Schmidt

FREDERICK THE WISE

After the portrait by Lucas Cranach in the Grand Ducal
Museum at Weimar

ing him to see that something additional was given him on his return home. A small matter this, but it illustrates his thoughtfulness for others. He was generous to a fault, and when, as frequently happened, he had nothing left to give, he would go to any amount of trouble and write numberless appeals for those in need.

Letters of introduction from the elector, couched in the warmest terms, were given our traveler, addressed to prominent persons along the route, and he was everywhere received hospitably and with marked consideration. The Bishop of Würzburg, a man of humanistic sympathies, went out of his way to do him honor and afterward wrote Frederick, urging him to stand by his professor, whatever happened, and to allow no harm to come to him.

The trip was of great benefit to Luther. He got away from the anxiety and solicitude of the Wittenberg circle, and found himself treated with respect and his conduct applauded by men of position and influence both within and without his order. The fears of his own prior were not shared by the members of the convention, and he could count, as he discovered, on the warm support of many of his brethren. He was appointed to conduct the disputation held as usual on such occasions, and carefully avoiding the subject of indulgences, took the opportunity to expound and defend his Pauline and Augustinian theology, to the admiration of his hearers. One of them, the young Dominican Martin Bucer, himself later a reformer, describing the affair in a letter to a friend, spoke of Luther's "wonderful suavity in replying and incomparable patience in listening," traits, it should be remarked, not always observed in him. The same auditor declared enthusiastically that the Wittenberg professor agreed in all things with Erasmus, but surpassed him in teaching openly and freely what Erasmus only insinuated. Though not altogether correct, there was some truth in this opinion, and before long it was shared by many others, to the great annoyance of the eminent humanist.

Writing to Spalatin of his Heidelberg stay, Luther said:

The most illustrious prince Wolfgang, Count Palatine, with Master Jacob Symler and the court chamberlain Hazius, treated me uncommonly well. For he entertained me with Father Staupitz and our Lang, now district-vicar, and we had a good time together, conversing pleasantly and agreeably, eating and drinking, and viewing all the treasures of the little chapel, as also the instruments of war, and most of the beauties of the truly royal and remarkable castle. Master Jacob could not say enough about the letters of our prince, exclaiming in his Neckar dialect, "You have, by God, a splendid recommendation." Nothing was lacking which kindness could suggest. The doctors also heard my disputation with pleasure, and debated with me so modestly that they made themselves very dear to me. For although the theology seemed strange to them, they discussed it acutely and skilfully, with the exception of the fifth and youngest doctor, who drew a laugh from everybody when he said, "If the peasants were to hear such things, they would surely stone you to death."

Luther was particularly pleased with the enthusiastic support of a number of the younger monks and began to realize that the hope of reform lay in the rising generation rather than in those grown old in the traditional system. He returned home greatly cheered and strengthened, looking better, according to his friends, than he had for a long time, and ready to take up the campaign with new vigor. The effect upon his

Wittenberg acquaintances and colleagues was also marked. They began to be proud of what he had done as they saw what others thought of him, and to rally to his support with a heartiness hitherto quite lacking.

The circle of his intimates was enlarged before the end of the summer, when there came to Wittenberg from the University of Tübingen a young man, scarcely more than a boy, who was to be his most valued associate and principal helper in his great work. Philip Melanchthon was a grand-nephew of the humanist and Hebraist Reuchlin, and one of the most precocious geniuses of that precocious age. He was already an accomplished classical scholar and a humanist of considerable repute when, at the age of twenty-one, he was called to the University of Wittenberg to become its first professor of Greek. There he speedily fell under the domination of Luther's stalwart personality and threw himself into his cause with all the enthusiasm of youth. Invaluable services he performed for the new faith, and though not always fully in sympathy with his greater colleague or duly appreciative of him, for the most part he proved himself a most efficient aide. He was of special use at first in drawing the attention of his fellow-humanists to Luther and his work. With many of them his support of the new movement counted for a great deal, and tended to offset in some degree Luther's oft-expressed contempt for human reason and his rough-and-ready methods in controversy. One of the greatest scholars and teachers of the century, Melanchthon immensely enhanced the fame of the university, and his class-room was thronged with students of many nationalities. His title of Praeceptor Germaniae was fairly won, for he did more than any other man to reform the educational system of the country.

Nothing could be more striking than the contrast between the two colleagues, closely associated for more than a quarter of a century—the robust, fearless warrior, man of action, and leader of men, and the delicate, cautious, almost effeminate scholar, naturally a student and recluse, dragged into the arena of conflict against his will, and never quite at home in it. Luther himself draws an apt comparison in the following words: "I was born to fight with mobs and devils, and so my books are very stormy and warlike. I must remove trees and stumps, cut away thorns and thickets, and fill up quagmires. I am the rough woodsman who must blaze the way and clear the path. But Master Philip comes along gently and quietly; builds and plants, sows and waters, with joy, according to the gifts God has richly bestowed upon him."

Luther's lifelong affection for Melanchthon is one of the most beautiful things about the great reformer. Older by fourteen years, and of far more massive and heroic mold, he yet felt an admiration for the younger man which he was never tired of expressing. "This little Greek surpasses me even in theology," he wrote his friend Lang in 1519, and similar praise was continually upon his lips. It speaks more for his personal affection, and the simplicity and generosity of his nature, than for his penetration, that for some time he regarded Melanchthon as a greater man than himself and thought of him as the coming prophet for whose work he was only preparing the way, declaring even as late as 1529 that he was not worthy to unloose the latchet of his shoe. The event proved his mistake. He had gained a useful lieutenant, but his was still the commanding figure, and he remained sole leader till the end.

CHAPTER VIII

THE BEGINNING OF THE CONFLICT WITH ROME

WHILE Luther was attending quietly to his duties as professor and preacher, the Dominicans, traditional rivals of the Augustinians, and old-time watchdogs of the orthodox faith, were bestirring themselves at Rome, endeavoring to induce the pope to proceed with vigor against the audacious monk. The efforts of the Augustinian general to silence him had proved unavailing. Luther stood so well with Staupitz and other leading Augustinians in Germany that the machinery of the order could not easily be employed against him. An ecclesiastical procedure therefore seemed necessary, both the financial situation and the importunity of the Dominicans making decisive action of some sort imperative.

In May the master of the papal palace, Sylvester Prierias, was called upon for a preliminary report. Instead of presenting a dispassionate statement of the case, he prepared and published an elaborate scholastic reply to the theses, filled with bitter personal abuse of Luther, and setting forth in most uncompromising fashion the high papal theory already defended by Tetzel. He looked upon the Wittenberg professor with great contempt, and boasted that his book, evidently expected to crush him completely, had been written in three days. Referring to the matter long afterward Luther said:

The pope never caused me unhappiness except at the beginning, when Sylvester wrote against me and put on the title-page of his book, "Master of the Sacred Palace." Then I thought, "Horrors! will it come to this, that the affair will be brought before the pope?" But our Lord God gave me grace, for the bacchant wrote such poor stuff I could only laugh at it.

As a matter of fact, the book was not in the least fitted to break the force of Luther's strictures upon indulgences, and could carry no weight except with those already in sympathy with the extreme views of its author. The pope himself is reported to have expressed his dissatisfaction with it and the wish that Prierias had taken three months instead of three days for it.

Not to be outdone by his Italian antagonist, Luther wrote a reply in two days. It was a brief and scornful document, and made short work of the theory of papal absolutism. It closed with the contemptuous words:

Behold, my reverend Father, I have composed this reply hastily and in two days, for the things brought forward by you seemed very trifling. I have therefore written without premeditation whatever came into my head. If you wish to respond again take care to bring your Thomas better armed into the arena, lest perchance you may next time be received less mildly than now. For I have controlled myself that I might not render evil for evil. Farewell.

A few days later he wrote Staupitz:

If Sylvester, that sylvan sophist, goes on and provokes me with another attack, I will not jest again, but will give my brain and my pen free course, and will show him there are those in Germany who understand him and his Roman wiles. This I hope may soon happen.

About the same time he published the long-delayed commentary on the theses, containing many statements more radical than any hitherto made. The work was dedicated to Leo in a letter couched in terms of humble submission. "Wherefore, blessed Father, prostrate at the feet of thy Blessedness I offer myself with all I am and have. Restore to life, kill, call, recall, approve, reprove, as it shall please thee. Thy voice I will recognize as the voice of Christ, presiding and speaking in thee."

The contrast between this and the brusque declaration in the body of the work, "I am not moved in the least by what pleases or displeases the supreme pontiff; he is a man like others," need not cause surprise. In Luther's situation such a divided state of mind was entirely natural, at one moment humbly submissive, at the next, when thinking only of his own opinions, boldly defiant. But looking back in later years upon these early days of conflict he deeply regretted what he called his weakness and ignorance in showing himself submissive to the pope and addressing him so bashfully and reverently.

Whatever the writer's state of mind, the dedicatory letter counted for nothing when the book itself denounced unsparingly that particular doctrine of the papacy which was coming to be looked upon as a necessary article of faith. The conflict had begun with an attack on indulgences, but it was rapidly developing into a war against papal authority. Not that Luther thought as yet of attacking the papacy,—he was still a devout and loyal subject of the pope,—but, like many others, he was strenuously opposed to a theory destroying all independence, either of thought or action, for the church as a whole. Unfortunately, the theory was shared by the pope himself and by the Roman authorities, and, as the event proved, they were bound to crush any one openly attacking it.

Anticipating possible excommunication, Luther preached in the late spring, and published some weeks afterward, a sermon on the ban, declaring that exclusion from the church could harm no one provided he retained his Christian faith and character, for the true communion of the church is spiritual and internal, and no one can be put without its pale except by his own act. Referring to it in a letter to his old friend Wenceslaus Link, he remarked:

I have recently preached a sermon to the people concerning the force of excommunication. In it I attacked in passing the tyranny and ignorance of that most sordid crowd of officials, commissaries, and vicars. All wonder they have never before heard such things, and now we are all waiting to see what farther harm will come to me because of the new fire I have kindled. Thus it goes with the word and the sign of the truth, when it is contradicted. I wanted to take up the subject in a public disputation, but the report of it got abroad and so troubled many great people that my superior, the Bishop of Brandenburg, sent a messenger requesting me to postpone the debate. This I did, and still do, especially since my friends also advise it. See what a monster I am, whose very attempts are intolerable!

The sermon made him many enemies particularly in the ruling classes. It was widely felt that he was undermining the safeguards of society. Even the Emperor Maximilian, usually tolerant enough, although he had recently told Frederick's counselor Pfeffinger that Luther's theses were not to be despised and the elector would better take good care of him, for he might some day be useful, now wrote the pope urging

him to silence the dangerous monk before he did worse
damage.

In September, Spalatin, who was at the Diet of
Augsburg in attendance upon the elector, wrote
Luther:

I cannot tell you how much harm your work concerning the ban has done you, and what hatred it seems to
have caused. I greatly wonder it should have been sent
here, all the more because there was subjoined to it a
most bitter epigram against Roman avarice—I speak of
my own knowledge. When this reached here it was put
into the hands of both the apostolic legates, and I fear
has been transmitted to Rome to your great detriment.
But God will be present to aid his own. Nevertheless,
have a care that you do not stir up the hornets too much
by discourse, debate, and published writings.

Formal proceedings against Luther were finally set
on foot at the papal court, and on the seventh of
August he received an imperative summons to appear
in Rome within sixty days to answer the charge of
heresy. The situation was now becoming serious. It
was quite evident he could not expect even justice in
Rome. The trial must prove a farce, and inevitably
result in his condemnation. Indeed, one of the three
judges appointed to try his case was his antagonist
Prierias. Luther realized the gravity of the situation
and at once wrote as follows to Spalatin:

Greeting. Your good offices, my Spalatin, I am now in
especial need of, as for that matter the honor of almost
our whole university is too. What I ask is this, that
you labor with the most illustrious Prince and Doctor
Pfeffinger to have our Prince and His Imperial Majesty
secure from the supreme Pontiff my remission or the
transfer of my case to Germany, as I have written our
Prince. For you see how craftily and maliciously the

Dominicans, my murderers, work for my destruction. I have written to the same effect to Lord Pfeffinger that by his own good offices and those of his friends this favor may be secured from his Imperial Majesty and the Prince. It is necessary to act quickly. They have given me very little time, as you will see from this Lernæan citation, with its hydras and monsters. Therefore if you love me and hate iniquity, you will see to it that the counsel and aid of the Prince are sought at once, and will inform me, or rather our reverend Father Vicar, John Staupitz, who is perhaps already with you at Augsburg, or will be soon. For he is staying at Salzburg and has promised to be at Nuremberg for the Feast of the Assumption. Finally, I beg you not to be troubled or distressed about me. The Lord with the temptation will provide a way of escape.

Again a fortnight later, he wrote:

I do not yet see how I can escape the threatened judgment unless the Prince comes to my aid. On the other hand, I should much rather remain under perpetual censure than have the Prince gain an evil name on my account. Believe, therefore, that as I offered myself before I am still ready, and persuade any others you think best to believe the same. I will never be a heretic. I may err in disputation, but I wish to assert nothing, nor hereafter to be taken captive by the opinions of men. It seems advisable to our learned and wise friends that I should ask from our Prince Frederick a safe-conduct, as it is called, through his dominions. When he refuses it, as I know he will, I shall have an excellent excuse, so they say, for not going to Rome. If therefore you are willing and will procure from the most illustrious Prince in my name a written reply, refusing me a safe-conduct and leaving me to go if I wish at my own risk, you will best serve me.

In a letter written about the same time to his superior Staupitz, he said: "See how insidiously I am attacked. Everywhere I am hedged about with thorns; but Christ lives and reigns yesterday, and to-day, and forever. . . . Pray for me that in this time of temptation I be not too joyful and too confident." A very human touch this last! Joy in battle he always felt, and was never so happy as when in the midst of the fray.

Meanwhile, moved perhaps by Luther's sermon on the ban, and by reports of the growing radicalism of his utterances, the pope decided not to wait until the sixty days were gone, but to have him arrested at once and held for trial, and the elector was called upon to turn him over to Cardinal Cajetan, the papal legate at the Diet of Augsburg. This Frederick was unwilling to do. Though he disclaimed all sympathy with heretics and heresy, he was yet determined that his most famous professor, the chief ornament of his university, should enjoy fair play. He therefore endeavored to have his case transferred to Germany, where there was more likelihood of securing justice. His support was of incalculable benefit to Luther. Without it he would have been destroyed at the very beginning, before his great reforming work was fairly under way. Frederick was the most highly respected and influential prince in Germany, and the pope, particularly just at this juncture, could ill afford to offend him. The Emperor Maximilian was endeavoring to secure the imperial succession for his grandson Charles, but Leo, foreseeing that his own power would be greatly curtailed if the King of Spain, already possessed of large territory in Italy, should also become Emperor of Germany, supported the candidature of Francis I of France as the lesser of two evils. In these circumstances it was of the utmost importance to remain on friendly terms with so influential an elector as Frederick. He

therefore yielded so far at least as to commission Cajetan, one of the leading theologians of the day, to hear
Luther's case at Augsburg instead of arresting him
and sending him to Rome unheard.

Luther was accordingly directed by the elector to
appear at Augsburg and answer for himself before the
legate. This was not what he had wished. He had
hoped for a trial before some German tribunal, not
already prejudiced against him, and his friends urged
him not to go, warning him that the whole thing was a
ruse and he would certainly be arrested and forfeit his
life. But he felt in duty bound to obey the elector's
mandate, and, though he was far from well, made the
journey on foot, arriving in Augsburg on the seventh
of October, and putting up in the Carmelite monastery
of St. Anne, the prior of which was a former Wittenberg student. His mood during the journey is shown
by the following passage in a letter written from
Nuremberg: "I have found some men so pusillanimous
in my cause that they have even undertaken to tempt
me not to go to Augsburg. But I continue firm. The
will of the Lord be done. Even at Augsburg, even in
the midst of his enemies, Jesus Christ reigns. Let
Christ live, let Martin die, and every sinner." Years
afterward he remarked that he saw only the stake before him when he set out from Wittenberg, and was
troubled to think what a disgrace he would be to his
dear parents.

In Augsburg he was warmly received by some of the
leading men of the town and was entertained at dinner
by the city councilor Conrad Peutinger, a humanist
of patrician birth, whose fame among his brother
humanists was great and whose library was one of the
wonders of the age. Augsburg, an important imperial
city, was then at the height of its prosperity. It was

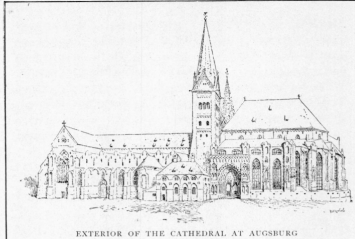

EXTERIOR OF THE CATHEDRAL AT AUGSBURG

CLOISTERS OF THE CATHEDRAL AT AUGSBURG

the home of the Fuggers, the principal financial magnates of the day, the bankers of emperors and popes,
and the fiscal agents in charge of all the great indulgence campaigns of that age. According to tradition
the papal legate made the palatial residence of Jacob
Fugger, the head of the house, his stopping-place, and
Luther appeared before him there.

A few days after his arrival he wrote his colleague
Melanchthon :

> Nothing new or wonderful is happening here, except
> that the city is full of my name, and everybody desires to
> see the Herostratus who has kindled so great a fire. Play
> the man as you are doing, and teach the young rightly.
> I am going to be sacrificed for you and them, if it please
> the Lord. I prefer to perish and even to lose forever your
> most delightful companionship—a thing most grievous
> to me—rather than revoke what I have rightly said, and
> be an occasion of loss to the best studies. With these
> most ignorant and bitter enemies of literature and educa-
> tion Italy has fallen into palpable Egyptian darkness. For
> they are all ignorant of Christ and his affairs. These
> men, nevertheless, we have as lords and masters in faith
> and practice.

The impatience of Roman rule thus expressed is
very significant. It was already wide-spread in Germany, and Luther's awakening sense of the situation
was prophetic of what he was yet to do for his native
land. At the Diet of Augsburg, which had closed
shortly before he arrived in the city, hostility to the
papacy found most emphatic utterance. It was no new
thing. For many generations the avarice of the
Roman curia had provoked the complaints of Christendom. In all sorts of ways, and by the most devious
paths, money flowed to Rome, and the wealth of the
nations was drained for its support. Sovereign of the

states of the church, a small territory able at best to sustain only a modest court, the pope was at the same time a world ruler and kept up the pomp and circumstance of the greatest of potentates. To Christendom at large he must look for funds to meet the needs of his government and of the thousands of retainers thronging his court. It was inevitable that the veneration naturally felt toward the head of the church should be tempered with impatience at a foreign power whose maintenance heavily taxed the peoples of Europe. No country felt the burden more than Germany. With its historic devotion to the holy see, with its numerous and wealthy ecclesiastical states, with the conflicting interests of its various principalities, and with the weakness of its central government, making common action impossible, it offered abundant opportunities for spoliation.

It had long been growing clear to German princes and people that they were being exploited by a race which despised them for their very submission, and national pride was beginning to take fire everywhere. At the Diet of 1510 a long and ominous list of grievances against the papacy was formulated, and at Augsburg, in 1518, the bitterness was equally marked. The old plea that money was needed for the defense of Christendom against the Turks was urged both by emperor and pope, but the Diet was obdurate, believing that so far at least as the pope was concerned the plea was only a pretext, and the money would go to line the pockets of his relatives and retainers. In these circumstances it was hardly to be expected that Luther should find the papal legate in particularly good humor, or disposed to treat him with leniency. It would seem as if the temper of the Diet might have warned him of the necessity of handling the case of the Wittenberg

professor with circumspection; but he evidently did
not realize the gravity of the situation and did not
dream, as, for that matter, Luther did not, that the
affair would yet assume national importance.

Luther's interviews with him proved exceedingly
unsatisfactory. The cardinal refused to enter into the
merits of the case, insisting quite in the spirit of
Prierias and Tetzel that it was the monk's duty to
submit unquestioningly to the authority of the pope
and to recant unconditionally. This Luther naturally
refused to do, and when he undertook to defend his
positions, a protracted and heated discussion ensued,
which served only to confirm him in his own views and
to convince the legate of his obduracy and heresy. The
remark attributed to Cajetan by an early biographer
of Luther is probably apocryphal: "I do not wish to
talk further with this beast, for he has deep eyes, and
his head is full of amazing speculations"; but his impression of the Wittenberg professor was very unfavorable, as is shown by his account of the affair sent to
the Elector Frederick, and Luther's opinion of the
cardinal is recorded in a letter written from Augsburg
to his colleague Carlstadt. "He is perhaps a famous
Thomist, but he is an obscure and ignorant theologian
and Christian, and therefore as well fitted to manage
this affair as an ass to play the harp." Long afterward Luther declared his break with the pope might
have been avoided had a more conciliatory policy been
adopted by the legate, and a papal ambassador is reported to have accused Cajetan of ruining the cause by
using violence instead of diplomacy. But neither remark does justice to the fundamental difference of
principle between Luther and the papacy—a difference
fully apparent only some time later, but already realized
by Cajetan. As a convinced and consistent supporter

of the theory of papal absolutism he really followed the only course possible in the circumstances when he demanded unconditional submission.

Successive interviews having proved quite futile, Luther was finally dismissed with the command not to appear again until he was prepared to recant. In response to the request of his superior Staupitz, and his boyhood friend Wenceslaus Link, whom Cajetan induced to labor with the refractory monk, he then wrote the cardinal a letter of apology:

Most reverend Father in Christ, I confess, as I have confessed before, that I was certainly too indiscreet, as they say, and too bitter and irreverent toward the name of the supreme Pontiff. And although I was most strongly provoked to this irreverence, nevertheless I now know I ought to have handled the case more modestly, humbly, and reverently, and not answered a fool according to his folly. I am most sincerely sorry and beg pardon, and I will make it known to the people from the pulpit, whenever I have opportunity, as I have already often done, and will henceforth take care to act and speak differently by the mercy of God. I also promise most willingly not to deal with the subject of indulgences, and to be silent when the present affair is ended, provided similar speech or silence be imposed also on those who incited me to this tragedy.

But at the same time he again refused to recant, declaring:

So far as concerns the truth of my opinions I would most gladly revoke everything in accordance with your command and advice as well as my vicar's, if my conscience in any way permitted it. For I know I ought to be persuaded by no precept, counsel, or kindness to say or do anything against my conscience.

Nothing came of the letter, and when Staupitz found

From the painting by Christopher Amberger

CONRAD PEUTINGER, THE AUGSBURG HUMANIST

him fully determined not to yield he absolved him from his vow of monastic obedience, whether for Luther's sake, or to relieve himself and the Augustinian order from responsibility for the dangerous monk, is not clear. After waiting a few days for further developments, Luther was smuggled out of the city by his friends, who had heard rumors of his impending arrest, and made his way hurriedly back to Wittenberg on horseback. At the close of the first day's ride of nearly forty miles, completely exhausted by the unaccustomed exercise, he tumbled half dead on the floor of the stable. As he later said, he rode "without trousers, boots, spurs, or sword," to the great amusement of Count Albert of Mansfeld, whom he visited at Gräfenthal on his way home. He arrived at Wittenberg on the last day of October "full of joy and peace," as he wrote Spalatin the same day, "so that I wonder this trial of mine should seem so great a thing to many great men." He left behind him in Augsburg another letter to the cardinal and an appeal duly signed and executed from the pope-ill-informed to the pope-to-be-better-informed, demanding that the process against him be begun anew and unprejudiced judges be substituted for those already named.

That the seriousness of the situation did not wholly absorb him, or dampen the buoyancy of his spirits, is shown by the following playful note to Melanchthon, written shortly after his return home apropos of a dinner he gave as dean of the theological faculty to a newly made doctor.

To Philip Melanchthon, Schwarzerd, Greek, Latin, Hebrew, German, never barbarian. Greeting. To-day you despised both me and the new doctor, so-called. May the Muse and Apollo forgive you for it. Although it was not altogether my affair, I have pardoned you. But unless you show yourself punctually to Dr. Andrew Carlstadt and Licentiate Amsdorf, and especially to the Rector, not even Greek will be able to excuse you, much less the little brother Martin, as Cajetan calls me. The new doctor thinks, as he says jestingly, that as a barbarian he is held in contempt by a Greek. Take care what you do, for I have promised you will surely come this time. You will do me a kindness if you come, but I should very much like to have you bring with you Dr. Veit and John Schwertfeger, for this evening I shall be host to my best and dearest friends. Use your influence and my command, if the little brother counts for anything, that they may come with you. Farewell.

Little brother Martin Eleutherius.

Within a week after the dinner, on November 28, expecting speedy condemnation from Rome, he drew up another formal appeal, this time from the pope to a general council. The appeal was a master stroke of policy. It arrayed upon his side opponents of papal absolutism whatever their attitude toward indulgences. From time immemorial a general council had been regarded as supreme in the church, the only final and infallible authority in faith and practice. But during the later Middle Ages papal absolutism had steadily grown, and in the early fifteenth century, in the struggle between the papacy and the great reforming councils, the former had won a complete victory. Discredited as the conciliar party was in Luther's time, the general council still remained the one hope of all deprecating the unlimited power of the pope. To appeal from pope to council was to put oneself on the side of multitudes of devout Catholics of the highest standing, particularly in Germany and France; and inevitably Luther's case at once assumed in many eyes the aspect of a struggle between the newer papal claims and the older principle of representative government. As a result, the particular reform interesting Luther was widely lost sight of in the larger issue, and the bold professor came to be regarded as a champion of the rights of the church against the usurpations of the pope. In such a struggle, loyal and orthodox Catholics were as likely to be with him as against him. His appeal served to rally and consolidate forces of Catholic devotion long existent, but for some time past without the power of effective and concerted expression.

Greatly annoyed at the outcome of the Augsburg interview, Cajetan wrote a sharp letter to Frederick, assuring him Luther's teachings were heretical, reminding him of his duty as a loyal son of the church, and calling upon him to deliver the refractory professor to the Roman authorities or expel him from his dominions. The elector referred the letter to Luther, who immediately returned it, with his own version of the Augsburg interview, and with the request that he be not sent to Rome, where his life would scarcely be safe for an instant. He offered to leave Saxony, if Frederick felt embarrassed by his presence, but suggested that the cardinal be told to put his proofs in writing and not content himself with merely denouncing Brother Martin as a heretic. In an admirably firm and temperate reply to Cajetan, the elector followed Luther's suggestion, writing in part as follows:

There are many scholars in our principality, in the university and elsewhere, from whom we have not yet been able to learn with certainty that Martin's teaching is impious, unchristian, and heretical, though there are some who have opposed him on private grounds, because his learning has injured them pecuniarily; but even they have as yet proved nothing against him. For if we had adequate evidence that Martin's teaching were impious and unsettling, we should ourselves know by Almighty God's help and grace what to do without being exhorted and admonished. For we are determined in this whole affair to act as becomes a Christian prince who desires to consult both his honor and his conscience with the aid of God. . . . Since Martin offers to submit his case to the judgment of certain universities, and to stand trial in some safe place, and to surrender himself obediently for instruction and guidance, when his cause has been heard, we think he ought to be allowed to do so, or at least that his errors should be indicated in writing. This we also ask, that we may know on what ground he is to be regarded as heretical, and may be able to proceed accordingly. For we think that when he is not yet convicted, he ought not to be reputed and written down a heretic. Finally we would not willingly permit ourselves to be drawn into error or to be counted disobedient by the holy apostolic see.

Opposition to the papal absolutism of the Roman party, which made the mere word of the pope sufficient to determine heresy, here speaks in decided though respectful terms. Against such absolutism Frederick could evidently be counted on to stand firm, whatever his views as to the right or wrong of his famous professor's reforming efforts.

Luther was delighted with the elector's reply, as he might well be. With such a prince to see he had fair play, he could feel the ground firm beneath his feet; and Frederick's attitude made it clear enough to the Roman authorities that to crush Luther summarily was quite out of the question.

Force having failed, diplomacy was resorted to. The papal chamberlain Carl von Miltitz, a Saxon nobleman and agent of the Saxon princes in Rome, was despatched to Germany to discover how the land lay, and, if possible, induce the elector to yield to the wishes of the pope. His instructions gave him considerable latitude. He was to seize Luther and send him to Rome if he could, but if not, to accomplish the desired end in some more indirect fashion. He was commissioned to bestow upon the elector the golden rose, the most coveted decoration in the gift of the pope. Apropos of this, Luther repeats a tale brought from Rome, that when it was proposed to offer Frederick the golden rose on condition he surrender the monk, one of the cardinals angrily exclaimed: "Are you all children or idiots that you propose to buy the monk from the prince?" and tore up the document containing the proposal. Whether the report was true or not, at any rate the gift just at this juncture might easily be construed as an attempt to bribe the elector; and though he had long desired it, he accepted it now with marked coolness.

Arrived in Germany, Miltitz speedily discovered the situation to be much more serious than had been imagined at Rome. He found the whole country stirred up over Luther's case, and not more than one German out of every four on the pope's side. An army of twenty-five thousand men, he confessed, would be insufficient to carry Luther off to Rome. It was quite evident the time for suppressing him by force or threats had passed, and the adroit envoy, interpreting his mission more broadly than had been intended, at once decided that the only course was to gain him by flattery and promises of favor. He apparently let it be known quietly to Luther's friends that ecclesiastical preferment, possibly even a bishopric, would be his reward if he yielded. At least Pfeffinger, who was with Miltitz in Nuremberg, was sure the Wittenberg professor might have any dignity he wished, as Christopher Scheurl was careful to inform Luther in a very interesting letter of the twentieth of December. A couple of years later, it may be added, at the Diet of Worms, the Elector Frederick told some of his fellow-princes that he knew to a certainty Martin could have a rich archbishopric, or a cardinal's hat, if he would only recant.

Finding such hints of no avail, early in January, 1519, Miltitz secured a personal interview with Luther himself. He met him with assurances of respect and protestations of affection, and succeeded in persuading him to agree to have his case submitted to the Archbishop of Trêves, and to abide by his decision. Luther further promised, as he had already offered to do at Augsburg, to say no more upon the subject of indulgences, and to refrain from all controversy if his opponents would do the same. The one thing the curia most desired was to put an end to the discussion. The more public attention was called to the matter, the worse for the indulgence traffic, so long unpopular in many quarters. If the Wittenberg professor could not be induced to retract, the next best thing, as Miltitz rightly saw, was to secure his silence; and out of consideration for the peace of the church Luther entered cheerfully into a conditional agreement to remain quiet. He was prevailed upon at the same time to write a humble letter to the pope, though it was apparently never sent, perhaps because not submissive enough to suit Miltitz, and he also published a pamphlet for circulation among the people, warning them against putting too radical an interpretation upon his utterances and exhorting them to loyalty and obedience.

To call all this a retraction on Luther's part, and to accuse him of cowardice or undue regard for his own

EXTERIOR OF THE FUGGER HOUSE AT AUGSBURG

From a wood-engraving by Hans Burkmair

JACOB FUGGER OF AUGSBURG

safety is entirely to misunderstand him. The situation
was very natural and reveals the genuine humanness
of the Wittenberg monk. It was never difficult to
work upon his feelings, and the wily German knew
how to make an effective appeal to his ingrained devotion and his long-time habit of cloisteral obedience. It
was a monastic principle that chief regard must always
be had to the good of the church, and for its sake
even the truth must often remain unspoken. When
Luther was assured that the welfare of the institution
he loved was threatened, naturally enough everything
else shrank for the moment into insignificance. Like
many another man of his temperament, he could never
be driven, but he could very easily be led. Miltitz,
despite the questionable reputation he enjoyed, was the
only person who showed any understanding of the
man he was dealing with.

It is a further evidence of the papal envoy's appreciation of the situation that he recognized the need of
publicly admitting the justice of Luther's criticisms and
doing something to mend the evils he had attacked.
Tetzel, he decided, must be made a scapegoat of, and
so he summoned him to appear and answer for his
conduct. The pope, according to Scheurl, had already
expressed his indignation at some of the most offensive utterances attributed to the indulgence preacher,
and whether rightly or wrongly, the Roman authorities
from this time on held him accountable for all the
trouble.

When Tetzel informed Miltitz that the wrath of the
people made it unsafe for him to obey the summons,
the papal envoy sought him out in Leipsic, where he
had sheltered himself in a monastery, and passed condemnation upon him for immorality of long standing
and for alleged dishonesty in connection with the in-

9

dulgence funds. Tetzel felt his disgrace keenly, and
did not long survive. It was like Luther to write him
a letter of sympathy before his death, telling him not
to take the matter too much to heart; the fault was not
his, for "the child had another father altogether." The
responsibility for the abuses attaching to the indulgence traffic, formerly attributed to Tetzel, or at worst
to Archbishop Albert, he now began to see belonged to
the papacy itself. Possibly his recent stay in Augsburg, where the anti-papal attitude of the Diet was
on everybody's lips, had opened his eyes to the real
situation. At any rate, thenceforth he laid the fault at
Rome's door, and held the pope himself, or the curia,
chiefly responsible for the evils he condemned.

The diplomatic success scored by Miltitz proved,
after all, only temporary. When the impressions of
the interview had somewhat faded, and he had leisure
to think the matter over calmly by himself, Luther
reverted not unnaturally to his earlier state of mind.
He became aware once more of the gravity of the
issue, and began to feel with considerable chagrin
that under the spell of the courtly nobleman's blandish-
ments—his "Judas kiss and crocodile tears" as he ir-
reverently called them in a letter to a friend—he had
gone too far and yielded too much. When his opponents, paying no attention to Miltitz's efforts, gave
him the opportunity to break silence, as they soon did,
it is not surprising he entered the arena again more
determined and more radical in his views than ever.

CHAPTER IX

THE LEIPSIC DEBATE

THE summer of 1519 witnessed two events each in its way of cardinal importance for the career of Luther and the progress of the Reformation—the election of an emperor of Germany and the Leipsic debate.

The Emperor Maximilian died unexpectedly on the twelfth of January. The two most prominent candidates for the imperial throne were his grandson Charles, King of Spain and the Netherlands, and King Francis I of France. Maximilian had already been laying the wires for Charles's election, but the pope favored the candidacy of Francis. The election lay in the hands of three ecclesiastical and four secular princes, the archbishops of Trêves, Mayence, and Cologne, the electors of Brandenburg and Saxony, the Count Palatine, and the King of Bohemia. Large sums of money were spent by the candidates and their supporters in forwarding their interests, and Frederick the Wise was apparently the only one of the seven who was above accepting bribes. It looked for a time as if the prize would go to the highest bidder, but as the possibility of Francis's election became imminent, national feeling asserted itself, and demanded an emperor of German blood. Pressure proved too strong to be resisted, and when the supporters of Francis found it impossible to secure his election, they compromised on Frederick the Wise, easily the most influential and respected of German princes, and the pope's original choice for the position. Feeling his resources unequal to the task, Frederick declined the proffered crown and threw the weight of his influence upon the side of Charles, who was elected on the twenty-eighth of June.

Not for centuries had such power been lodged in the hands of a single man. Inheriting the crown of Spain and the Netherlands and large possessions in Italy from his Spanish mother, his Hapsburg father brought him Austria and Burgundy, and now the empire of Germany was added. Great things were expected of him by his new subjects, particularly by the members of the young German party. Their watchword was "Germany for the Germans," and they hoped for the creation of a strong and united nation, sufficient unto itself and independent of all foreign control. In Germany, as in many other parts of Europe, the new spirit of nationalism was running high, and everywhere it gave rise to a growing impatience with the papacy, for the latter's cosmopolitanism seemed to many the greatest obstacle to national development. The pope's support of the candidature of Francis only made matters worse and increased the hostility to his interference in German affairs.

The election of Charles was hailed with enthusiasm, and hope everywhere ran high. But those who expected much were doomed to disappointment. Instead of putting himself at the head of the national movement and devoting his energies to the building up of a strong and independent empire, he treated Germany only as an appanage of Spain, where alone his heart lay. Though German blood flowed in his veins, he was by temperament and training far more Spanish than German. He had little understanding of his Teu-

tonic subjects, or sympathy with them, and to their
new hopes and aspirations he was altogether blind.
Germany was hardly more than a pawn in his political
game, and when he needed the support of the papacy,
he was quite willing to use his power to suppress heresy
and schism in the empire, as he was equally ready,
even though a devout and orthodox Catholic, to permit
both to flourish when he wished to bring the pope to
terms.   The Lutheran movement thus proved frequently of no little advantage to him, but of real
sympathy with it he never showed a trace, and his
general policy was hostile to it.

At the time of Charles's election, Luther shared the
common mood, and his countrymen's enthusiasm for
the young ruler was reflected in his writings. Over
and over again not only then, but years afterward, he
spoke in terms of warm admiration of the emperor,
and it was long before he could bring himself to believe
that he would disappoint the nation's hopes.

In the meantime, while the intrigues preceding the
election were distracting the attention of the princes of
Germany, Luther was preparing himself all unconsciously to fill the place of popular leader declined by
Charles. As yet his work was almost exclusively religious and theological, and its wider implications were
nowhere understood, but as the event proved the structure ultimately reared was the more permanent because
of the solidity and depth of the foundations he was
laying. His break with the papacy, a necessary step in
his progress toward national leadership, was becoming
more and more imminent during the early months of
1519, and was greatly hastened by the second of the
two notable events of that year, the Leipsic disputation.

The ablest Catholic theologian of the day in Germany was Dr. John Eck of the University of Ingol-

stadt. Some three years younger than Luther, he took his master's degree at the University of Tübingen at the early age of fourteen, while Luther was still only an undergraduate. Interested in mathematics, geography, physics, philosophy, and law, as well as theology, he was a man of uncommon learning and extraordinary attainments in many fields. For a time he was generally reckoned a member of the growing humanistic party, and was on terms of intimacy with many of its leaders. Luther spoke of him with marked respect in some of his earlier letters, and frequently sent him greetings through common friends. But the appearance of the ninety-five theses led to a permanent break and the alinement of Eck upon the side of reaction. He criticized them severely in a paper intended for private circulation called "Obelisks." Outraged that a man he supposed his friend should attack him without giving him any warning, Luther replied with considerable asperity in a similar paper entitled "Asterisks." Thenceforth, although the forms of friendship were observed for a while, there was growing enmity between the two men.

In May, 1518, Luther's friend Carlstadt, who had some time before committed himself publicly and enthusiastically to the Augustinian theology of his younger colleague, assailed Eck in an extended series of theses, and the controversy, thus opened, was carried on vigorously for months. The Wittenberg faculty finally invited Eck, an experienced, one might almost say a professional, disputant, to meet Carlstadt in public debate, and after protracted negotiations Leipsic was agreed upon as the scene of the disputation.

In the winter Eck published the theses he purposed to defend, and sent a copy of them to Luther. Instead

POTENTISSIMVS·MAXIMVS·ET·INVICTISSIMVS·CÆSAR·MAXIMILIANVS
QVI·CVNCTOS·SVI·TEMPORIS·REGES·ET·PRINCIPES·IVSTICIA·PRVDENCIA
MAGNANIMITATE·LIBERALITATE·PRÆCIPVE·VERO·BELLICA·LAVDE·ET
ANIMI·FORTITVDINE·SVPERAVIT·NATVS·EST·ANNO·SALVTIS·HVMANÆ
·M·CCCC·LIX·DIE·MARCII·IX·VIXIT·ANNOS·LIX·MENSES·IX·DIES·XXV
DECESSIT·VERO·ANNO·M·D·XIX·MENSIS·IANVARII·DIE·XII·QVEM·DEVS
OPT·MAX·IN·NVMERVM·VIVENCIVM·REFERRE·VELIT

From a carbon print by Braun & Co. of the engraving by Albert Dürer

MAXIMILIAN I, EMPEROR OF GERMANY

of dealing with the matters in dispute between himself and Carlstadt, they had to do wholly with Luther's teachings, showing it was he whom Eck wished to meet. Indeed, in the letter accompanying the theses he said:

As Carlstadt is your champion, but you are the principal, who have disseminated throughout Germany dogmas which seem to my small and feeble judgment false and erroneous, it is fitting that you also should come and either defend your own positions or disprove mine. . . . You see from the inclosed document that the propositions have been aimed not so much at Carlstadt as at your teachings.

Luther felt much aggrieved at this new and public attack, made as it was under cover of the approaching debate with Carlstadt and despite renewed protestations of friendship. In deference to Miltitz, he had maintained strict silence, and had even allowed a recent pamphlet of Prierias to pass unnoticed; but Eck's assault was too serious to be ignored. He was the first German theologian of any importance to come out in open opposition, and Luther felt that his own honor and the honor of the university required him to meet his antagonist in debate. Considering himself absolved from his promise of silence by what had happened, he decided to join Carlstadt in the approaching disputation, leaving to his colleague the defense of the Augustinian theology, and devoting himself to the points specifically impugned in Eck's theses.

He found considerable difficulty in getting Duke George's permission to take part. It seemed almost an affront to the papal see to allow him to appear in Leipsic and defend propositions he had already been called upon to recant. But he was very eager, and wrote a number of urgent letters to the duke. Finally, Carlstadt was authorized to bring with him such friends as he pleased, and under cover of this indirect permission, Luther appeared and bore his share in the debate.

Like Tetzel and Prierias, Eck was a believer in papal absolutism and infallibility, and he took occasion in his final thesis to declare the pope successor of Peter and universal vicar of Christ, thus challenging Luther to debate the question of his supremacy. The matter, as Luther saw clearly enough, was of fundamental importance and its discussion sooner or later inevitable. He therefore spent the months preceding the debate in the most diligent study of the whole topic. As he gathered his material, he became convinced of the nullity of the papal claims. He discovered the untrustworthiness of many of the documents appealed to in their support, and was led to the conclusion that the whole structure was based on fraud and was of comparatively recent growth. The conclusion, as a matter of fact, was quite unwarranted. Papal supremacy was much older than he thought, and was due in no small part to natural causes. But his opinion was not surprising in the circumstances, and was shared by many others. As a consequence, his bitterness steadily increased, and it became more and more difficult for him to distinguish between the current theory and the papal institution itself. Writing to his friend Lang on the third of February, he said:

Our Eck is waging new wars against me, and it will come to pass that I shall do with Christ's aid what I have long had in mind; namely, attack sometime the Roman scarecrows in a serious book. For hitherto I have only sported and played with the Roman affair, although they complain loudly as if it were real earnest.

Before the end of the month he wrote Christopher Scheurl:

Our Eck, after beautifully hiding his madness against me until now, has finally let it be seen. Behold what kind of a man he is! But God is in the midst of the gods, and knows what He purposes to bring out of this tragedy. Neither Eck nor I can serve our own ends in this affair. The counsel of God, so I believe, will be accomplished. I have often said that hitherto I have been playing; now at length serious things against the Roman pontiff and Roman arrogance are under way.

The same day he wrote the humanist Willibald Pirkheimer:

The Lord drags me and not unwillingly do I follow. If the Roman curia has mourned over dying indulgences what will it do when its decretals, if God will, are expiring? Not that I would boast before the victory, trusting in my own powers, but I have faith that the mercy of God will be wroth at human traditions. The power and majesty of the supreme pontiff I will guard and defend, but I will not bear corruptions of the sacred scriptures.

A few days later he declared in a letter to Spalatin:

I am studying the papal decretals in preparation for my disputation, and, between us, I am ignorant whether the pope is antichrist himself or his apostle, so miserably is Christ—that is, the truth—corrupted and crucified by him in his decretals.

Already in December, in writing to his friend Link about the meeting with Cajetan at Augsburg, he had said:

I send you my account of the Augsburg interview, couched in sharper terms than the legate wished; but my pen is already pregnant with much greater matters. I do not know where my ideas come from. The affair, in my judgment, is not yet begun, much less is it nearing its end, as the Romans hope. I will send you my trifles, that you may see whether I rightly divine that the antichrist, of whom Paul speaks, reigns in the Roman curia. I think I am able to show that he is worse to-day than the Turk.

The idea was not a novel one. In the Middle Ages the word "antichrist" was frequently used by disputants as a term of opprobrium for political or ecclesiastical opponents of whatever sort, and long before Luther's time it had been repeatedly applied to the pope by those who saw in the political power and worldly interests of the papacy the profanation of a holy office and the betrayal of Christ. This it was that led Luther to the same condemnatory judgment. Not the personal character of the popes, but the secularization of the papacy chiefly aroused his resentment. As he discovered how consciously and deliberately and often by what devious means its political power had been attained, his anger waxed hot within him. In another letter to Spalatin, written about the same time, he says:

Many things I suppress and hold back for the sake of the prince and our university. If I were elsewhere, I should vomit them out against Rome, or rather Babylon, the devastator of Bible and church. The truth about the Bible and the church, my Spalatin, cannot be discussed without offending this beast. Therefore do not hope that I shall be quiet and undisturbed unless you wish me to give up theology altogether. Let our friends think me mad. This affair will not have an end, if it be of God, until all my friends desert me, as his disciples and acquaintances deserted Christ, and truth be left alone,

From a carbon print by Braun & Co. of the painting by Clouet in the Louvre

FRANCIS I OF FRANCE, DEFEATED CANDIDATE FOR THE IMPERIAL
THRONE OF GERMANY

which will save itself by its own power and not by mine nor thine nor any man's. This hour I have expected from the beginning. . . . If I perish, the world will lose nothing. The Wittenbergers, by the grace of God, have already progressed so far they do not need me at all. What will you? I, worthless man that I am, fear I may not be counted worthy to suffer and die for such a cause. That felicity belongs to better men, not to so vile a sinner.

He evidently realized the seriousness of the outlook. Insubordination to the pope, it was generally believed, could have only one result, the condemnation and death of the rebel. He was hastening on, it seemed, to certain destruction. His friends were in terror, and urged him to be careful. Carlstadt, radical and impetuous as he was, tried to hold him back. He was ready and eager to defend the Augustinian theology, but was not prepared to attack the pope, and his younger colleague's course sorely alarmed him.

But Luther was not to be dissuaded. Expediency meant little to him, his own reputation and safety still less. When once convinced that a certain evil needed mending, no other consideration, however important, could long hold him back. He would often restrain himself for the sake of others when he would not for his own, but the restraint could be only temporary, and the deed had at length to be done, whatever it cost either them or him.

The great Leipsic debate began on the twenty-seventh of June in the hall of the Pleissenburg, Duke George's palace, in the presence of the duke himself and many other distinguished personages. A number of professors and two hundred students from Wittenberg were in attendance, and the latter kept the town well stirred up with their noisy and not always orderly demonstrations in support of the Wittenberg champions.

Peter Mosellan, a Leipsic professor of humanistic sympathies, gives us a vivid description of the participants in the debate. The following pen-picture of Luther, then thirty-five years old, is worth quoting:

Martin is of medium height and slender form, with a body so wasted both with cares and study that you can almost count all his bones. He is just in the prime of life, with a clear and penetrating voice. His learning and his knowledge of Scripture are admirable, and he has almost everything at command. He knows enough Greek and Hebrew to decide between different interpretations. Nor is he wanting in matter, for he has a great forest both of ideas and words. Judgment, perhaps, and discretion you might miss in him. In his life and manners he is polite and affable, not in the least stoical or supercilious, and he is able to adapt himself to all occasions. In company he is a gay and merry jester, alert and good-humored, everywhere and always with a bright and cheerful face, however terribly his enemies threaten him, so that you find it difficult to believe the man could undertake so arduous a task without divine aid. But there is one thing nearly all count a vice in him: he is a little more imprudent and biting in reproof than is either safe in one who goes new ways in theology or decorous in a theologian, a fault which I am not sure does not attach to all that have learned late.

During the first week the debate was between Eck and Carlstadt, and Luther entered the fray only on the fourth of July. It was for this both Eck and the spectators had been eagerly waiting, and the disputation now assumed for the first time the aspect of a real and serious struggle. The disputants began at once

with the fundamental question of the nature of papal
authority. Luther was very careful and moderate in
his utterances. He did not deny the supremacy of the
pope. He claimed only that he ruled by human, not
divine, right, and a Christian might therefore be saved
even if he refused to submit to his authority. This,
Eck at once declared, sounded very like the opinion of
John Hus, who had been condemned by the Council of
Constance and burned at the stake a hundred years
before.

The spread of Hus's views in Bohemia, his native
land, had led to civil war and cost Germany much blood
and treasure. The Bohemian heresy had become the
synonym of riot and revolution, and to accuse Luther
of sympathy with it was to hold him up to general
execration. He felt the gravity of the accusation, and
at first repelled it angrily. "Never," he retorted, "have
I taken pleasure in any schism whatsoever, nor will
I to the end of time. The Bohemians have done wrong
in voluntarily separating from our communion, even
if they have divine right on their side; for the highest
divine right is love and unity of the Spirit."

But after thinking the matter over, he declared, "It
is certain that among the articles of John Hus and the
Bohemians are many most Christian and evangelical,
and these the universal church cannot condemn."

This was the climax of the debate. Luther's words
were heard with horror by his enemies and with consternation by his friends. From the duke they elicited
an angry oath audible to the whole assembly. Seeing
the effect produced, Luther tried to qualify his statement and make it less offensive; but he had expressed
his real opinion, as everybody saw, and explanation
did not help the matter.

A couple of days later, in response to Eck's continued appeal to the authority of the Council of Constance, he declared: "I shall not be moved until the most excellent doctor proves that a council is unable to err, has not erred, and does not err. For a council cannot make divine right of what is not by its nature such, nor can it make that heresy which is not against divine right."

To which Eck replied: "The Reverend Father begs me to prove that a council cannot err. I am ignorant what he means by this unless he wishes to throw suspicion on the praiseworthy Council of Constance. This I say to you, Reverend Father, if you believe that a council lawfully assembled errs and has erred, you are to me as a heathen and a publican."

Eck was fully justified in taking this position, for to deny or doubt the infallibility of a general council was to reject the one ultimate authority depended upon for centuries by Catholic Christians. That Luther took his stand upon the Bible did not help the matter. According to Catholic belief, the church alone could properly interpret the Bible, and to set the teaching of the one in opposition to the other was nothing less than heresy.

The remainder of the debate, dealing with purgatory, indulgences, penance, and related matters, was of little importance, and the attention of the spectators flagged. It is significant of the change wrought in a year and a half that the discussion of indulgences aroused scant interest. Eck was quite ready to admit the justice of many of his opponent's strictures upon the practice, and Luther declared there never would have been any trouble if the ecclesiastical authorities had taken this attitude in the beginning. The conflict had been carried so much further, and had come to involve so much graver things, that agreement or disagreement about the matter originally in dispute counted for little. Luther had been driven by his opponents, and led by his own study and reflection, to positions so radical as to make his earlier criticism of abuses seem of small importance. He might be orthodox in every other respect, and accept without question all the doctrines and practices of the church, but to deny its infallible authority was to put himself outside the Catholic pale. Unless he repented and recanted, his excommunication was a foregone conclusion.

The debate from Luther's point of view was not a success. He had hoped much from it, and returned home greatly disappointed. Despite his own and his supporters' claims, the victory was really Eck's, not his, and it was fairly won. No other outcome was possible, and the result might have been foreseen. Luther made a much better showing against the powerful and resourceful debater than Carlstadt, but even his skill was unequal to the task of defending an essentially indefensible position. He committed the mistake of supposing that the radical views reached under the influence of his own religious experience were in harmony with the faith of the church. It is a common mistake. Some men, when they find themselves out of sympathy with the prevailing beliefs of the institution wherein they have been born and bred, at once turn their backs upon it. Others of a more sanguine temperament, or with more of the reformer's instinct, read its faith in the light of their own opinions, and endeavor to call their fellows back to what they believe its real platform. When, as is very apt to happen, a conflict comes and they try to defend as orthodox what they were originally led to accept as true, they only invite defeat. Luther maintained at Leipsic not merely that his interpretation of the papacy was correct, but that it was orthodox, and in this, as Eck showed, he was wrong. There remained only the alternative of abandoning his interpretation and accepting the traditional view or of foregoing the claim of orthodoxy. Consciously and deliberately he chose the latter course, and in doing so broke decisively with all his past.

Eck repeatedly protested that he held all his opinions subject to correction by the ecclesiastical authorities, but Luther avowed submission to no one. Only to the clear teaching of the divine word would he bow, and he would read it with his own and not with other men's eyes. In his attack on indulgences he had appealed from the indulgence-venders to the pope; at Augsburg, from the pope-ill-informed to the pope-to-be-better-informed; and soon afterward from the pope to a council. Now, when the decision of a council was cited against him, he declined to be bound by it, and took his stand upon the sole authority of the Scriptures. But even this was not final. The Bible itself, he maintained, has to be used with discrimination, for parts of it do not teach Christian truth. He really substituted for all external authorities the enlightened conscience of the individual Christian. The Bible he read for himself and admitted the claim of no council or body of men to read it for him. This, in principle, though he never fully realized it, and seldom acted upon it, meant the right of private judgment in religious things, and in it lay the promise of a new age.

It was not skepticism or indifference to religion that enabled Luther thus to stand upon his own feet. Rather it was the vividness of his religious experience, making him sure of acceptance with God. Because of this he found it possible to dispense with the traditional authorities. Had he not come into conflict with the rulers of the church, he might have lived to the end

From the painting by Lucas Cranach

DUKE GEORGE OF SAXONY

of his days quite unaware of any difference between himself and his fellow-Christians. Many another had passed through a religious experience similar to his and had lived and died content in the communion of the Catholic Church. There was nothing in his faith to cause a break. But when it became impossible to speak his mind about abuses and remain within the Roman fellowship, he discovered his faith was such that he could get along outside. He justified his attitude not by declaring the church unnecessary,— even when most radical he was still conservative,— but by interpreting it as the community of Christian believers wherever found and however governed. Greeks, Bohemians, and others condemned by Rome he now regarded as members of the universal church, and in their communion he felt it possible to enjoy all the blessings of Christianity. He did not for a moment imagine that the Roman Church was not a true church, but he came to feel that it was not the only one, and if forced without its pale, he would still be a member of the Christian family.

The significance of the Leipsic debate for Luther's own development it is impossible to exaggerate. It meant the final parting of the ways. It showed him clearly where he stood and emancipated him once and for all from the delusion that he was in harmony with the papal Church and could remain permanently within it. His condemnation he saw must follow in due time, and while Miltitz was still hopeful, and was industriously laying plans for compromise and conciliation, Luther himself was preparing for the break he knew could not long be delayed.

It shows the distance traveled and the lessons learned from the experiences of the last two years that he was neither crushed nor apparently greatly distressed by

10

the outlook. His development had been gradual, and he was fully prepared to take the final step when confronted by it. He had not foreseen the outcome, and, as he often said, would never have dared to begin had he known whither he was going; but he was driven against his will from point to point, and could not turn back without denying his faith. History presents no more striking example of the iron logic of events.

CHAPTER X

THE DEVELOPING CONTROVERSIALIST

THOUGH startled when he first discovered his agreement with Hus, as he did at the Leipsic disputation, Luther soon recovered his equanimity, and was heartened rather than dismayed by the discovery. During the summer he received letters from prominent Bohemians expressing their joy in him and his work and likening his place in Saxony to that of Hus in Bohemia. Instead of denying all sympathy with the condemned heretic, as he would have done a few weeks before, he acknowledged the letters with thanks, and after reading for the first time some of Hus's writings, declared, with his usual impulsiveness and frank generosity: "Hitherto I have unconsciously held and taught all the doctrines of John Hus. John Staupitz has also taught them in like ignorance. Briefly we are all Hussites without knowing it." Evidently he had come to look upon the generally hated Bohemians as allies, and felt confirmed in his own position rather than frightened from it because it was shared by them.

The same sympathy with outsiders appeared in the Leipsic debate itself, when he referred to the Eastern Church in support of his contention that submission to the pope was not necessary to salvation. Most of the Greek fathers either knew nothing of papal supremacy or consciously rejected it. In them he found kindred spirits, and thenceforth was always fond of

appealing to them. His attitude was not a sign, as is
often said, of his native breadth of view,—liberality
was not one of his virtues,—but of the instinctive feeling of comradeship with others like himself in opposition. He began to think of himself not merely as a
single individual engaged in a petty contest of his own,
but as one of a long line of fighters against ecclesiastical tyranny and corruption. His consciousness ex-
panded, and his work came to seem of national and
even world-wide meaning.

He always had an uncommonly vivid sense of fulfilling the divine will in everything he undertook. Now
the conviction dominated him more completely than
ever. Henceforth he believed himself one of God's
chosen instruments, called to carry on the labors of the
great leaders who had fought and fallen in earlier days.
Martyrdom he was in constant expectation of, looking
forward to the fate that had overtaken so many. But
he was inspired rather than oppressed by the thought,
and rejoiced in the opportunity to suffer as they had
suffered.

He also saw more clearly than before the difficulties of the task he was engaged in. Others had tried
to do what he was now attempting, and had failed.
Even this did not dishearten him. He believed the
times were fast growing ripe. Either he or some one
else for whom he was preparing the way—his colleague Melanchthon, for instance—he was sure would
yet accomplish the hitherto impossible. Fantastic notions that the end of the world was at hand, notions
very common in that day, began to find lodgment in his
mind, and were never afterward altogether abandoned.
It was a time of feverish excitement, not altogether
conducive to calm and deliberate thought.

The months succeeding the Leipsic disputation were

very busy ones. His mental powers were at their height and he worked to the very limit of his strength. He was more active with his pen than ever, continually sending pamphlets to the press and occasionally books of considerable bulk. The titles of his publications for the year 1519 number nearly thirty, many of them to be sure only sermons or brief tracts, but among them two large Scripture commentaries and a sizable book on the power of the pope. In one of his letters he complained of his inability to publish as rapidly as he wished because of the limitations of the printing-office, and a little later informed a friend that he kept three presses going all the time. It was his habit to send copy to the printer day by day, and he was nearly always reading the proof of the earlier pages of a book while writing the later. Often the preface was in type before the work itself was even begun. It is surprising not that much of his published work bears the marks of haste, but that so many of his writings still richly repay reading after the lapse of four centuries.

Newspapers were then unknown and the place they now occupy was filled by brief pamphlets. Since the recent invention of printing the latter had multiplied rapidly and were read with great avidity. Of this means of reaching the public ear Luther made most effective use, becoming in a short time the most active and influential pamphleteer in Germany and giving a tremendous impetus to the new form of popular literature. He had, as he once remarked, a quick hand and a ready memory, and all he wrote flowed from his pen without effort. His speed was the despair of friends and foes alike. It is amusing to see how often, when requested by Spalatin or the elector or some other anxious sympathizer to refrain from a publication likely to make trouble, he replied that their protests were too late, for the deed was already done. The physical and mental vitality of the man was one of the most amazing things about him and one of the secrets of his tremendous power.

He was indefatigable in controversy, determined to let no attack go unanswered. Hearing that the University of Erfurt, which had been asked, with the University of Paris, to pass judgment on the Leipsic debate, was about to give a decision against him, he wrote his old friend Lang in October:

The Leipsic people assert that your Erfurters have reached a conclusion adverse to us and favorable to Eck. If this be so I hope it will prove of advantage to you that your people have meddled without cause in a matter that is none of their business. I have resolved in a Latin and German defense to brand their judgment with infamy before the whole world, and for the sake of protecting the truth I will publicly show its injustice or its ignorance as soon as it is announced, and in doing so I shall be innocent of their blood. My mind is made up not to leave a single syllable of my theses undefended. The will of God be done.

A little later, learning that the report was incorrect and the university had declined to pronounce any judgment, he wrote Lang again:

I am glad your Erfurters have refused to render a decision. For it is already in vain we have disputed, and even a judgment from the Parisians will accomplish nothing except to give me an opportunity of speaking against the Roman antichrist with the aid of God.

The attacks upon him during these months were many and severe. Though he frequently expressed regret at being obliged to waste so much time in controversy and interrupt more important work, he really welcomed the attacks as invitations to let his views be known, and many a reply was rather a statement of his own doctrines than an answer to his antagonists. For the latter, he often contented himself with personal abuse instead of reasoned argument. "Never," he politely assured one of his assailants, "have I seen a more ignorant ass than you, though you particularly boast of having studied dialectics for many years. I greatly rejoice to be condemned by so obscure a head."

His treatment of opponents, which grew more bitter with the passing years, has always been a ground of offense to his enemies and of confusion to his friends. After the not uncommon fashion of the day, error in opinion was taken as a sign of moral obliquity, and the inexhaustible stores of his rich and racy vocabulary were freely drawn upon to portray the characters of those venturing to oppose him. From the beginning profoundly convinced of his own divine call, he identified his cause with God's and always attributed the hostility of his enemies to the promptings of Satan, who filled their hearts with hatred for God and all His works. In these circumstances the outbreaks of his fiery temper were justified as heaven-sent. In 1531, more than ten years after his final break with Rome, in a pamphlet entitled "Against the Traitor at Dresden," he wrote:

This shall be my glory and honor, and I will have it so, that henceforth they will say of me that I am full of bad words, of scolding and cursing against the papists. I have often humbled myself for more than ten years, and used the very best language, but have only increased their wrath, and the peasants have been the more puffed up by my supplications. Now, however, because they are obdurate and have determined to do nothing good, but only evil, so that there is no longer any hope, I will hereafter heap curses and maledictions upon the villains until I go to my grave, and no good word shall they hear from me again. I will toll them to their tombs with my thunder and lightning. For I cannot pray without at the same time cursing. If I say, "Hallowed be Thy name," I have to add, "Cursed, damned, reviled be the name of the papists and of all who blaspheme Thy name." If I say, "Thy kingdom come," I have to add, "Cursed, damned, destroyed be the papacy, together with all the kingdoms of the earth, which oppose Thy kingdom." If I say, "Thy will be done," I have to add, "Cursed, damned, reviled, and destroyed be all the thoughts and plans of the papists and of every one who strives against Thy will and counsel." Thus I pray aloud every day and inwardly without ceasing, and with me all that believe in Christ. And I feel sure that my prayer will be heard. Nevertheless I have a kind, friendly, peaceable, and Christian heart toward every one, as even my worst enemies know.

His violence has been excused by appealing to the prevailing tone of contemporary polemics, but the excuse is insufficient. Though his form of expression might have been different in another century, the man he was would have been violent and vituperative in any. Passionate and high-tempered, to speak or write calmly about an antagonist was an impossibility to him. As he once remarked in a letter to a friend: "That I am vehement is not to be wondered at. If you were what I am you too would be vehement." Anger he always recognized as his greatest fault, but he believed it a very good thing in its place. He liked to be angry in a good cause, he once remarked. It refreshed him like a thunderstorm, and he could write much better for it. As a matter of fact, he seldom deliberated over his controversial productions, but dashed them off while his wrath was at its hottest, and, printing always as he wrote, he never had the opportunity or took the pains to revise and moderate his language after the first flush of indignation had passed.

When Spalatin found fault, in 1520, with the strong language of a reply to the Bishop of Meissen, he wrote:

Greeting. Good God! how excited you are, my Spalatin! You seem even more stirred up than I and the others. Do you not see that my patience in not replying to Emser's and Eck's five or six wagon-loads of curses is the sole reason why the framers of this document have dared to attack me with such silly and ridiculous nonsense? For you know how little I cared that my sermon at Leipsic was condemned and suppressed by a public edict; how I despised suspicion, infamy, injury, hatred. Must these audacious persons even be permitted to add to these follies scandalous pamphlets crammed full of falsehoods and blasphemies against gospel truth? Do you forbid even to bark at these wolves? The Lord is my witness how I restrained myself lest I should not treat with reverence this accursed and most impotent document issued in the bishop's name. Otherwise I should have said things those heads ought to hear, and I will yet, when they acknowledge their authorship by beginning to defend themselves. I beg, if you think rightly of the gospel, do not imagine its cause can be accomplished without tumult, scandal, and sedition. Out of the sword you cannot make a feather, nor out of war, peace. The word of God is a sword, war, ruin, destruction, poison, and, as Amos says, it meets the children of Ephraim like a bear in the way and a lioness in the woods.

I cannot deny that I have been more vehement than is seemly. But since they knew this, they ought not to have stirred up the dog. How difficult it is to temper one's passions and one's pen you can judge even from your own case. This is the reason I have always disliked to engage in public controversy; but the more I dislike it, the more I am involved against my will, and that only by the most atrocious slanders brought against me and the word of God. If I were not carried away thereby either in temper or pen, even a heart of stone would be moved by the indignity of the thing to take up arms; and how much more I, who am both passionate and possessed of a pen not altogether blunt! By these monstrosities I am driven beyond modesty and decorum. At the same time, I wonder where this new religion came from, that whatever you say against an adversary is regarded as slander. What do you think of Christ? Was he a slanderer when he called the Jews an adulterous and perverse generation, the offspring of vipers, hypocrites, sons of the devil? And what about Paul when he used the words dogs, vain babblers, seducers, ignorant, and in Acts xiii so inveighed against a false prophet that he seems almost insane: "Oh, thou full of all deceit and of all craft, thou son of the devil, enemy of truth"? Why did he not gently flatter him, that he might convert him, rather than thunder in such a way? It is not possible, if acquainted with the truth, to be patient with inflexible and ungovernable enemies of the truth. But enough of this nonsense. I see that everybody wishes I were gentle, especially my enemies, who show themselves least so of all. If I am too little gentle, I am at least simple and open, and therein, as I believe, surpass them, for they dispute only in a deceitful fashion. Farewell, and be not afraid.

Twenty years and more later, referring to one of his bitterest and most scathing invectives, he remarked:

I have read my book over again, and wonder how it happened that I was so moderate. I ascribe it to the state of my head, which was such that my mind was prevented from working more freely and actively.

His violence was not merely a matter of temperament but also of deliberate choice. As he once remarked, when criticized for his sharp words:

Our Lord God must begin with a pelting thunderstorm, afterward it rains gently and so soaks into the ground. A willow or hazel twig you can cut with a bread-knife, but for a hard oak you must have an ax and then you can hardly fell it and split it.

He was better acquainted than most men with the common people of his day, and he knew strong language was needed to move and arouse them. He was working not to win a reputation, but to stir up a nation, and while many others were appealing to a small and select circle of the cultured, vast multitudes were hanging on his words. His fiercest onslaughts carried terror and joy to the ends of Christendom, and by them no less than by his inimitable appeals to the finer sentiments he swayed and dominated the masses. Often he went beyond all reason and broke the canons of good taste recognized even in that free-spoken age; but he was not engaged in a parlor exhibition, and he would have cared as little for our criticisms of his style of fighting as he did for the criticisms of his contemporaries. Had he been other than he was, he might have been better liked by many a delicate soul, but he could not have wielded the influence he did. He needs no apologies from us. As well apologize for the fury of the wind as for the vehemence of Martin Luther.

But if we would do justice to this extraordinary

man, it must be remembered that the conflict he was engaged in did not keep him from performing his ordinary duties with his accustomed vigor and effectiveness. He did more than a man's full work quite apart from his controversy, though the latter, it would seem, was alone enough to absorb all his attention and tax all his powers. He preached regularly in the city church and the convent, lectured as usual in the university, and gave a surprising amount of attention to administrative matters, concerning himself even with the pettiest details of faculty business. He also worked steadily upon the interpretation of the Bible, continuing the publication of his careful and laborious exposition of the Psalms, which excited the admiration even of an Erasmus, and issuing in the autumn his famous commentary on Galatians, designed particularly to bring his new interpretation of the gospel to the attention of the learned world. In addition he printed many moral and religious pamphlets, containing no trace whatever of the stress and strain of conflict, and wrote beautiful letters and tracts for the solace and inspiration of the sick and suffering.

A couple of brief passages may be quoted from his quaint little book, entitled "Tesseredecas," because containing in two contrasted tables seven pictures of the evils Christians are called on to suffer and seven of the blessings with which God consoles them. It was written in September, in the midst of battle and under the pressure of strenuous labors, for the comfort of the Elector Frederick, who was lying grievously ill.

When you regard as sacred relics, and love, kiss, and embrace the coat, the vessels, the water-jars, and all the things Christ touched and used, why do you not much more love, embrace, and kiss pains, worldly evils, ignominy, and death? For these he not only made sacred, but bathed and blessed them with his blood, enduring them with willing heart and deepest devotion.

When Jacob heard that his son Joseph was a ruler in Egypt, like one awaking out of deep sleep he believed it not until the wagons sent by Joseph proved the truth of all his sons told him. Thus it would be indeed difficult to believe so great blessings are given us unworthy creatures in Christ, if he had not revealed himself to his disciples in manifold ways, and taught us also to believe by use and experience as if we saw the very wagons. A wagon bringing rich comfort it is that Christ has been made to us by God righteousness, sanctification, redemption, and wisdom. For I am a sinner, but I am borne in his righteousness given to me; I am impure, but his holiness is my sanctification wherein I sweetly ride; I am foolish, but his wisdom carries me; worthy of damnation I am, but his liberty is my redemption, a wagon most secure.

Luther showed the simplicity of his nature when he soon afterward asked the manuscript of this tract back from Spalatin, hoping to derive from its perusal consolation in his own troubles.

CHAPTER XI

THE NATIONAL REFORMER

WHILE enemies were springing up on all sides to denounce Luther for his attitude toward papacy and church his fame was rapidly growing and his friends and supporters were steadily multiplying. Particularly important was the recognition received from leading humanists both at home and abroad. They were the liberals of the day, devoted to the new culture of the age and eager to welcome anything promising release from the yoke of ecclesiastical bigotry and theological obscurantism. As early as the autumn of 1518, speaking of Albrecht Dürer, Lazarus Spengler, and other celebrated lights of Nuremberg, Christopher Scheurl remarked: "Nearly all the conversation at table concerns a certain Martin. Him they celebrate, adore, and champion. For him they are prepared to endure everything." A few months later he wrote Eck, expostulating with him for his attack on Luther:

You are bringing upon yourself, unless I am mistaken, the strong disfavor and hatred of most followers of Erasmus and Reuchlin, nearly all friends of learning, and even modern theologians. I have recently traveled through a number of important dioceses and everywhere found a great many adherents of Martin. The clergy's love for the man is astonishing. They are flying to him in flocks, like jackdaws and starlings. They subscribe to his opinions, they applaud him, they bless him.

About the same time Luther received letters from John Froben, the publisher of Basel, and from Wolfgang Capito, a well-known humanist, informing him that he had many warm and influential friends in Switzerland and along the Rhine, and that his books were widely read not only there, but also in Italy, France, Spain, and England.

Even the great Erasmus spoke of him in a friendly way, and guarded as his utterances were, for he early realized the difference between Luther's spirit and his own, his attitude was generally interpreted as sympathetic, and greatly enhanced Luther's credit with men of modern tendencies.

The Leipsic debate still further increased his reputation. The humanist Mosellan had expected to hear only old and threadbare themes discussed in traditional scholastic fashion, and was surprised and delighted at Luther's attitude, as he was careful to inform his correspondents. Luther's enemies, humanists everywhere now began to realize, were theirs and his struggle a renewal of the Reuchlin conflict between the representatives of the old and the new learning. In such a battle it could not be doubtful where their sympathies would lie.

In October he received a couple of notable letters from an acquaintance of his Erfurt student days, the humanist Crotus Rubeanus, principal author of the famous "Letters of Obscure Men." Crotus was in Italy at the time, and gave Luther first-hand information of the efforts there on foot to crush him. He also hailed him in enthusiastic terms as a father of the fatherland, "worthy of a golden statue and an annual feast."

This recognition of the national importance of Luther's work, taken with the unconcealed contempt for the Roman curia which breathes in the letters of Crotus, was full of significance. It foreshadowed an alliance between Luther and another group of Germans who were chiefly interested in economic and political reform. The leading spokesman of the group was Ulrich von Hutten, one of the most interesting and picturesque figures of the age. Son of a poor knight, and, on account of his delicate physique, destined for the priesthood, he early ran away and spent the remainder of his brief life in wandering from place to place, at times in abject poverty, again enjoying the favor and protection of the great. He was a poet of no mean gifts and an enthusiastic humanist. While in Italy, in 1517, he ran across Lorenzo Valla's significant work on the Donation of Constantine which proved that famous document a forgery. For centuries canonists had made the Emperor Constantine's alleged gift to Pope Sylvester one of the bases of the papal claim to political sovereignty over the western world. To show the gift a mere fiction was to strike a severe blow at the prestige of the papacy. Upon Hutten Valla's work made a great impression. He republished it with a fiery preface of his own, and was thenceforth one of the most active opponents of the Roman see. Germany's subjection to it, he became convinced, was the principal cause of all the ills of his native land, and he exchanged the career of a mere litterateur for that of a political agitator. Before long he was widely recognized as the most influential member of the young German party and the chief leader in the movement for throwing off the Roman yoke.

At Augsburg, in 1518, Hutten did much to arouse the enmity of the members of the diet to the holy see. He had no interest as yet in Luther or his cause. He looked with contempt upon the whole thing as a mere monk's quarrel. But after the Leipsic debate, perhaps under the influence of his old friend Crotus, he saw in the Wittenberg professor the most formidable opponent the papacy had yet encountered and thought of him as a possible ally. At the time he was in the service of Archbishop Albert of Mayence and there were difficulties in the way of forming an acquaintance with Luther; but he sent him greetings, and in the spring of 1520, through the intervention of common friends, the two men got into communication with each other, and, though only temporary, their friendship, while it lasted, was of great importance for them both. It opened Hutten's eyes to the religious issues involved in the national movement, and Luther's to the importance of that movement for his own cause. Hitherto, while not blind to the economic and social evils of the day, as many passages in his earlier writings show, Luther's thought was largely occupied with educational and religious questions. Now he began to concern himself with other matters altogether, and to dream of a reformation which should affect every phase of national life.

Hutten's friendship for Luther also brought the reformer the support of many other German noblemen, and gave him a feeling of personal security and independence quite unknown before. In his letters of 1520 he referred frequently and with great satisfaction to his new allies. Writing to Spalatin in July he said:

I inclose a letter from the Franconian knight, Sylvester Schaumberg, and should be glad, if it is not too much trouble, to have the prince mention it in his communication to the Cardinal of St. George, that they may know, even if they drive me out of Wittenberg, with their detestable attacks, they will accomplish nothing, but will only make their case worse. For now not merely in

11

Bohemia, but in the heart of Germany itself, there are those able and willing to protect the exile in spite of them and all their thunders. There is danger that, once under their protection, I shall be much more severe in attacking the Romanists than if I remain under the dominion of the prince, engaged in the work of teaching. This without doubt will occur unless God prevents. I shall not then be obliged to consider the prince, whom I have hitherto respected on many occasions, even when provoked. Let them know I frequently refrain from attacking them not because of my own modesty or their tyranny or merit, but because of the name and authority of the prince, as well as the common good of the Wittenberg students. As for me, the die is cast. Rome's fury and favor are alike despised. Never will I be reconciled, or commune with her.

Not simply Schaumberg, but also no less a person than Franz von Sickingen, friend and protector of Hutten, and the most powerful and widely feared knight of Germany, offered the reformer an asylum and assured him of his warm interest. Sickingen and Schaumberg, Luther wrote to Spalatin, had freed him altogether from the fear of men.

Under the influence of his newly formed connection with such warriors as these, Luther even went so far as to give expression to sentiments of a decidedly violent sort. In June, referring to a new attack by Prierias, he wrote:

It seems to me, if the fury of the Romanists goes on in this fashion, no remedy is left except for emperor, kings, and princes to arm themselves and attack these pests of the whole world, and settle the affair no longer with words, but with the sword. For what do these lost men, deprived even of common sense, say? Exactly what was predicted of antichrist, as if we were more

irrational than blockheads. If we punish thieves with
the halter, brigands with the sword, heretics with fire,
why do we not still more attack with every sort of
weapon these masters of perdition, these cardinals, these
popes, and all this crowd of Roman Sodom, who corrupt
the church of God unceasingly? Why do we not bathe
our hands in their blood that we may rescue ourselves
and our children from this general and most dangerous
conflagration?

And in a letter to Spalatin written on the thirteenth
of November he expressed the wish that Hutten's plan
to intercept and capture the papal legates on their way
to the Diet of Worms might have been carried out.

To be sure, too much should not be made of such
utterances. They are exceptional in Luther's writings.
As a rule, he earnestly deprecated physical violence and
armed revolution. In January, 1521, he declared
himself entirely out of sympathy with Hutten's warlike
plans, writing to Spalatin:

You see what Hutten desires. I do not wish to battle
for the gospel with violence and murder, and I have
written the man to that effect. By the word the world
has been conquered and the church preserved, and by
the word it will be repaired. Antichrist also, as he began
without violence, will without violence be overthrown by
the word.

And a little later:

I am without blame, for I have striven to bring it
about that the German nobility should check the Romanists, as they are well able to do, with resolutions and
edicts, not with the sword. For to attack the unarmed
masses of the clergy would be like making war upon
women and children.

In 1522, in his bitter pamphlet "Against the so-called Spiritual Estate of Pope and Bishops," after declaring that every one who did what he could to uproot the episcopate and destroy its authority was a child of God and a true Christian, he added:

I do not mean that the bishops should be overthrown with fist and sword. They are not worth such punishment, nor would anything be accomplished by it. On the contrary, as Daniel teaches, the antichrist is to be overcome without force, every one using God's word against him until he falls into contempt and perishes of himself.

But in 1520 the reformer was evidently feeling the influence of his new friends and entering rather recklessly into their warlike ideas. Gradually he steadied himself again and realized that the cause he was interested in would only be hindered by violence and war. Thenceforth he was unalterably opposed to both.

THE most notable fruit of Luther's awakened interest in national reform was his famous "Address to the German Nobility," published in August, 1520. In the dedicatory letter to his colleague Amsdorf he says:

The time for silence is past and the time to speak is come, as the preacher Solomon says. In conformity with our resolve I have put together a few points concerning the reformation of the Christian estate in order to lay them before the Christian nobility of Germany in case it may please God to help His church by means of the laity, since the clergy whom this task rather befitted have grown quite careless. I send it all to your worship to judge, and to amend where needed. I am well aware that I shall not escape the reproach of taking far too much upon me in presuming, despised and insignificant

to her, the sacraments, it had been believed since the second century, were absolutely essential to salvation. As their validity depended ordinarily upon their performance by duly ordained priests, Christians were obliged to rely altogether upon priestly ministrations and were quite helpless alone. The authority of church and hierarchy over the faith and life of Christendom was rooted in this fact and to deny it was to attack Catholicism at its most vital spot. Deny it Luther did, and with emphasis. Every Christian, he claimed, is truly a priest in the sight of God, and need depend on no one else for divine grace. And what was more, the sacraments themselves, he insisted, are mere signs of the forgiving love of God in Christ. Unless their message be believed they are of no help, and if it be believed without them they may be dispensed with. Thus while recognizing their value as aids to faith he freed Christians from slavish dependence on them and on church and priesthood as well. Never was man more independent of external and factitious means, or franker and more fearless in declaring their needlessness. Splendidly regardless of consequences either to himself or to others he proclaimed his message of emancipation in ringing terms.

The work was a declaration of freedom such as alone made his own position tenable. It was of a piece with his sermon on the ban, published two years earlier, and in harmony with the religious point of view attained long before as a result of his youthful struggles in the convent. Out of despair due to a vivid sense of the wrath of God he had been rescued by the recognition of divine love, and the ensuing peace was the salvation he sought. A present reality it was, not simply a future hope, a state of mind and so the fruit of faith not of works. To one thus already saved sacraments and hierarchy were of secondary importance. Though Luther long remained unconscious of his inner independence of them, when the conflict came and he was threatened with their loss he discovered he could do without them, and the discovery proved a new charter of liberty for himself and in the end for multitudes of others.

That charter found its clearest and most beautiful expression in a wonderful little tract, one of the world's great religious classics, published almost immediately after the work on the sacraments and entitled The Freedom of a Christian Man. At its very beginning were placed the paradoxical statements:

A Christian man is a most free lord of all things and subject to no one; a Christian man is a most dutiful servant of all things and subject to every one.

What he meant by the former appears in such words as these:

Every Christian is by faith so exalted above all things that in spiritual power he is completely lord of all. Nothing whatever can do him any hurt, but all things are subject to him and are compelled to be subservient to his salvation. . . . This is a spiritual power ruling in the midst of enemies and mighty in the midst of distresses. And it is nothing else than that strength is made perfect in weakness, and in all things I am able to gain salvation, so that even the cross and death are compelled to serve me and work together for salvation. For this is a high and illustrious dignity, a true and almighty power, a spiritual empire, in which there is nothing so good, nothing so bad as not to work together for my good if only I believe. . . . A Christian man needs no work, no law for salvation, for by faith he is free from all law and in perfect freedom does gratuitously all he does, seeking

man as I am, to address such high estates on such weighty subjects, as if there were no one in the world but Dr. Luther to have a care for Christianity and to give advice to such wise people. I offer no excuse. Let who will blame me. Perhaps I still owe God and the world another folly. This debt I have now resolved honestly to discharge, if I can, and to be court fool for once. If I fail, I have at least one advantage, that no one need buy me a cap or shave my poll. But it remains to be seen which shall hang the bells on the other. I must fulfil the proverb "When anything is to be done in the world a monk must be in it were it only as a painted figure."

I beg you to excuse me to the moderately wise for I know not how to deserve the favor and grace of the overwise. Often I have sought it with much labor, but henceforth will neither have nor care for it. God help us to seek not our glory but His alone.

The work itself was a ringing appeal to the German Emperor, princes, and nobility to take in hand the reformation of Germany, religious, ethical, social, and economic. Because of the claim of pope and hierarchy that the civil power had no jurisdiction in the matter, and no one but they could reform the church, a terrific onslaught was made upon them. The current criticisms of the avarice and extortion of the curia and the current impatience at its spoliation of Germany were given passionate expression. "Do we still wonder," he exclaimed, "why princes, noblemen, cities, convents, land, and people grow poor? We should rather wonder that we have anything left to eat." "Oh, noble princes and lords, how long will you suffer your land and your people to be the prey of these ravening wolves?"

The incompatibility between the spiritual office and temporal power of the pope was also depicted in vivid fashion:

How can the government of the empire consist with preaching, prayer, study, and the care of the poor? These are the true employments of the pope. Christ imposed them with such insistence that he forbade to take either coat or scrip, for he that has to govern a single house can hardly perform these duties. Yet the pope wishes to rule an empire and remain pope.

Luther conceded that the bishop of Rome might still be the spiritual head of Christendom whom all should honor and obey in spiritual things so long as he was true to Christ. But he would have his temporal power brought altogether to an end and would deprive him of all administrative authority over the church in Germany. The management of its affairs, the appointment and deposition of its officials, the trial of ecclesiastical cases, the granting of dispensations and the like, he would put into the hands of the German ecclesiastical authorities presided over by the primate of Germany, the Archbishop of Mayence. The new national feeling, growing rapidly in Luther's day, here found utterance. In religion, as in everything else, the nation, he believed, should manage its own affairs and live its own life.

But freedom from a foreign yoke was not, in his opinion, all Germany needed. The false claims of the clergy must be exposed and their usurped power taken from them. They possessed no prerogatives not belonging of right to all Christians. They were only ministers appointed to serve in religious things, and were subject to the people, not lords over them. Civil rulers "ordained of God for the punishment of the bad and protection of the good" were supreme in their own lands and the clergy were as completely under their jurisdiction as anybody else. If the existing ecclesiastical authorities failed to do their duty and left the

From an old print

ULRICH VON HUTTEN

church unreformed, the civil rulers must take the matter in hand and force a reformation in spite of hierarchy and pope. Liberty from the domination of the spiritual power, from dependence upon its offices and from dread of its penalties, was one of the watchwords of the book. In it a new age was foreshadowed.

No less important was Luther's declaration of freedom from bondage to exclusively religious duties. Perhaps the most extraordinary thing about the book is its complete break with what may be called the monastic ideal of life. As in his important "Sermon on Good Works," published some months before, he complained again of the over-emphasis of religion. It sounds strange enough to hear a monk insisting that such common human virtues as find play in the ordinary relationships of life are far more important than any religious exercises. This difference in the estimate of life was more decisive than any difference of doctrine between Luther and the Roman Church, at this or any subsequent time. In it was wrapped up the promise of a new world.

The Address to the German Nobility was not simply an appeal for reformation and an attack upon the forces that were hindering it, but also a program of reform on a large scale. All sorts of evils were dealt with, and the range of topics was very wide. Amazement has often been expressed that a monk should possess so extensive a knowledge of men and things. The amazement is misplaced. Luther had long been a public man in touch with the movements of the day and in correspondence with leaders of thought in many parts of Germany and abroad. It would have been surprising had he not known what men were thinking and talking about. As a matter of fact, he said little that was new. More than any other of his important works the Address to the Nobility reflected the ideas of his contemporaries. Not Hutten alone, but many besides, had attacked the evils of the day, religious, ecclesiastical, social, and economic, as severely and as intelligently as he. And so far as his constructive program went it was as vague and unpractical as any of theirs. There was much homely good sense in his proposals of reform—the abolishment of the mendicant orders, the reduction of festivals and holidays, the abandonment of enforced clerical celibacy, the improvement of schools and universities, the regulation of beggary, and the like—but some of his suggestions were quite impracticable and revealed a vast ignorance particularly of economics and politics.

He wanted to put a bridle on the Fuggers, the great money-lenders of the day.

How is it possible that in a single man's lifetime such great and kingly wealth can be collected together if all be done rightly and according to God's will? I am not skilled in accounts, but I do not understand how a hundred gulden can gain twenty in a year or how one can gain another, and that not from the soil or cattle, where success depends not on the wit of men but on the blessing of God.

In this he was only giving voice to the common and oft-expressed sentiment of the knights and nobles, the rural magnates of the age, whose prosperity and prestige were threatened by the extension of trade and the growth of cities. Like them, he was opposed to commerce and in favor of agriculture, and he supported his position as he always did by appealing to the Bible.

This I know well, it were much more godly to increase agriculture and lessen commerce, and they do best who, according to the Scriptures, till the ground to get their living. As is said to all of us in Adam, "Cursed be the earth. When thou workest in it it shall bring forth thistles and thorns to thee, and in the sweat of thy face shalt thou eat thy bread."

The greatest misfortune of the Germans he believed was the growing custom of mortgaging their property.

But for this many a man would have to leave unbought his silk, velvet, jewelry, spices, and all sorts of luxuries. The system has not been in force more than a hundred years and has already brought poverty, misery, and destruction on almost all princes, foundations, cities, nobles, and heirs. If it continue for another hundred years Germany will be left without a farthing, and we shall be reduced to eating one another. The devil invented this system and the pope has done injury to the whole world by sanctioning it.

The reigning extravagance in food and dress likewise troubled him, and he wished to see it controlled by legislation. At the same time he thought the nation could do without its elaborate system of laws and could best be governed by wise princes using only the Bible as their guide.

He always had great confidence in the ability of civil rulers to set everything right in the social and economic sphere if they only had the inclination. In 1539, when the price of food stuffs was unwontedly high in Wittenberg, and there was much complaint in consequence, he wrote the elector urging him to come to the rescue and fix lower prices by law. In 1524, in a very interesting little book on Trade and Usury, he depicted in detail what he regarded as the worst evils in the commercial life of the day, complaining of international trade, which only impoverishes a country, and denouncing monopolies, corners, trusts, buying and selling on margins, and the like, in language that sounds very familiar to-day. The remedy, he thought, lay wholly in the hands of the government.

Kings and princes should look into the matter and prevent such practices by law. But I hear they have a share in them, as is said in Isaiah, "Your princes have become the companions of robbers." They hang the thieves who have stolen a gulden or less, while they are hand and glove with those who rob the whole world, according to the proverb, "Great thieves hang little thieves."

In all this there is a curious mixture of wisdom and naïveté which is perhaps only what we might expect. Keen sighted as he was for the evils of the day his training and experience had not fitted him to play the rôle of a statesman or economist and he showed his limitations very clearly. Society he rightly saw was all too little governed by Christian principles, but like many another he had an implicit faith in the possibility of righting all wrongs by legislation and fondly imagined every evil could be mended by restoring the more primitive conditions of an earlier day.

For all his lack of worldly knowledge he had one merit not shared by all venturing into unfamiliar fields. He recognized his own ignorance. "I know," he wrote, "that I have sung a lofty strain, that I have proposed many things that will be thought impossible and attacked many points too sharply. But what was I to do? I was bound to say it. If I had the power, this is what I should do." Thus he closes his discussion, and the words from such a man are very signifi-

THE RUINS OF EBERNBURG, THE STRONGHOLD OF
FRANZ VON SICKINGEN

FRANCISCVS·VON·SICKINGEN

ALLEIN·GOT·DI·ER·LIEB
DEN·GEMEINEN·VCZ·BESCH
IRM·DI·GERECHTIKEI

From an old print

FRANZ VON SICKINGEN

cant. Ordinarily he was sure enough of himself and let it be known to everybody. Evidently his confidence was not mere self-conceit, the fond persuasion that he was always right. It was a confidence felt only in his native sphere and justified by his long and hard experience therein.

The Address to the Nobility produced a tremendous sensation and had an enormous sale. Most of its ideas had been expressed many times before, but Luther had his own inimitable way of putting things, and the very fact it was he who said them meant a great deal for the circulation of the book. Men were already listening eagerly to all he had to say, and his venture into the field of national reform met with a wide and instant response. It is not recorded that the work brought him reputation as a statesman and led princes to seek his counsel in political affairs, but it did show them he was a power to be reckoned with, and it gave new standing to the cause of national independence and regeneration.

CHAPTER XII

THE PROPHET OF A NEW FAITH

AT the end of his Address to the German Nobility Luther remarked: "I know still another song concerning Rome. If they wish to hear it I will sing it and will pitch it high. Do you understand, dear Rome, what I mean?"

This new work appeared a few weeks later under the title "The Babylonian Captivity of the Church." It dealt with the traditional sacramental system, representing it as a bondage from which Christendom must be freed if the needed reformation were to come. Unlike the former work, it was written in Latin, as befitted a theological discussion, and appealed primarily to theologians instead of the general public. Doctrinally it was far and away the most radical book Luther had yet published, and was alone enough to make his condemnation for heresy imperative. None of his other works so excited the hostility of Catholic theologians, or drew so many replies from them. Even King Henry VIII of England thought it worth while to write an answer to it, for which he was rewarded by the pope with the title of Defender of the Faith and by Luther with one of the most scathing and insulting rejoinders ever addressed to a king.

The sacramental system was the very heart of traditional Catholicism. Supernatural means by which alone the Church dispensed the divine grace intrusted

neither profit nor salvation, but only what is well-pleasing to God, since by the grace of God he is already satisfied and saved through his faith.

And what he meant by the second of his paradoxical statements appears with equal clearness in the following passages:

Though he is thus free from all works yet he ought again to empty himself of this liberty, take on the form of a servant, be made in the likeness of men, be found in fashion as a man, serve, help, and in every way act toward his neighbor as he sees that God through Christ has acted and is acting toward him. All this he should do freely and with regard to nothing but the good pleasure of God; and he should reason thus: Lo, to me, an unworthy, condemned, and contemptible creature, altogether without merit, my God of His pure and free mercy has given in Christ all the riches of righteousness and salvation, so that I am no longer in want of anything except faith to believe this is so. For such a Father therefore, who has overwhelmed me with these inestimable riches of His, why should I not freely, gladly, with a whole heart and eager devotion, do all that I know will be pleasing and acceptable in his sight? I will therefore give myself as a sort of Christ to my neighbor, as Christ has given himself to me, and will do nothing in this life except what I see to be needful, advantageous, and wholesome for my neighbor, since through faith I abound in all good things in Christ. . . . Man does not live for himself alone in this mortal body, in order to work on its account, but also for all men on earth; nay, he lives only for others and not for himself. For to this end he brings his own body into subjection that he may be able to serve others more sincerely and freely. . . . It is the part of a Christian to take care of his body for the very purpose that by its soundness and well-being he may be able to labor and to acquire and save property for the aid of those who are in want, that thus the strong member may serve the weak, and we may be sons of God, thoughtful and busy one for the other, bearing one another's burdens and so fulfilling the law of Christ. Behold, here is the truly Christian life, here is faith really working by love, when it applies itself with joy and love to the work of freest servitude, in which it serves others freely and spontaneously, itself abundantly satisfied with the fullness and riches of its own faith.

The chief fault of traditional Catholic ethics was its divided ideal. It too taught devotion to others and self-sacrificing labor for their good, but it made this simply a part of the Christian's duty. Holiness and righteousness were also demanded of him, and frequently the two parallel and independent ideals seemed to clash and one had to be sacrificed to the other. The great significance of Luther's ethical teaching, so clearly enunciated in the passages just quoted, was his subordination of all human duties to the one end of human service. He did not for a moment lose sight of the other moral virtues. Purity, righteousness, temperance, frugality, all had their place, but as means not end. That one may better serve his fellow-men, for this he strives to be a better man.

The effects of this principle were epochal. For centuries the ideal Christian life had been commonly identified with that of the monk or nun, who lived apart from the distractions and pleasures of the world in religious devotion and in the exercise of rigorous self-discipline. To be in the midst of society, to engage in worldly occupations, to marry and enjoy the delights of home, all this was legitimate, but less noble than a life of celibacy and seclusion. Other-worldliness was the dominant note of traditional Christian piety. Not to make a man a good citizen of this world, but to pre-

pare him for citizenship in another was thought to be
the supreme aim of Christianity; and hence the more
unworldly this life could be made the more Christian
it seemed.   In opposition to this Luther taught the
sanctity of ordinary human callings.   The Christian
is already a saved man, and his life on earth is as
sacred as in heaven.   He may express as truly here
as there his character as a son of God, not by with-
drawing from the world and giving himself wholly to
religious practices, but by doing the daily task faithfully and joyfully, with trust in God and devotion to
His will.

In how practical and homely a fashion Luther applied this principle to every-day life is seen in such
passages as the following, culled from one or another
of his sermons:

What you do in your house is worth as much as if you
did it up in Heaven for our Lord God.   For what we do
in our calling here on earth in accordance with His word
and command He counts as if it were done in heaven for
Him. . . . In whatever calling God has placed you do
not abandon it when you become a Christian.   If you are
a servant, a maid, a workman, a master, a housewife, a
mayor, a prince, do whatever your position demands.
For it does not interfere with your Christian faith and
you can serve God rightly in any vocation. . . . Therefore we should accustom ourselves to think of our position and work as sacred and well-pleasing to God, not on
its own account, but because of the word and the faith
from which our obedience flows.   No Christian should
despise his position if he is living in accordance with the
word of God, but should say, "I believe in Jesus Christ,
and do as the ten commandments teach, and pray that
our dear Lord God may help me thus to do."   That is a
right holy life, and cannot be made holier even if one
fast oneself to death. . . . It looks like a great thing

12

when a monk renounces everything, goes into a cloister, lives a life of asceticism, fasts, watches, prays and the like. Works in abundance are there. But God's command is lacking, and so they cannot be gloried in as if done for Him. On the other hand it looks like a small thing when a maid cooks, and cleans, and does other housework. But because God's command is there, even such a lowly employment must be praised as a service of God, far surpassing the holiness and asceticism of all monks and nuns. Here there is no command of God. But there God's command is fulfilled, that one should honor Father and Mother and help in the care of the home.

The theme of Luther's tract on Christian freedom was not even liberty as an ultimate end, as though it were a good in itself, without regard to the use made of it, but liberty as a means to the service of others. Just because a Christian is a most free lord of all and subject to no one, he can be a most dutiful servant of all and subject to every one. It was a profound observation of Luther's, based upon his own monastic experience, that so long as one is troubled and anxious about one's own fate single-minded devotion to others is very difficult. To be freed from concern for oneself, he felt, was the first requisite of genuine Christian living, for the Christian life meant not chiefly growth in character and piety, but unselfish labor for others' good. As he said later in one of his sermons: "What is it to serve God and do His will? Nothing else than to show mercy to one's neighbor, for it is our neighbor needs our service, God in heaven needs it not."

Religion he saw, as commonly understood, had added burdens instead of removing them. From such burdens he would set men free, making religion wholly subservient to common human duty and service. And he would set them free not only from the trammels of religious obligation—skepticism and unbelief might do that equally well—but also from anxiety about the present, by giving them faith in their Father God, whose world this is and in whose hands all things are working for His children's good. Freedom from the fear both of present and of future was Luther's gospel, a freedom making possible the living of a serene and confident and wholesome life of usefulness.

The contrast between all this and traditional Catholic thought was as wide as the poles. Catholicism proceeded on the assumption that man is naturally bad and needs to be held under strict control to keep him from expressing his badness in wicked deeds. To become confident, to gain the assurance of salvation, to be set free from fear of eternal punishment was regarded as the most dangerous thing in the world. That life here is a probation for the life to come must be kept constantly before the minds of men lest they grow careless and indifferent. Fear, not peace, is alone safe for fallen and corrupt humanity.

To Luther, on the contrary, a state of fear and apprehension made true Christian living, ideal living of any kind, quite impossible. Virtue must be disinterested, or it is not true virtue. The man who is righteous for the sake of gaining reward or escaping punishment is not really righteous. Such selfish motives may be necessary for the natural man, but the Christian is moved by an altogether different impulse. Having seen the vision of God's gracious love in Jesus Christ he is eager to show his gratitude in service. He does not need the pressure of fear to keep him right; he needs to be liberated from fear in order that he may be able to give himself unselfishly and undividedly to the doing of God's will. From such fear the gospel of a present salvation through faith in

God had set Luther himself free, and he preached it to the world as the great liberator from bondage of every kind.

Control to keep men from being themselves Catholicism offered; freedom to be themselves Luther preached. Not trust in man led him thus to set man free, but trust in the gospel. He retained the traditional estimate of the native depravity of the human race, but he had so tremendous a confidence in the power of the revelation of God in Jesus Christ that he was sure where it was apprehended men would haste to do God's will. The experiences of later years did much to weaken this confidence. The great disillusionment of his life was the discovery that the preaching of the true gospel often left men no better than it found them. But he never lost faith in the gospel itself, and to the end of his days he regarded it as his great work and his supreme duty to bring it to the knowledge of men in ever clearer and more convincing form.

Not in the national reformer but in the religious prophet we are to see the real and permanent Luther. While he might concern himself with questions of moral, social, and economic reform, the one thing which always interested him most was his gospel of a present salvation through faith in God, bringing peace and confidence and spiritual freedom. To the end of his life he was above all the prophet of this faith.

AETHERNA IPSE SVAE MENTIS SIMVLACHRA LVTHERVS
EXPRIMIT AT VVLTVS CERA LVCAE OCCIDVOS

· M · D · X · X ·

From a copperplate engraving by Lucas Cranach

LUTHER IN 1520
HIS EARLIEST KNOWN LIKENESS

CHAPTER XIII

THE FINAL BREAK WITH ROME

THE year 1520, which saw the publication of Luther's greatest reformation tracts, witnessed also his complete and permanent break with the Roman Church. At the Leipsic debate he had shown himself sharply at variance with it, and while Miltitz and others were still hoping for reconciliation Eck saw the hope was vain and no course left the church but to condemn the dangerous heretic. Early in the spring of 1520 Eck betook himself to Rome with the express purpose of convincing the authorities of the need of decisive action. With devotion to the faith was perhaps associated, as many of his contemporaries believed, the desire for personal glory and aggrandizement, but his conduct was consistent throughout and much more to his credit than the vacillating and temporizing policy of the holy see. To be sure it was possible for him as a mere theologian to disregard considerations that must weigh heavily with the Roman authorities. They too knew that Luther was a heretic, but he had the backing of the most important prince in Germany and of an aroused public sentiment not to be lightly disregarded. Month after month they waited, hoping that by the use of pressure of one kind and another they might yet succeed in forcing him to recant, or that his growing radicalism might bring reaction in Germany and cost him the elector's support. Finally formal process was once more instituted and condemnation definitely settled upon. Realizing the gravity of the situation the curia went about the matter in the most careful way. No such summary proceedings as had been indulged in a couple of years before were now thought of. Nothing could better show the strength of the feeling against the papacy in Germany than the hesitation of the Roman authorities at this time. Even after a carefully selected commission was at work upon the matter, as late as May, 1520, its sessions were suspended, when a report reached the Vatican that there was still some hope of an easier way out of the difficulty, and the decisive step was finally taken only in June, when the hope was seen to be groundless.

The papal bull Exurge Domine, published on the fifteenth of that month, condemned forty-one propositions drawn from Luther's writings, forbade the reading of his books and called upon Christians everywhere to burn them, threatened with the ban everybody who should support or protect him, suspended him from the ministry, and announced his definitive excommunication, if he did not repent and recant within sixty days after the publication of the bull in Germany. As is apt to be the case, the document gave little hint of Luther's real interest or of the fundamental differences between him and the church. Propositions concerning the sacraments, indulgences, excommunication, the authority of the pope, the condemnation of Hus, free will, purgatory, and the mendicant orders, were condemned, as was also Luther's statement that to burn heretics is against the will of the Spirit. The list of errors might easily have been made more formidable by any one intimately acquainted with the reformer's writings, but it seemed to the papal commission quite sufficient for the purpose.

The bull clearly reflected the difficulties of the situation. In its phraseology it was a mild document, in striking contrast with Luther's heated denunciations of the holy see. Full of pathos it was too, and almost apologetic in tone:

> So far as concerns Martin himself, good God, what have we omitted, what have we not done, what have we neglected of paternal charity, that we might recall him from his errors? After we had summoned him, desiring to deal more mildly with him, we urged and exhorted him, through our legate and by letter, to renounce his errors, or to come without any hesitation or fear—for perfect love should cast out fear—and after the example of our Saviour and the blessed Apostle Paul, talk not secretly but openly and face to face. To this end we offered him a safe conduct and money for the journey. If he had done this he would certainly, we believe, have seen his errors and repented. Nor would he have found so many evils in the Roman curia which, relying upon the empty rumors of its enemies, he vituperates much more than is seemly. We should also have taught him more clearly than light that the holy Roman pontiffs, though he abuses them beyond all modesty, have never erred in their canons or constitutions.

Luther's disobedience and contumacy were then recited and his appeal to a future council was condemned with special emphasis in accordance with a constitution of Pius II and Julius II threatening any one thus appealing with punishment for heresy.

With a singular disregard for the demands of the situation, betrayed not infrequently in the curia's dealings with Luther, Eck was appointed one of two commissioners to publish the bull in Germany. At best it was bound to be unpopular there, and Eck's connection with it served only to discredit it the more, giving currency to the belief that it was a partizan document, wrung from the papal see by Luther's principal antagonist. To make matters worse Eck was given authority to insert in the bull the names of a limited number of Luther's supporters, an opportunity he used to revenge himself upon some of his own antagonists, among them the famous humanist Willibald Pirkheimer, author of the stinging satire "Der abgehobelte Eck."

As might have been expected, the reception accorded the bull in Germany was far from cordial. Coming "bearded, bulled, and moneyed," as Luther put it, Eck found himself almost everywhere an object of hatred and contumely. In many places the bull was treated with open contempt, in others its publication was delayed or prevented altogether on technical grounds of one kind and another.

To be sure, there were those who welcomed it warmly, and here and there its provisions were put into immediate effect. Whole wagon-loads of Luther's books were burned at Cologne, Mayence, and some other towns. It had also the desired effect in leading not a few of his adherents, real or supposed, to renounce all connection with him. Eck had the satisfaction, for instance, of seeing Pirkheimer, Spengler, and others of the Nuremberg group sue humbly for pardon and seek his good offices in their behalf.

Staupitz, although not named in the bull, had to suffer for his known sympathy with the Wittenberg heretic. The relations between the two had been strained for some time. Luther's radicalism greatly distressed the older man and led to a growing estrangement. Already in the spring of 1519 the reformer complained in a letter to Lang that Staupitz had completely forgotten him, and in the fall of the same year he appealed to his beloved superior in the following affecting words:

You forsake me too much. I have sorrowed for you like a weaned child for its mother. I beseech you praise the Lord even in me a sinner. Last night I dreamed of you. I thought you were leaving me, and as I was weeping and lamenting most bitterly, you waved your hand and told me to be quiet for you would return.

For a time, indeed, communication was resumed between the two old friends but was soon interrupted again. In August, feeling unequal to the strain put upon him by his position as vicar in the troublous days upon which the Augustinian order had fallen, Staupitz resigned his office, and soon afterward retired to Salzburg, where he ultimately joined the Dominicans. He hoped his retirement would bring him peace, but he was not allowed to escape so easily. The pope called upon him to join in the condemnation of Luther's heresies. Sorely stricken by the necessity laid upon him, he wrote pathetically to his successor, Wenceslaus Link, "Martin has undertaken a dangerous task and is carrying it on with high courage under the guidance of God. But I stammer, and am a child in need of milk."

Finally he yielded, at least so far as to declare his complete submission to the pope, and with this the curia was satisfied. The following protest from Luther shows how deeply the younger man was grieved by the weakness of his old superior:

This is no time for fear, but for crying aloud, when our Lord Jesus Christ is condemned, cast off, and blasphemed. As you exhorted me to humility I exhort you to pride. You have too much humility as I have too

much pride. The affair indeed is serious. We see Christ
suffering. If hitherto we were obliged to be silent and
humble, now when our most excellent Saviour, who has
given himself for us, is mocked in all the world, I beseech
you shall we not fight for him? Shall we not expose our
lives? My father, the danger is greater than many suppose. Here the gospel word applies, Whosoever confess-
eth me before men, him will I also confess before my
Father.

How little Luther was himself disturbed or thrown
off his balance by the pope's condemnation is shown
by the fact that his beautiful tract on The Freedom of
a Christian Man, in all its noble serenity, was written
just at the time Eck was publishing the papal bull in
Germany. The tract was dedicated to the pope in a
long and remarkable letter penned at the solicitation
of Miltitz, and at his request dated back from October
to September 6 that it might not seem to have been
called forth, as it actually was not, by the bull itself.
The letter was of a very different tone from the two
previously addressed to the pope. While protesting
his regard for Leo's own person, Luther spoke in
sharp terms of the corruption of the papal see, and of
the evils it was bringing upon Christendom. The
humble monk had traveled far who could calmly address the supreme head of the church, the world's
greatest potentate, in such words as the following:

Therefore, Leo, my father, beware of listening to those
sirens who make you out to be not simply a man, but
partly a god, so that you can command and require whatever you will. It will not happen so, nor will you prevail. A servant of servants you are, and above all men
in a most pitiable and perilous position. Let not those
deceive you who pretend you are lord of the world; who
will not allow any one to be a Christian without your

authority; who babble of your having power over heaven, hell, and purgatory. They are your enemies and are seeking your soul to destroy it, as Isaiah says, "My people, they that call thee blessed are themselves deceiving thee." They are in error who raise you above councils and the universal church. They are in error who attribute to you alone the right of interpreting Scripture. All these are seeking to set up their own impieties in the church under your name, and alas, Satan has gained much through them in the time of your predecessors. In short, believe not those who exalt you, but those who humiliate you.

The arrival of the papal bull in Wittenberg was greeted with joy by Luther and taken as a summons to renewed conflict. On the twentieth of October he wrote a friend:

You would scarcely believe how pleased I am that enemies rise up against me more than ever. For I am never prouder or bolder than when I dare to displease them. Let them be doctors, bishops, or princes, what difference does it make? If the word of God were not attacked by them it would not be God's word.

At first he pretended to think the bull a forgery of Eck's and poured out the vials of his wrath upon it in a tract entitled "The New Eckian Bulls and Lies." A little later, accepting it as genuine, he commented upon it briefly in a pamphlet, "Against the Bull of Antichrist," and at the elector's request, at greater length, in his important "Ground and Reason of all the Articles unjustly condemned in the Roman Bull." In the latter work he said:

Even if it were true, as they assert, that I have put myself forward on my own responsibility, they would not be excused thereby. Who knows whether God has called and awakened me for this? Let them fear Him and beware lest they despise God in me. . . . I do not say I am a prophet, but I do say they have all the greater reason to fear I am one, the more they despise me and esteem themselves. If I am not a prophet I am at any rate **sure** the word of God is with me and not with them, for **I** always have the Bible on my side, they only their own doctrine. It is on this account I have the courage to fear them so little, much as they despise and persecute me.

Both of these pamphlets appeared in Latin as well as German, and in referring to the longer one, in a letter to Spalatin, Luther defended the greater severity of the Latin version with the remark that it seemed necessary "to introduce a little salt for Latin stomachs."

On November 17 he renewed his appeal from the pope to a general council declaring, in his usual violent fashion, that the former was an unrighteous judge, a heretic and apostate, an enemy of the Holy Scriptures, and a slanderer of church and council. He also called upon emperors, princes, and all civil officials to support his appeal and oppose what he styled the unchristian conduct of the pope.

Finally, on December 10, he broke permanently with the papal see and gave dramatic expression to his renunciation of the pope's authority by publicly burning the bull and the canon law in the presence of a large concourse of professors and students. Melanchthon announced the event in the following placard, posted upon the door of the City Church:

Whoever is devoted to gospel truth, let him be on hand at nine o'clock by the Church of the Holy Cross, outside the walls, where according to ancient and apostolic custom the impious books of papal law and scholastic theology will be given to the flames. For the

From a carbon print by Braun & Co.

PHILIP MELANCHTHON. FROM A CRAYON DRAWING BY HANS HOLBEIN

audacity of the enemies of the gospel has gone so far as to burn the devout and evangelical books of Luther. Come, reverent and studious youth, to this pious and religious spectacle, for perhaps now is the time when antichrist shall be revealed.

In a defense published soon afterward Luther justified the burning of the canon law because it taught among other things the supremacy of the pope and his absolute authority over Bible, church, and Christian conscience. Again, as so often, there was revealed the kinship in principle between his revolt and the many other uprisings against unlimited and unconstitutional monarchy through which freedom has been won for the modern world.

Luther's bold act was not the result of a sudden and hasty impulse. He had announced his intention months before, and though the project was known to the elector and many friends, no objection seems to have been made by any of them. Writing about it to Staupitz he said he had done the deed in trembling and prayer, but after it was over felt more pleased than at any other act of his life.

Speaking of the matter to the students the next day, he told them, according to the report of one of his hearers, that salvation was impossible for those submitting to the rule of the pope; and in March he wrote a friend: "I am persuaded of this, that unless a man fight with all his might, and if need be unto death, against the statutes and laws of the pope and bishops, he cannot be saved." This soon became a common feeling among his adherents. From the assurance that salvation is possible apart from the pope both he and they went on to the still more radical belief that it was impossible with the pope. The latter was not a logical deduction from the former. It was only the instinctive repayment of condemnation by condemnation. But it found its justification in the conviction, long growing and now full blown, that the pope was antichrist. The basis was thus given, not for the possibility merely, but for the necessity of a new church. Catholic exclusiveness was matched by Lutheran, and the new movement was prepared to meet the old on its own ground. Protestants have happily long outgrown the bitterness and narrowness of the early days, but it may well be doubted whether anything less would have sufficed then to stand the strain.

On January 3, 1521, the period of grace named in the previous bull having more than elapsed, the pope took formal action against Luther in the bull Decet Romanum Pontificem, pronouncing him excommunicate, declaring him guilty of the crime of lese-majesty, and condemning him to all the spiritual and temporal penalties imposed upon heretics by the canons of the church.

CHAPTER XIV

THE DIET OF WORMS

IN excommunicating Luther the pope had done his worst. It remained to be seen whether his action would be given effect by the civil power. In ordinary circumstances there would have been no doubt. To be condemned as a heretic meant certain death at the hands either of the ecclesiastical or civil government. But the present case was unusual. Luther had the backing of the most important prince in Germany, the support of a large body of nobles, the confidence of many of the lower clergy, and the devotion of great masses of the population. Quite apart from sympathy with him and his views it was widely felt that his appeal from the pope to a council should have been heeded, and there were those who doubted whether the pope after all had the right to condemn any one for heresy without conciliar support. The situation was very complicated. The outcome was by no means certain, all the less so in view of the diverse political interests represented in the empire. It was just the kind of a case, beset sufficiently with doubt, to offer the best possible excuse for political bargaining, and the emperor and princes made good use of the opportunity.

In January, 1521, the first imperial diet of Charles's reign met in the free city of Worms, one of the most ancient and famous towns of Germany, situated on the left bank of the upper Rhine. There is still extant a remarkable series of despatches addressed to the Vice-Chancellor at Rome by the papal legate Jerome Aleander, containing a vivid account of the diet itself and an interesting picture of the general situation. The following facts and impressions reported by Aleander are perhaps worth repeating. Legions of poor noblemen under Hutten's lead were enlisted against the pope, and the great majority of lawyers, canonists, grammarians, poets, priests, and monks, together with the masses of the common people, in fact, nine tenths of all Germany, were on Luther's side, and the other tenth against the curia. Even where the Wittenberg professor was not understood, he was supported because of the general hatred of Rome. Multitudes thought they could remain good Christians and orthodox Catholics while renouncing allegiance to the pope. Even those opposed to Luther, including the greatest princes and prelates, dared not come out against him for fear of Hutten and Sickingen, everywhere recognized as his allies. No books but his were sold in Worms, and his picture was everywhere to be seen, often with the Holy Ghost hovering over his head. The people thought him sinless and infallible and attributed miraculous power to him. Only the emperor was on the side of Rome. If he were to yield in the least all Germany would fall away from the papacy. And even he hesitated to bring pressure to bear upon the princes out of consideration for the Elector of Saxony and from a desire to retain in his own hands the means of inducing the pope to yield to his wishes in other matters.

We are reminded in this connection that some time before, while Charles was still in the Netherlands, his ambassador at Rome advised him to show favor to a certain Martin Luther whom the pope greatly feared.

We get also in these despatches a frank account of
the negotiations carried on and the devious means employed by Aleander and his fellow legate Caracciolo
in their efforts to secure Luther's condemnation and
maintain the authority of Rome. Flattery, threats,
and bribery were freely used, and Aleander did not
hesitate to avow his own falsehoods for the good of
the cause. A most interesting picture it is of the skilful use of political methods such as have been employed
in every age of the world and for all sorts of ends.

Aleander complained frequently of his own unpopu-
larity and the shabby treatment accorded him by the
populace, causing him often to fear for his life. At
the same time he felt called upon to defend himself
against the accusation of living voluptuously and luxu-
riously, averring that he was so poorly housed as nearly
to freeze to death and had had no new clothes for ten
years. In general his reports, at least during the
earlier part of his stay in Worms, were gloomy and
despondent enough. It may well be that he exaggerated the difficulties in order to enhance the value of his
services, but his account bears for the most part the
marks of truth and is a fairly accurate picture of the
situation from a Roman point of view.

The despatches also contain some interesting pen
portraits of the leading actors in the great events of
those weeks. Luther, the antichrist, as Aleander calls
him, is of course spoken of with uniform hatred and
contempt. A hard drinker, and too much of an igno-
ramus to be the author of the books ascribed to him,
he is represented as merely a tool of Hutten and his
associates, like them interested to overthrow all authority, civil as well as ecclesiastical. Hutten himself would
like to be the chief leader of the whole movement if he
could only count on the support of the people as Luther

can. The real motive underlying all his efforts and those of his followers is the desire to seize for themselves the property of the clergy. Sickingen, a man of unusual ability, is greatly feared by everybody and is really king in Germany. Albert of Mayence is a good Catholic and at heart loyal to the pope, but sadly lacking in firmness and courage. The Elector Frederick, at first spoken of as an excellent prince, pious and devout, but with councilors more Lutheran than Luther himself, is later called "the infamous Saxon," and inelegantly compared to a fat hog, with the eyes of a dog, which rarely look any one straight in the face. He is also dubbed a basilisk and a fox who supports Luther only because of the fame and prosperity he brings the university and town of Wittenberg. The frankness of the despatches makes them interesting reading, and the bitter prejudice of the legate, preventing him from seeing any good in Luther and his friends, need not be wondered at. Indeed his attitude was in no way different from Luther's own. The latter too was seldom able to see any good in his opponents.

Late in November, in response to the Elector Frederick's insistence that Luther be not condemned without a hearing, the emperor requested him to bring his professor to the diet and let him answer for himself before a commission of learned and judicious men. Luther was eager to appear and defend his cause. When the elector inquired through Spalatin if he were willing to go, he wrote the latter on the twenty-first of December:

If I am summoned I will do what in me lies to be carried there sick, if I cannot go well. For it is not to be doubted, if the emperor summons me I am summoned by the Lord. If they use force, as is probable, for they do not wish me to come that I may be instructed, my cause shall be commended to the Lord, for He lives and reigns who preserved the three children in the furnace of the Babylonian king. If He is unwilling to preserve me my life is a small thing compared with Christ's, who was wickedly slain to the disgrace of all and the harm of many. . . . Expect anything of me except flight or recantation. I will not flee, much less recant. So may the Lord Jesus strengthen me.

In the meantime, fearing the effect of Luther's presence in Worms, and incensed at the proposal to give a condemned heretic the opportunity to defend his views, Aleander induced the emperor to withdraw his request and deny Luther a hearing. For a long time it was uncertain what would be done. But when the members of the diet persistently refused to assent to various measures the emperor had at heart until Luther was permitted to appear before them, the case was finally compromised in spite of Aleander's protests. The excommunicated professor was to be summoned and required to recant his doctrinal heresies. If he refused he was to be condemned without further ado. If he consented his criticisms of ecclesiastical abuses were to be considered by the diet and such action taken as might seem advisable.

Accordingly an imperial summons was issued on March 6 requiring him to appear within six weeks and guaranteeing him safe conduct both in going and returning. To Aleander's disgust the summons was phrased in respectful terms, and an imperial herald, of known Lutheran sympathies, was despatched to Wittenberg to escort the heretic to Worms in state. The honorable treatment accorded the reformer was an acknowledgment of the important position he occupied in the eyes of Germany.

The herald found him ready and eager to go, and
in spite of the dangers attending the journey, for imperial safe-conducts had been violated before, and in
spite of the serious issues hinging upon it, he left
Wittenberg for Worms on April 2, 1521, in good
spirits and with a light heart.

He was accompanied by his colleague Nicholas Amsdorf, an Augustinian brother, John Petzensteiner, and
one of his students, a young Pomeranian nobleman,
Peter Swaben. Instead of traveling on foot as he
usually did, he rode in state with his companions in a
covered wagon. The city magistrates provided the con-
veyance and the university added funds for the journey. Condemned heretic though he was, town after
town showed him distinguished honor as he passed
through. According to the papal legate Aleander his
entire journey was nothing less than a triumphal procession. At Leipsic the city council sent him a gift of
wine. At Erfurt, where his old friend Crotus was rector of the university, he was met outside the walls by
an imposing deputation, and was greeted with an ora-
tion by the rector and a poem by Eoban Hess, the
most celebrated poet of the day.

Early in his journey he was unpleasantly surprised
to learn of the imperial mandate requiring the seques-
tration of his books. He was alarmed, he says, and
trembled at the news, for it showed that the emperor
was against him and he could hope for little from his
own appearance at the diet. But his resolution to
proceed remained unshaken.

According to his friend Myconius, when warned that
he would be burned to ashes by the cardinals and
bishops at Worms, and reminded of the fate met by
Hus at Constance, he replied, "Even if they kindled a
fire as high as heaven from Wittenberg to Worms, I

LVCAE · OPVS · EFFIGIES · HAEC · EST · MORITVRA · LVTHERI ·
AETHERNAM · MENTIS · EXPRIMIT · IPSE · SVAE ·
M · D · X · X · I ·

From a copperplate engraving by Lucas Cranach

LUTHER IN 1521

The second earliest known likeness of Luther

would appear in the name of the Lord, in obedience to the imperial summons, and would walk into behemoth's mouth, between his great teeth, and confess Christ." Though Myconius is not a very trustworthy reporter, the words have a genuine ring.

Equally characteristic of another of Luther's familiar moods was his laughing reply to a similar prophecy, recorded by another friend and biographer, Ratzeberger: "Nettles would n't be so bad, one could stand them, but to be burned with fire, yes, that would be too hot."

From Frankfort, where he stopped over night, Luther wrote Spalatin, who was already at Worms with the elector:

We are coming, my Spalatin, although Satan has tried to stop me with more than one sickness. The whole way from Eisenach here I have been miserable and am still in a way not before experienced. Charles's mandate I know has been published to frighten me. But Christ lives, and we will enter Worms in spite of all the gates of hell and powers of the air. I send a copy of the imperial letter. I have thought it well to write no more letters until I arrive and see what is to be done, that Satan may not be puffed up, whom I am minded rather to terrify and despise. Arrange a lodging for me therefore. Farewell.

A year later, in a letter to the elector, he remarked: "The devil saw clearly the mood I was in when I went to Worms. Had I known as many devils would set upon me as there were tiles on the roofs, I should have sprung into the midst of them with joy." Long afterward, in talking about his journey, he repeated the same words, and added: "For I was undismayed and feared nothing, so foolish can God make a man! I am not sure I should now be so joyful."

At Oppenheim, some thirty miles from Worms, he was met by Martin Bucer, the young Dominican whose enthusiastic admiration he had won at Heidelberg. Bucer brought a message from Franz von Sickingen inviting Luther to stop over at his castle, the Ebernburg, for an interview with the emperor's confessor Glapion, who had been sent thither for the purpose. What Glapion's exact design was is uncertain. The papal legates and imperial counselors feared the effects of Luther's presence at the diet and would have liked to prevent his coming. Glapion perhaps hoped to induce him to remain away altogether, or, as Luther believed, simply to delay him until his safe-conduct had expired. At any rate the traveler declined the invitation and sent the confessor word that if he had anything to say he could see him at Worms.

He reached his journey's end about ten o'clock on the morning of Tuesday, the sixteenth of April. His coming was announced by a trumpeter, and though it was the hour of the midday meal, the whole town poured out to see him. Aleander sent one of his attendants to witness the great heretic's arrival, and afterward wrote the papal vice-chancellor:

About a hundred horsemen, presumably Sickingen's, accompanied him to the city gate. Sitting in a wagon with three companions, he entered the city, surrounded by some eight riders, and took up his lodging in the neighborhood of his Saxon prince. When he alighted, a priest threw his arms about him, touched his garments three times, and went away exulting, as if he had handled a relic of the greatest of saints. I suspect it will soon be said he works miracles. This Luther, as he stepped from the wagon, looked about with his demoniac eyes and said, "God will be with me." Then he entered a chamber where many gentlemen visited him, with ten or twelve

of whom he dined, and after dinner everybody ran in
to see him.

In spite of the pressure he was under, Luther took
time the next morning to visit a sick nobleman who
had expressed the desire to see him. After offering
him spiritual consolation, he heard him confess, and
administered the sacrament. It was a thoroughly characteristic act, for he was never too busy to heed such
calls. Always to the end of his days he remained a
devoted and self-sacrificing pastor and spiritual guide.

At four in the afternoon he appeared before the
diet, sitting at the time in the bishop's palace, where
the Emperor Charles and his brother Ferdinand were
staying. The hall was filled with a large and distinguished company of princes, noblemen, high ecclesiastics, representatives of the various states and free
cities of Germany, and ambassadors of foreign powers,
including two from England. It was an impressive
occasion, fraught with consequence not only for Luther himself, but for the empire and the world as well.
The case of the condemned monk, it is true, was only
one of many items of business to engage the attention of the diet, and doubtless most of the members
were far more interested in other matters of local or
national concern. Few realized the seriousness of the
situation, and fewer still appreciated the world-wide
significance of his appearance before the German emperor and estates. But all were curious to see and
hear the man who had made such a stir, and it is not
surprising that the hall was crowded, as well as the
streets outside.

Aleander was scandalized to see the Wittenberg
monk enter the hall with a smiling face and let his
eyes rove over the assembled company instead of

exhibiting the humility and fear appropriate to one in his situation. The humanist Peutinger, a delegate from the city of Augsburg, where he had entertained Luther at the time of his appearance before Cajetan, happened to be standing near and was greeted cheerily with the words, "What, you here, too, Herr Doctor?" Peutinger afterward saw him frequently during his stay in Worms, and reported to the Augsburg authorities that he found him always in excellent spirits.

As soon as he had reached his place, Luther was peremptorily required to say whether he acknowledged as his own a pile of some twenty books collected by the diligence of Aleander and arranged upon a table before him, and whether he would retract the whole or any part of their contents. He wondered, as he later remarked, where so many of his writings had been picked up; but when their titles had been read, he promptly acknowledged them as his own, adding that he had written many others besides. In reply to the second question, he asked for time to consider the matter, since faith and salvation and the divine word were involved, and to answer without premeditation might work injury to the word and endanger his own soul. The papal legates and imperial counselors were surprised and annoyed, but after some hesitation he was granted a delay of twenty-four hours.

Much speculation has been indulged in as to the reason for this request. In one of the many extant reports of the occasion from the pen of the Frankfort representative, Fürstenberg, Luther is said to have spoken in a low voice, as if he were frightened and confused. This has led to the common assumption that he was overawed by the august assembly and too much upset to take a firm stand such as might ordinarily have been expected of him. It would perhaps not be surprising

if he were. For the first time face to face with the
leading princes of the empire and the greatest sovereign of the world, almost any man might be pardoned if he were dazzled by the spectacle and discon-
certed by the hostility shown in the abrupt demand for
a retraction. But the evidence is insufficient to support the conclusion. No one else, so far as we are
aware, shared Fürstenberg's opinion that Luther was
frightened, though many who have left reports of the
occasion had a much better opportunity than he to observe the monk's attitude.

We must not be misled by the dramatic contrasts of
the scene—a poor monk of peasant birth standing
alone against the world. If he had been standing alone,
the emperor and diet would never have wasted their
time with him. He was no mere individual, on trial
for his life, but the champion of a great and growing
party, of political, as well as religious, importance.
Nor was he a simple-minded, inexperienced monk,
thrust suddenly into the lime-light of publicity, but a
seasoned warrior, long aware of the national significance of the battle he was engaged in. At Worms he
had a host of influential supporters, and was surrounded by sage counselors. It is impossible to suppose he entered the hall ignorant of what he had to
expect and without a carefully arranged plan of procedure. Apparently the plan did not altogether please
Luther himself, for he frequently complained in later
days that under the influence of his friends he was
milder at Worms than he would have liked to be.
Doubtless his supporters were greatly divided as to
the best way to meet the situation, and many of them
must have hoped some compromise could be reached
whereby the crushing of the whole movement might be
prevented. Very likely he was induced to ask for

delay until there was time for further discussion, in the light of the impression made by his first appearance. During the following night we are told he was in constant consultation with his friends, so that he got no sleep at all. And when he appeared before the diet the next day, firm as his final answer was, it was phrased very carefully, and in such a way as to give as little offense as possible.

Speaking in a louder voice than at his first appearance, so as to be heard by everybody in the hall, he apologized for any lack of respect he might have shown the members of the diet the previous day, through ignorance of the forms and customs of the great world, and then gave his answer to the crucial question at considerable length, first in German and afterward in Latin.

His writings he divided into three groups. Some of them, he said, concerned faith and morals, and were so simple and evangelical that even his enemies confessed them harmless and worthy to be read by Christian people. Others attacked the pope, and these he could not retract without giving support and encouragement to his abominable tyrannies. Still others were directed against individuals who opposed his gospel and defended the papacy. In these he confessed he had often been more violent than was seemly, for he did not claim to be a saint; but if he withdrew them, impiety under his protection would prevail more widely than ever. At the same time, repeating the words of Christ, "If I have spoken evil, bear witness of the evil," he professed himself ready to submit and recant provided he were proved wrong. If his teachings were out of harmony with the Bible, he would be the first to throw his books into the fire.

When reproved for not speaking to the point, and

asked to give a categorical answer without horns, whether he would recant or not, he replied:

Since, then, your Majesty and Lordships demand a simple response, I will give one with neither horns nor teeth to this effect. Unless convinced by the testimony of Scripture or by clear reason—for I believe neither pope nor councils alone, since it is certain they have often erred and contradicted themselves,—having been conquered by the Scriptures referred to and my conscience taken captive by the word of God, I cannot and will not revoke anything, for it is neither safe nor right to act against one's conscience. God help me. Amen.

A discussion ensued touching the authority of councils, when the emperor, as it was already growing late, interrupted the colloquy and abruptly closed the session.

Arrived at his lodgings, Luther threw up his hands, according to the report of an eye-witness, and cried with joy, "I am through, I am through!" The strain must have been tremendous even for him, and his relief that it was all over and he had held his ground without flinching was proportionately great. A few days later, in a letter to his friend Lucas Cranach, he made the following characteristic comment upon the whole affair: "In my opinion the emperor ought to have gathered a number of doctors and conquered the monk by argument. Instead of that, I was simply asked, 'Are the books yours?' 'Yes,' 'Will you recant them?' 'No.' 'Then begone.' Oh, we blind Germans, how childishly we act and how contemptible we are to allow the Romans to make such fools of us!"

The impression made by Luther upon the members of the diet was very diverse. The Venetian ambassador wrote: "Martin has hardly fulfilled the expectations which all had. He appears neither blameless in life nor gifted with wisdom. He is uneducated and has nothing to distinguish him except his rashness." According to Aleander's report, written at the close of the first day, many even of those friendly to him, after seeing him, thought him crazy or possessed, while others considered him a pious man, full of the Holy Spirit. Later the legate wrote that his coming had had excellent results. The emperor saw in him only a dissolute and demented man, and exclaimed disdainfully, "He will never make a heretic of me." In fact, his appearance and conduct had destroyed altogether the reputation he had hitherto enjoyed.

On the contrary, according to another eye-witness, Luther conducted himself so bravely, Christianly, and honorably that the Romanists would have been very thankful if he had not come.

The Elector Frederick was delighted with him, and said privately to Spalatin, "The father, Dr. Martin, spoke well before the emperor and all the princes and estates of the realm in Latin and German. He is much too bold for me."

In pursuance of the agreement reached before he was summoned, the emperor wished to have sentence at once passed upon the refractory heretic; but some of the influential members of the diet thought it possible, in view of his promise to retract if he were convinced of his errors, that he might yield to instruction or persuasion. At any rate, to condemn him without making an effort to show him wrong, it was felt, would lead the populace to think him unfairly treated. There were those, too, who hoped his great influence might be used to promote the reformation of ecclesiastical abuses. As at previous diets, impatience with the exactions of the curia found frequent expression at Worms, and even

THE LUTHER MEMORIAL AT WORMS

About Luther, the central figure, are seated four precursors of the Reformation: Hus, Savonarola, Wyclif, and Peter Waldo; the standing figure at the right of Luther is Melanchthon, and a figure of Reuchlin, at the left, is hidden by the statue of Frederick the Wise, at the corner, with uplifted sword; the outside figure, at the right, is Philip the Magnanimous of Hesse.

THE CATHEDRAL AT WORMS, WHICH WAS STANDING IN LUTHER'S TIME

so good a Catholic as Duke George of Saxony presented a long list of grievances. A committee appointed to consider the matter drew up a document containing a hundred and two gravamina against the papacy and clergy, and, though never acted upon by the diet, it showed clearly enough the temper of many of the members. With Luther's doctrinal innovations few of them were in sympathy. They had little enough idea of what they were, but they feared their unsettling effects and were sure they ought not to be tolerated. Hus and the Bohemian uprising were constantly before their minds, and the dread of similar trouble in Germany acted continually as a check.

With Luther himself the situation was reversed. He was willing to yield in the matter of ecclesiastical abuses, and keep silent for the sake of the peace of the church, but he would not dissemble his doctrinal beliefs. He had attacked the pope, he said, not because of his bad life, but of his false teaching. The word of God, he insisted, must not be bound, and preach it he would as he understood it, whatever the consequences might be. With such convictions it was quite impossible for him to enter into the sort of compromise many of the princes wished. Matters in their opinion of minor concern he considered of fundamental importance, and they ultimately discovered, to their great disgust, that he was quite intractable. So long as there was hope that he could be controlled and made use of, they were anxious to protect him, but when it became evident that he would go his own independent way and bring about changes they did not like, they dropped him altogether.

But, in the meantime, the emperor having finally consented, in spite of Aleander's protests, to grant a brief delay, negotiations with Luther were carried on

under the lead of the Archbishop of Treves, a liberal
and fair-minded prelate and a personal friend of
the Elector Frederick. A series of interviews was
held, which must have proved more trying to Luther than his appearance before the diet. Every
form of persuasion was brought to bear upon him.
His patriotism, his loyalty to the emperor, and his love
for the church were appealed to. Theological argument was tried and biblical scholarship invoked, but
all to no purpose. At one time it was believed he was
about to yield, and the archbishop was much encouraged; but the belief was due to a misunderstanding,
and it was soon discovered that nothing could be done.

From the pen of John Cochlæus, a Frankfort theologian, later one of Luther's principal opponents and
author of the first unfriendly biography of the reformer, we have a long and interesting account of a
protracted discussion he had with Luther and his
friends. Visiting them in their lodgings, he attempted
single-handed to meet the whole company in debate,
and was obliged to submit to considerable banter and
to suffer some hard knocks from those present. The
interview was enlivened by a tilt between Cochlæus and
the Wittenberg Augustinian Petzensteiner. When
Cochlæus addressed him contemptuously as "Little
Brother," and asked him disdainfully if he thought
there were no wise men except in Wittenberg, Luther,
who happened to enter the room at the moment, quieted
the threatened disturbance with the jocose remark,
"My brother thinks he is wiser than all of us, especially
when he has been drinking hard." The words brought
a laugh and restored the company's good humor.

At another point Cochlæus asked Luther whether
he had received a revelation, and after some hesitation the reformer replied in the affirmative, to the no

small scandal of the Frankfort theologian, who accused
him of contradicting himself and asserting at one moment what he denied at another.   As a matter of fact,
the question was not an easy one to answer.   Luther
firmly believed his gospel came from God, and yet he
naturally hesitated to claim supernatural illumination,
and as a rule was careful not to do so.   But all his conduct was that of a man believing in divine inspiration
and aware of his own divine call.   The two disputants
finally separated in a friendly spirit, but Cochlæus
assured Luther of his intention to write against him,
and the latter promised to answer him to the best of
his ability.

After a week of futile effort on the part of the Archbishop of Treves and others called in to assist him, the
reformer begged to be allowed to depart, and on
Friday, the twenty-sixth of April, left Worms with
an imperial safe-conduct good for twenty days.   He
was ordered not to preach on the way home, but refused to be bound by the prohibition.

After his departure, Aleander was intrusted by the
emperor with the task of preparing an edict of condemnation.   That the papal legate should be called
upon to do this was an interesting indication of
Charles's attitude.   The young sovereign was a devout
Catholic, and though in political matters he might deal
with the pope as with any other civil ruler, when legal
effect was to be given the papal condemnation, he recognized the pope's representative as the proper person
to formulate the decision.   The result was not a brief
and summary state document, but an elaborate account
of Luther's errors and of the means employed to bring
him to reason.   Particular stress was laid upon his
alleged anarchical principles and his incitement of the
masses to uproar, bloodshed, and war.   Evidently the

need was felt, as in the bull Exurge Domine, of justifying the action before the people of Germany, whose
devotion to Luther had been the chief obstacle in the
way of his condemnation.

The edict put Luther unconditionally under the ban
of the empire, and thenceforth to the end of his life
he remained an outlaw. He was to be seized wherever
found and sent to the emperor, or held in safe-keeping
until his fate was decided upon. All his books were
ordered burned, and to publish, sell, buy, or read any
of his writings was strictly forbidden. To support or
follow him was to involve oneself in his guilt, and to
befriend or hold communication with him openly or
secretly was to commit the crime of lese-majesty. The
document was approved by the emperor on the eighth
of May and received his signature on the twenty-sixth
of the month. It was not submitted to the diet, but
it had the assent of the leading princes still on the
ground, the Elector of Saxony having left Worms
some time before, and in view of the earlier decision
to condemn Luther if he did not recant, its proclamation was entirely in order.

Aleander was overjoyed at the outcome of the difficult and complicated affair. He had spent many anxious months over it, and when it was finally brought
to a successful completion, his exultation knew no
bounds. He even broke into poetry in the despatch
announcing the final decision, and his satisfaction
with the emperor was expressed in glowing terms. "I
cannot refrain," he exclaimed, "from adding a few
words about this most glorious emperor, whom I have
always spoken of in my despatches as the best man in
the world. As appears more clearly day by day, he is
superior to every one else in wisdom as well as in
goodness. Daily can be seen in his acts a judgment

more than human." Though Charles had purposely postponed the adoption of the edict and had often acted as if opposed to the wishes of the pope, Aleander declared it was simply in order to secure the assent of the princes to other matters of the utmost importance. The delay, he thought, had really proved of great benefit, and the effect of the edict was far better than if it had been published at the opening of the diet.

CHAPTER XV

AT THE WARTBURG

LUTHER'S appearance at Worms, to which he had looked forward as a splendid opportunity to proclaim his gospel before the princes and lords of Germany, and from which, in his faith in the power of the spoken word, he had expected great things, apparently resulted in a complete victory for his enemies and in the destruction of the cause he had at heart. Condemned by church and state, it looked as if the end had come both for him and for his work. His only possible course, it would seem, was to flee the country and make his way to some land like Bohemia, where neither emperor nor pope held sway, and whence he might easily continue his agitation and scatter his writings over Germany. This Aleander and many others actually feared he would do; but the Elector Frederick, true to his policy of supporting his professor without too openly incurring blame for his heresies, formed other plans for him. According to Spalatin, while Frederick was fond of Luther, and would have been very sorry to see any harm befall him, he was at this time somewhat faint-hearted and unwilling to incur the anger of the emperor. He therefore conceived the idea of concealing his condemned professor for a time, and secured his assent before he left Worms, though Luther would much have preferred to remain in the open.

Writing from Frankfort on the morning of Sunday, the twenty-eighth of April, to his friend Lucas Cranach, Luther remarked, "I am allowing myself to be shut up and hidden; I don't know where. Though I should rather have suffered death at the hands of the tyrants, especially the raging Duke George of Saxony, I must not despise the advice of good people until the hour comes."

The same evening, after arriving at Friedberg, he wrote, at Spalatin's request, a long letter in Latin to the emperor and in Germany to the electors, princes, and estates of the realm, explaining and defending his course. As so often before, he asserted again his readiness to yield if he were convicted out of the Scriptures, and expressed in the warmest terms his love for the Fatherland and his conviction that he was acting for its good. This conviction, indeed, did much to sustain him during all the troubles of these years. "I was born for my Germans," he once exclaimed, "and them I serve."

He was received by one after another of the towns through which he passed as warmly as on his way to Worms. At Hersfeld he was welcomed by the city council and handsomely entertained by the Benedictine abbot, who insisted on his preaching in the convent, although Luther warned him it might cost him his position. He also preached at Eisenach, where the parish priest, fearing possible consequences to himself, went through the formality of filing a protest before a notary, privately excusing himself to Luther for doing so.

After being hospitably treated in the little city where he had spent the happiest years of his boyhood, he left, on the third of May, to visit his relatives in the near-by village of Möhra, his father's birthplace, where many of his kindred still lived. The next afternoon he started on again, taking a road through the forest in the direction of Waltershausen and Gotha. Shortly before dark, not far from the castle of Altenstein, the travelers were suddenly set upon by a company of armed horsemen. Most of Luther's companions, including the imperial herald, had already been got rid of on one or another pretext, and only Amsdorf and Brother Petzensteiner were with him. The latter at once took to his heels and made his way on foot to Waltershausen. Amsdorf, who had been forewarned of what was to happen, was permitted to return with the driver to Eisenach. Luther himself was taken back through the forest by devious paths to the Wartburg, one of the strongholds of the Elector Frederick, where he arrived late at night, half dead from fatigue.

The large and imposing castle, already more than four hundred years old and crowded with historical memories and legendary tales, stood upon the wooded heights just beyond the confines of Eisenach, commanding the town itself and the beautiful Thuringian country for many miles round. There, in honorable captivity, Luther made his home for nearly a year, while the great movement which owed so much to him went on without him.

His disappearance was the signal for a tremendous outcry in all parts of Germany. In the absence of accurate information, rumors flew thick and fast. Many believed he was held in confinement by his enemies. Some thought he had been carried off by Sickingen, others that he had been murdered, and circumstantial tales were told of the finding of his body in this or that spot. When the news reached Albrecht Dürer, who was traveling at the time in the Netherlands, he made a long entry in his diary expressing in impas-

From a photograph by the Berlin Photographische Gesellschaft, of the painting by
Lucas Cranach in the City Library at Leipsic

LUTHER'S APPEARANCE
WHILE SECLUDED IN THE WARTBURG

sioned terms his devotion to Luther and his sorrow at his death. "O God, is Luther dead, who will henceforth proclaim the gospel so clearly to us? O God, what might he not still have written for us in ten or twenty years!"

According to a report repeated by Luther himself, a Romanist wrote the Archbishop of Mayence, "We are rid of Luther, as we wished to be; but the people are so stirred up that I suspect we shall scarcely escape with our lives unless with lighted candles we seek him everywhere and bring him back."

Aleander, as well as many others, guessed the truth, but neither he nor any one else knew where the condemned monk was hidden. Even the elector remained in ignorance of his whereabouts, that he might be able publicly to deny all knowledge of what had become of him.

The identity of the captive was carefully concealed. He allowed his hair and beard to grow, put on the costume of a knight, wore a gold chain, carried a sword, and engaged occasionally in the sports and occupations of a young nobleman. He went by the name of Junker Georg, and was generally supposed to be a knight living in temporary retirement. He had some difficulty in maintaining the character he had assumed, and in his rides and walks the attendant who always accompanied him frequently had much ado to keep him from betraying himself by his interest in books, so foreign to one of his supposed class, and by his tendency to enter into theological discussion with those he happened to meet.

His letters to his friends dated from "the region of the birds," from "the desert," or from "the Island of Patmos," show how lonely he was and how eager for news of the progress of events in Wittenberg and elsewhere. To be set aside as he was, and unable to go on with the great work, was a sore trial. He wrote to Melanchthon, begging to know what he thought of his retirement, and expressing fear lest it be supposed he had fled from the conflict in cowardice. To his friend Agricola he wrote: "I am an extraordinary captive, sitting here willing and unwilling at the same time. Willing, because the Lord wills thus; unwilling, because I should prefer to stand publicly for the•word, but not yet am I worthy."

At first he was very impatient, but gradually, amazing as it seems in one like him, he grew accustomed to his enforced confinement, and even felt relief at being once more by himself, as in the earlier monastic days, and apart from the strife and turmoil of recent years. "What is going on in the world I care nothing for," he wrote Spalatin. "Here I sit in quiet."

The largeness and generosity of his nature were strikingly shown in his complete freedom from petty jealousy and from regard for his own importance. His letters, frank as they are, reveal no trace of annoyance because the movement he had started was going on as prosperously under the lead of others. On the contrary, he was continually rejoicing to find himself unnecessary to it, and when his friends lamented his absence and longed for his return, he kept assuring them with unmistakable sincerity that the cause was better off without him. "I rejoice so greatly in your fullness," he wrote Amsdorf, "that I bear my absence most tranquilly. For I see it is not you who need me, but I who need you." To Spalatin he wrote:

I am pleased with the news from Wittenberg, and give thanks to Christ who has raised up others in my place so that I see they now have no need of me, though Philip gives way too much to his affections and bears the cross more impatiently than becomes a disciple, still less such a master.

And to Melanchthon himself:

You are already full, you reign without me, nor do I see why you desire me so greatly, or what need you have of my labors. You seem to invent difficulties, for your affairs go better in my absence than when I am present. Although I should most gladly be with you, since you have all you need I should not be reluctant to go to Erfurt or Cologne or wherever else the Lord might think good to open a door for me to preach. How great is the harvest everywhere, and there are no laborers. But you are all laborers. We ought not to think of ourselves but of our brethren scattered everywhere, lest perchance we live for ourselves, that is, for the devil, and not for Christ.

The following passage from his "Warning against Uproar," written while he was still at the Wartburg, may be quoted in this connection:

I beg that my name may be passed over in silence, and that men will call themselves not Lutheran but Christian. What is Luther? My teaching is not mine. I have been crucified for nobody. Saint Paul would not suffer Christians to bear the name of Paul or Peter, but only of Christ. How does it happen that I, a poor stinking carcass, have the children of Christ called after my unholy name? Not so, dear friends! Let us root out party names and call ourselves Christians, for it is Christ's gospel we have.

Nevertheless, as was not unnatural, he began now to suffer a return of the mental depression of his earlier days. For some years he had apparently been almost free from it; but being again by himself and without absorbing activities, he fell frequently into deep despondency. Writing to Melanchthon but a fortnight after reaching the Wartburg, he exclaimed: "I congratulate Dr. Lupine on his happy death. Would that we too might live no longer! The wrath of God, which in my leisure I am daily observing more and more, is such that I doubt whether He will save anybody except infants from this kingdom of Satan. Our God has so deserted us!" But how rapidly his mood changed, as it always did, is shown by the beautiful words with which the letter closed: "Again farewell. Among the birds, singing sweetly in the branches, and praising God day and night with all their might."

Occasionally in his Wartburg letters he referred to the visitations of Satan he was called upon to endure. "You can believe that I am exposed to a thousand devils in this indolent solitude," he wrote his friend Nicholas Gerbel in November. Upon the basis of such casual remarks and of the somewhat highly colored tales recounted in later years to his credulous table companions, a whole crop of ghostly legends has grown up about the chambers he occupied in the lonely castle. Exaggerated as they are, the mental struggles they suggest were not altogether a fiction. Doubts and fears about the wisdom of his course he could not wholly escape. What if he were all wrong and were deceiving and leading to perdition the multitudes who were looking to him for leadership? "Are you alone wise, and has all the world gone wrong until you came to set it right?" was a taunt that caused him not a few anxious hours. Though his letters contain many splendid expressions of faith, the unwavering confidence of later years he had apparently not yet attained.

Relief and recreation he found frequently in out-of-door excursions, in the course of which he now and then visited the surrounding towns and mingled unrecognized with the crowds in market-place and inn. On one occasion he even took part in a two-days' hunt. His description of it in a letter to Spalatin is beautifully characteristic:

Last week I followed the chase for two days that I might taste that bitter-sweet pleasure of heroes. We caught two hares and three poor little partridges—a worthy occupation indeed for men of leisure! Even there among the nets and dogs I reflected upon theology, and great as was the pleasure of the scene, I was made sorrowful and wretched by the thoughts it suggested. For what else did it signify than the devil, who pursues these innocent little beasts with his snares and impious dogs of teachers, the bishops and theologians? Only too sensible I was of this sad picture of simple and believing souls. A still more dreadful symbol followed. When by my exertions a little hare had been preserved alive, and concealing him in my sleeve I had withdrawn to one side, the dogs found the poor beast and bit it through my coat, breaking its leg and strangling it. Thus the pope and Satan rage that they may destroy even saved souls regardless of my efforts. I have had enough of such hunting. It is sweeter, in my opinion, to slay with darts and arrows bears, wolves, wild boars, foxes, and impious teachers such as these. But I comfort myself with the thought that it is a symbol of salvation when hares and harmless beasts are caught by a man rather than by bears, wolves, rapacious hawks, and similar bishops and theologians. For in the latter case they are devoured, as it were, for hell, in the former for heaven. I have written this pleasantry to remind you that you hunters at court will also be hunted in paradise whom Christ, the best of hunters, shall scarcely with the greatest effort seize and save. When you are having sport in the chase, it is you who are sported with.

Relief from mental distress Luther found still oftener in work. Though he was continually complaining of his indolence and lack of occupation, and though he suffered much from ill health, due probably to the unaccustomed richness of his fare, he really did an enormous amount of study and writing. "Here I sit with nothing to do, like a free man among prisoners," he wrote Amsdorf; but for an idle man he accomplished extraordinary things. Though his place of concealment was kept a secret from the world at large, he did not hesitate to publish freely on all sorts of questions, and it was not long before enemies and friends alike knew the reformer was still alive and in touch with all that was going on.

His writings were of various kinds,—devotional tracts, popular sermons, Scripture expositions, and polemic pamphlets. In a critique of another papal bull, which had included him with many notable heretics of the past in a common condemnation, he attacked both the office and person of the pope in the coarsest and most abusive fashion. It was evidently his deliberate intention to give the German people courage to break with Rome by pouring scorn and contempt upon the papacy. And yet, with all his bitterness, he showed his conscientiousness and a somewhat remarkable fairness of mind when there came into his hands, early in 1521, a book by a young Bohemian scholar attempting to prove that Saint Peter was never in Rome. Greatly as the acceptance of this thesis would have strengthened his polemic, Luther rejected it as unproven.

One of the most interesting incidents of his stay at the Wartburg was his tilt with Archbishop Albert of Mayence. Made bold by Luther's disappearance from the scene, the archbishop ventured to open a new sale of indulgences at Halle, where he had gathered an extraordinary collection of relics, beside which the treasures of the castle church at Wittenberg paled into insignificance. From the proceeds of this new traffic he hoped to replenish his exhausted exchequer and also to build a university at Halle to rival the one at Wittenberg. When the matter came to Luther's knowledge, he sat down in the first flush of indignation to write a severe tract "Against the Idol at Halle," informing Spalatin of what he was doing. The elector promptly protested and ordered Luther to leave the Archbishop of Mayence alone. The one thing Frederick did not want was to have his professor get embroiled again with so prominent a prince of the realm. He was secretly defying the emperor and diet in protecting Luther, but he hoped the excitement would soon quiet down and the whole affair be forgotten. If the condemned monk were again to break the peace in such a fashion, Frederick's policy would be altogether shattered, and his position, he felt, would become intolerable. His command, communicated through Spalatin, drew from Luther the following fiery protest:

A more displeasing letter I have scarcely ever read than your last one, so that I not only put off answering it, but even determined not to reply at all. In the first place, I will not endure what you say, that the prince will not permit Mayence to be written against or the public peace disturbed. Rather I will lose you and the prince himself and every creature. For if I have withstood his creator the pope, why should I yield to his creature? Beautifully indeed you say that the public peace must not be disturbed while you suffer the eternal peace of God to be broken by the impious and sacrilegious acts of that son of perdition. Not so, Spalatin! Not so, Prince! For the sake of Christ's sheep, this most terrible wolf must be resisted with all one's powers, as an example to others. Therefore I send the little book against him, finished before your letter came. I have not been moved by what you write to make any alterations, although I have submitted it to the pen of Philip that he may change it as he sees fit. Beware you do not return the book to Philip, or dissuade him from publishing it. It is settled that you will not be listened to.

A few weeks later he took matters into his own hands and wrote Archbishop Albert one of his characteristic letters, threatening to pillory him before all the world if he did not at once put an end to his new indulgence campaign.

Your Electoral Grace perhaps thinks that, now I am off the scene, you are safe from me and the monk is smothered by his Imperial Majesty. However that may be, your Electoral Grace shall know that I will do what Christian love demands, regardless of the gates of hell, to say nothing of the unlearned, popes, cardinals, and bishops. . . . It has become so clear that indulgences are mere knavery and deception, and Christ alone ought to be preached to the people, that your Electoral Grace cannot excuse yourself on the ground of ignorance. Let me remind your Electoral Grace of the beginning. What a terrible fire was kindled by a little despised spark, when all the world felt so secure, and thought a single poor beggar was far too small for the pope, and was undertaking an impossible thing. But God pronounced his judgment and gave the pope and all his creatures quite enough to do, and contrary to everybody's expectation brought the game to such a pass that the pope's prosperity will hardly be restored, but affairs will daily grow worse with him, that God's work may be seen therein. . . . Therefore your Electoral Grace is hereby finally informed, if the idol is not done away with, I shall be unavoidably compelled, for the sake of divine

From a photograph by Verlagsanstalt Carl Jagemann, Eisenach

WESTERN SIDE OF THE WARTBURG

The building at the left is the Ritterhaus, at the right end of which are the Luther rooms

doctrine and Christian salvation, to attack your Electoral Grace openly as well as the pope, to denounce the undertaking merrily, to lay at the door of the Bishop of Mayence all the old enormities of Tetzel, and to show the whole world the difference between a bishop and a wolf. . . . I have no pleasure in your Electoral Grace's shame and humiliation, but if a stop is not put to the profaning and desecrating of God's truth, I and all Christians are in duty bound to maintain His honor, although the whole world, to say nothing of a poor man, a cardinal, be thereby disgraced. I shall not keep still, and even if I do not succeed, I hope you bishops will no longer sing your little song with joy. You have not yet got rid of all those whom Christ has awakened against your idolatrous tyranny. Within a fortnight I shall expect your Electoral Grace's favorable reply, for at the expiration of that time my little book "Against the Idol at Halle" will be issued if a public answer be not received.

The wholesome respect in which Luther's pen was held is shown by the complete submission of the frightened ecclesiastic. At the end of three weeks he wrote the irate monk an apologetic letter full of expressions of personal humility, assuring him that the traffic had been already stopped and promising to do nothing unbecoming a pious clergyman and Christian prince. His surrender led the reformer to suppress the book against him, and it was ultimately published only in a revised form and under another title as a general attack upon pope and bishops.

FAR and away the most important fruit of Luther's stay at the Wartburg was his translation of the New Testament, begun at Melanchthon's solicitation in December, and completed in less than three months. After a careful revision it was hurried through the press, and in September appeared in its first edition in a large folio volume embellished with many woodcuts. It was soon followed by a translation of successive books of the Old Testament, until, in 1534, the whole Bible was issued together. Even then Luther did not stop, but went on revising and improving until his death, and no fewer than ten editions of the complete work were published during his lifetime.

He was not the first to put the Scriptures into the German language. Vernacular translations were very common and had a wide circulation among the people. During the previous half-century, eighteen German editions of the whole Bible had been published, and some of Luther's own acquaintances were engaged in the task of translating before he began. Writing in December to his friend Lang, who had recently issued a German version of the Gospel of Matthew, he urged him to go on with the work, expressing the wish that every town might have its own translator, and thus the Bible be better understood by the people.

That he had many predecessors diminishes in no degree the importance of Luther's work. Though his was not the first German Bible, it soon won its way to general favor and crowded all others out of use.

The contrast with the earlier versions was very great. They were based on the Latin Vulgate, the official Bible of the Catholic Church, and smacked largely of their source. Written in a curious Latinized German, most of them were unattractive and sometimes almost unintelligible. Luther translated his New Testament direct from the Greek, and his Old Testament from the Hebrew. Besides getting nearer to the original, he was thus able to avoid the deleterious influence of the Latin, and produce a translation genuinely German in style and spirit.

His qualifications for the work were many. Though not one of the great philologists of the day, he had an excellent knowledge of both Hebrew and Greek, and a very unusual faculty, quite out of proportion to his grammatical attainments, for getting at the meaning of an author and divining the sense of obscure and difficult passages. After his return from the Wartburg he also had the constant assistance of Melanchthon and other eminent linguists of Wittenberg.

His long and intimate acquaintance with the Bible likewise stood him in good stead. Ever since his Erfurt days he had been a diligent student of it and had fairly saturated himself with its spirit and contents. His profound religious experience gave him a sympathy with it he could have gained in no other way. He found his own innermost feelings expressed in it, and his translation of many a passage was as truly the free and spontaneous expression of his own heart as the reproduction of the words of another. He doubtless had this in mind when he wrote: "Translating is not everybody's gift. It demands a genuinely pious, true, industrious, reverent, Christian, learned, experienced, and practised heart. Therefore I hold that no false Christian or sectary can translate correctly, as appears, for instance, in the Worms edition of the prophets. Great labor was employed in its preparation, and my German was closely imitated; but the translators were Jews, with little loyalty to Christ, and so their art and industry were vain."

His intimate contact in the confessional with the religious emotions, aspirations, and weaknesses of his fellows had also thrown light upon his own experiences and sharpened his insight into the hearts of men. He had a profound knowledge of human nature, as his letters, sermons, and tracts abundantly show, and it enabled him to understand as few have understood the most widely and variously human of all the world's books.

Most important of all was his extraordinary acquaintance with the German language. It is not often a writer of the first rank gives himself to the translation of another's work. Such a writer Luther was, and his version remains one of the great classics of the world. He had a command of idiomatic, racy, colloquial German seldom equaled and never surpassed, and he undertook to make the Bible really a German book.

In a tract on the subject of translating, defending his work against the strictures of his enemies, he remarked, "I have tried to talk German, not Latin and Greek"; and again, "You must not get your German from the Latin, as these asses do, but you must get it from the mother in the home, the child in the street, the common man in the market-place." The difficulties of the task he indicated in the words, "In translating I have always made the effort to write pure and clear German; and it has often happened that we have sought a fortnight or even three and four weeks for a single word, and then sometimes not found it." Writing to a friend in March, 1522, he said: "I also have undertaken to translate the Bible. It is good for me, for otherwise I might have died with the fond persuasion that I was learned." To Wenceslaus Link he wrote: "How great and laborious a task it is to force Hebrew writers to talk German! How they strive against it and rebel at being compelled to forsake their native manner and follow the rough German style! It is just as if a nightingale were made to give up its own sweet melody and imitate the song of the cuckoo, though disliking it extremely." And to Spalatin: "Job seems to endure our translating as little as the consolations of his friends."

Luther did not try to transport his readers back into Bible days, but to bring the Bible down to their own day. It was not a scholar's book he aimed to produce, done so literally that it might be retranslated into the original languages, but a people's book, so idiomatic and modern that its readers might forget it was written in a foreign tongue, in a distant land, and in an age long past. He therefore allowed himself many liberties with the text, to the great scandal of his critics, often substituting the name of a more for a less familiar object, and adding words freely where needed to bring out the sense, as he understood it, or to make the scene vivid and real. The result of his efforts was a Bible translation which, after the lapse of four centuries, still stands unapproached in its vital and compelling power.

Luther himself was not unaware of the merits of his work. Speaking of it on one occasion he remarked: "I do not want to boast—the work speaks for itself— but it is so good and precious that it is better than all the Greek and Latin versions, and you will find more in it than in all the commentaries, for we have cleared the stumps and stones out of the way that others may read in it without hindrance." But he underestimated its lasting popularity: "When I die every schoolmaster, every teacher, every parish clerk will want to make a translation of his own. Our version will no longer be used. All our books will be thrown away, Bible and postil as well. For the world must have something new."

The German employed by him was not his own creation, but it owed him much. The dialects of the day were many and various, so that people living only a few score miles apart, as he once remarked, could scarcely understand each other. But a common diplomatic language had already developed, and become the medium of official communication between all the principalities of the land. This he made the basis of his written German. "I use no special dialect of my own," he once said, "but the common German language, that I may be understood by all alike. I use the speech of the Saxon chancery, which is followed by all the princes and kings of Germany."

Formal, stilted, and clumsy enough it was as employed in the state documents of the day, but he greatly modified and enriched it, making it more flexible and colloquial, and enlarging its vocabulary from the language of the people, spoken and written. He had a wide knowledge of current literature, devotional and otherwise, and an enormous fund of popular saws and proverbs, and his style, as a rule, was not only simple and clear, but wonderfully vivid and picturesque. It was no exaggeration when a contemporary declared, "Dr. Martin is a real German Cicero. He has not only taught us the true religion, but has reformed the German tongue, and there is no writer on earth who equals him in it." His writings did much to promote the spread of the German he used and to give the whole country a common language. He was not the only agent in promoting this development, but he did more than any other single man, and above all books his German Bible contributed most.

Even more than the oneness of language promoted by it was the unity of sentiment to which it contributed. Divided the land was still, and torn for many a day with conflicts more bitter than it had ever known, but the Luther Bible went on generation by generation nourishing similar ideals and serving as few other agencies to unify the spirit of the German-speaking race.

Thus the reformer's enforced retirement bore rich fruit. Set aside from his active work as leader of the Reformation, he employed the quiet weeks of winter solitude in the lonely castle in a stupendous task, which, had he done nothing else, would alone have won for him the lasting gratitude of his native land.

CHAPTER XVI

THE CONFLICT WITH RADICALISM

WHILE Luther was in retirement at the Wartburg, events were moving rapidly in Wittenberg. Left to themselves, some of his associates and followers proceeded to put his principles into immediate practice and to break with traditional custom at many points. Hitherto, despite the radicalism of his utterances, the externals of the old system had remained untouched. But this state of things could not continue permanently. His doctrine of salvation by faith alone, making all efforts vain to win the divine favor by acts of special merit, his principle of Christian liberty, releasing believers from dependence on hierarchy and sacraments, and his denial that pope or council or any other ecclesiastical authorities had the right to lay upon Christians obligations not required in the word of God—all these could not fail to bear fruit in action.

The first break came in connection with the celibacy of the clergy, from time immemorial a rock of offense to would-be reformers. In the spring of 1521, certain priests among Luther's following ventured to marry, and in the summer his colleague Carlstadt published a book attacking not only clerical celibacy, but also monastic vows. Luther himself believed priests had the right to marry, if they chose, on the theory that celibacy was unjustly required of them by a tyrannical church; but he regarded monasticism in a different light. He remembered the solemnity of his own vow, taken freely and without compulsion, and though he had for some time looked with disfavor upon the monastic life, a voluntary promise, he felt, ought to be kept, be the consequences what they might.

But when led by the situation in Wittenberg to examine the matter more carefully, he soon came to the conclusion that monks were as free to marry as priests. The monastic vow, he decided, was itself wrong, and therefore not binding. It meant dependence upon works for salvation, neglect of the service of one's fellows, and permanent bondage to a law, thus violating Christian faith, love, and liberty. His condemnation of monasticism was undoubtedly far too sweeping, and his estimate of it unjust to many a devout and noble soul; but he was consistent in pronouncing the institution, with its irrevocable vows, fundamentally at variance with his gospel of Christian freedom, and its common emphasis out of line with his interpretation of the Christian life.

He defended his position in two series of theses, and a little later, when a number of monks left the Wittenberg convent and renounced monasticism, he wrote an elaborate work justifying their course and fortifying their consciences. The book was preceded by an interesting letter of dedication, addressed to his father, explaining and apologizing for his entrance into the monastery. He had taken the vow against his father's will, and hence, as he now confessed, in violation of his duty to God.

"And so," he exclaimed, "will you even now drag me out of monasticism? But that you may not boast, the Lord has anticipated you and has dragged me out Himself. For what difference does it make whether I wear cowl and tonsure, or lay them off? Do tonsure

and hood make the monk? 'All is yours,' says Paul;
'but ye are Christ's.' And shall I belong to the hood,
and not rather the hood to me? My conscience has
become free, and that is the most complete freedom.
Therefore I am a monk, and yet not a monk; a new
creature, not the pope's, but Christ's."

Meanwhile, at the instance of Carlstadt and other
radicals, among whom Gabriel Zwilling, an eloquent
and fiery inmate of the Augustinian convent, was the
most extreme and influential of all, there speedily followed many innovations in the religious services at
Wittenberg. While in themselves of no great importance, they were attended in many cases with uproar
and riot and outraged the feelings of the more sober
and conservative spirits in the town. Ominous they
were, too, because largely identical with changes made
in Bohemia under Hussite influence, thus seeming to
presage the same revolution and bloodshed as had
devastated that kingdom.

Early in December, while the movement was still in
its incipiency, the exiled Luther made a hurried and
secret visit to Wittenberg to see what was going on.
He found the situation less serious than he had feared,
writing Spalatin, "Everything I see and hear greatly
pleases me. May the Lord strengthen those who wish
us well." The students, he saw, were chiefly responsible for the riots, and he regarded all the troubles as
largely the result of a temporary excitement which
would soon spend itself.

But he thought it worth while, as he informed Spalatin, because of the many reports of the wide-spread
roughness of his followers, to write a vigorous tract
upon his return to the Wartburg, warning them against
uproar and violence. All changes in the existing system,
he insisted, must be made in an orderly fashion and by

From an old print

POPE HADRIAN VI

the civil authorities, not by private individuals. Uproar, he maintained, is always bad, and out of evil only evil comes. The devil was trying to discredit the new movement by inciting its adherents to such conduct. As for himself, Luther declared, he would support the side attacked, however bad it might be, rather than those who attacked it, however good their cause. Only with the word was the work of reformation to be accomplished. As the evils of the old system were exposed, they would disappear of themselves. "Pay no more money," he exclaimed, "for bulls, candles, bells, pictures, churches, but declare that the Christian life consists in faith and love, and keep doing it for two years, and you will see what happens to pope, bishop, cardinal, priest, monk, nun, bells, steeples, masses, vigils, cowl, cap, shaven poll, rules, statutes, and the whole swarm and rabble of the pope's government. They will vanish like smoke."

Late in December there appeared in Wittenberg certain fanatical spirits who claimed supernatural illumination, and upon the basis of what they thought divine inspiration preached the complete overturning of the existing system, religious, economic, and social. They came from the Saxon town of Zwickau, some eighty miles south of Wittenberg, not far from the Bohemian border. Probably under the influence of similar movements in Bohemia, Zwickau early became the center of a prophetic demonstration which spread widely and gained many adherents, especially among the lower classes. All social distinctions were decried, manual labor was insisted on as alone legitimate, education was denounced, and divine revelation, vouchsafed chiefly to the ignorant and untutored, was looked to as the sole guide of life. In Wittenberg even Melanchthon was deeply impressed by the newcomers, while

Carlstadt and others were completely carried away, and proceeded to put their principles into immediate practice, to the great scandal of many in town and university.

The town authorities had approved, more or less hesitantly, a number of the innovations urged by Carlstadt, but had not thereby succeeded in satisfying the most extreme radicals, and things were gradually getting beyond their control. Wittenberg was gaining a very bad name, and the university was losing many of its best and most sober-minded students. The theological faculty, to which Frederick turned for counsel, was all at sea. The innovators had much to say for themselves. Carlstadt was a prominent professor, and most of the radical leaders were men of devotion and exemplary piety. They appealed to the authority of the Scriptures or to the immediate illumination of the Spirit, and it was difficult to show them wrong. It was also dangerous, so many felt, including the pious elector himself, to resist what might be the will of God.

When Luther learned what was going on, with his usual good sense he wrote his colleague Amsdorf early in January:

Do not be too easily moved by the Zwickau prophets. The thirteenth chapter of Deuteronomy and the fifth of First John make it certain that you sin not if you put them off, and first prove their spirits whether they be of God. In the meantime, the Lord will show what is to be done. It seems to me at first sight strong cause for suspicion that they pretend to revelations from on high.

And to Melanchthon:

So far as the prophets are concerned I do not approve your timidity, for you are greater than I in spirit as well as in learning. First of all, when they bear testimony to themselves they are not immediately to be listened to, but are to be tested according to the advice of John. And if you are not able to prove them you have the counsel of Gamaliel to wait and see. For I have as yet heard of nothing said or done by them which Satan cannot do or imitate. Inquire for me whether they can show their credentials. For God never sends any one, not even his own Son, without giving him a commission through men, or approving him by visible signs. The prophets of old had their authority from prophetic law and order as we have ours through men. I will never acknowledge them if they claim to have been called by a mere revelation.

In February, learning of the perplexity and anxiety of the elector over the growing difficulties, he wrote him as follows:

For many years your Electoral Grace has been collecting sacred relics in every land. Now God has heard your wish and has sent you without cost or labor a whole cross with nails, spears, and scourges. I congratulate you on your new relics. Do not be frightened. Stretch out your arms trustfully. Let the nails pierce deep, and be thankful and glad. It must be thus with those who would follow God's word. Not only do Annas and Caiaphas rage, but Judas is among the apostles, and Satan among the children of God. May your Grace only be prudent and wise, and judge not according to the appearance of things. Be not faint-hearted. The matter has not yet reached the pass the devil desires. Though I am a fool, believe me a little. I understand such attacks of Satan. Therefore, I do not fear him, to his great sorrow. It is only the beginning. Let the world cry out and condemn. Let fall who may, even St. Peter and the apostles! They will come back on the third day, when Christ rises again.

Through one of his officials, the elector immediately replied, asking what Luther thought he ought to do in the circumstances, for he did not wish to attempt anything against the will of God and His holy word; but things were in the greatest confusion in Wittenberg, and nobody knew who was cook and who waiter. In the same connection he protested strongly against Luther's returning to Wittenberg, as the latter purposed to do. Much as he would hate to deliver him over to the emperor, if he appeared openly in Wittenberg, while still under the ban of the empire, he could not possibly refuse to do so without bringing serious evils upon his land and people.

Despite his protest, the reformer, who had in the meantime been urgently requested by the town council to return home, started for Wittenberg the day after receiving the elector's communication. On the way he replied to it in the following fashion:

Your Electoral Grace knows, or, if you do not, I now inform you, that I received the gospel not from men, but from Heaven alone, through our Lord Jesus Christ, so that I might boast and subscribe myself, as I henceforth will, a servant and evangelist. That I offered to be heard and judged was not because I was in doubt, but from over-humility, to win others. But now, perceiving that my humility will result in bringing contempt upon the gospel, and the devil will take possession of the whole place if I give him even a hand's breadth, I am compelled by my conscience to act otherwise. I have done enough for your Electoral Grace in yielding to you this year. For the devil knows very well that I have not done it out of fear. Looking into my heart, he saw clearly, when I went to Worms, that had I known as many devils would set upon me as there are tiles on the roofs I would have sprung into the midst of them with joy. . . . I write thus that you may know I come to Wittenberg under the protection of a far higher power than the elector, and I have no mind to seek shelter from your Grace.

From an old print

THOMAS MÜNZER

Indeed, I believe I can protect your Grace better than you can protect me. If I thought you could and would protect me, I would not come. No sword can help in this affair. God must act alone without man's care or aid. Therefore who believes most will be of most protection here. And since I suspect your Electoral Grace is still weak in faith, I can by no means regard you as the man who can guard or rescue me. Since your Grace desires to know what to do in this affair and fancies you have done too little, I answer respectfully that you have already done altogether too much, and should do nothing. For God will not and cannot endure either your care and effort or mine. He wishes it left to Him and to no one else. May your Grace act accordingly. If your Grace believes this, you will be secure and will have peace. If you do not, I do, and I must leave you to sorrow in your unbelief, as it becomes all unbelievers to suffer. Since I will not obey your Grace, you are excused in the sight of God if I am imprisoned or killed. Before men your Grace should conduct yourself as follows: as an elector you should be obedient to the higher powers and permit his Imperial Majesty to rule body and goods in your cities and lands in accordance with the law of the empire, and you should offer no opposition and interpose no hindrance if he tries to arrest or slay me. For no one ought to withstand the authorities save he who has appointed them. Else is it uproar and against God. I hope, however, they will have the good sense to recognize that your Grace was born in too lofty a cradle to be yourself my executioner. If you leave the door open and see that they are unmolested if they come themselves, or send their messengers to fetch me, you will have been obedient enough. They cannot demand more of your Electoral Grace than to know whether Luther be with you, and that they can learn without anxiety, trouble, or personal danger to your Grace. For Christ has not taught me to harm others by being a Christian. But should they be so lacking in intelligence as to ask your Electoral Grace to lay hands on me yourself, I will then tell your Grace what to do. I will keep your Grace safe from harm and danger to body, goods, and soul on my account, whether your Grace believes it or not. Herewith I commend your Electoral Grace to the grace of God. If necessary, we will very soon talk further. I have written this letter in haste that your Electoral Grace may not be distressed by the news of my arrival, for I must comfort everybody and harm nobody, if I would be a true Christian. It is another man than Duke George with whom I have to do. He knows me well, and I know him not ill. If your Electoral Grace believed, you would see the glory of God; but since you do not yet believe, you have as yet seen nothing. To God be love and honor forever. Amen!

The elector was obliged to content himself with a letter, written by Luther at his request, explaining the reasons for the return to Wittenberg and relieving Frederick from all responsibility. This he wished to show his fellow-princes in case he was blamed for his disregard of the Worms decree in allowing the condemned monk to go on with his work in Wittenberg. While desiring to protect Luther, he preferred to pose as incompetent rather than to avow his sympathy openly. But however he might veil his attitude, the important fact is that he continued to protect him. Eloquent testimony it was to his confidence in his heretical professor. Annoyed though he must have been at Luther's defiant return, he permitted him to resume his work and take up his old position in church and university as if nothing had happened. He could easily have stopped him by putting him under arrest. An outlaw, as the reformer was, and under the ban of the empire, it was only by the elector's grace he remained free at all. Had his prince's favor been withdrawn, his career would speedily have come to an end. But it was never withdrawn, and despite papal bull and imperial ban the bold monk went on unmolested.

Returning from the Wartburg, Luther stopped overnight in the Black Bear inn at Jena, where he was seen by two Swiss students on their way to Wittenberg to study theology. The following account of the scene, given by one of them, John Kessler, in a book on the Reformation, throws an attractive light on Luther's kindliness and affability:

In the inn we found a man alone at table with a book before him. He greeted us cordially and invited us to come and sit with him, for as our shoes were very muddy we were ashamed to enter the room and had set ourselves down on a bench by the door. He urged us to drink so that we could not refuse him. When we perceived his friendliness and amiability, we took seats at his table, as he had invited us to, and ordered a measure of wine that we might ask him to drink in return. We had no other idea than that he was a knight, for according to the custom of the country he wore a red cap, with hose and doublet, and had a sword at his side which he held by the hilt with his right hand while his left clasped the book.

Soon he asked where we came from, but after answering his own question—"You are Swiss"—he continued, "What part of Switzerland do you live in?"

We told him St. Gall. He went on, "If you are bound, as I understand, for Wittenberg, you will find some good countrymen there, Dr. Jerome Schurf and his brother Augustine."

We said we had letters to them. Then we asked him, "Do you know, sir, whether Martin Luther is now at Wittenberg, or where he is?"

"I have trustworthy information," he replied, "that he is not there at present, but will be soon. Philip Melanchthon, however, is there. He teaches Greek and there are others who teach Hebrew." He then advised us earnestly to study both languages, for they were especially necessary to an understanding of the Holy Scriptures.

"Thank God," we said, "for we are determined, if our lives are spared, to see and hear Luther. For we undertook this journey on his account, having been told that he wishes to destroy the priesthood together with the mass as a groundless superstition. As our parents brought us up from boyhood to be priests, we want to know what sort of instruction he will give us and by what right he proposes to do such things." . . .

Again he asked us, "What do they think of Luther in Switzerland?"

"There are many opinions, sir," we replied, "as everywhere else. Some cannot praise him enough and thank God truth has been revealed and error exposed through him. But some damn him as an intolerable heretic, particularly the clergy."

"I can well imagine," he remarked, "it is the clergy."

Conversing thus with us, he was so friendly that my companion picked up the book lying before him and examined it. As it proved to be a Hebrew Psalter he laid it down again, and we began to wonder who the man might be. . . .

After a little while the landlord called me to the door.

I was alarmed, thinking I had done something amiss. But he said, "I perceive you would really like to see and hear Luther; it is he who is sitting by you."

I took it as a joke and said, "Oh, come, Mr. Landlord, you wish to play the fool with me and satisfy my curiosity with Luther's phantom."

He replied, "It is certainly he, but do not act as if you recognized him."

Though I did not believe him, I let him have his way, and, returning to the room, told my companion what he had said. He too could not credit it and thought the landlord had perhaps said, "Hutten." As the knight's costume and bearing seemed more like Hutten than the monk

Luther, I let myself be persuaded, for the two names sound somewhat alike. I therefore talked the rest of the time as if he were Sir Ulrich von Hutten, knight.

Meantime two merchants came in to spend the night, and after taking off their wraps one of them laid an unbound book on the table. When Martin asked what book it was he answered, "It is Dr. Luther's interpretation of some of the Gospels and Epistles, which has just been printed. Have you not seen it?"

"I shall soon," Martin replied.

Then the landlord called us to supper, and when we asked him to let us have something by ourselves he replied, "Sit down with the gentlemen; I will treat you well." When Martin heard it he said, "Come on, I will pay for the supper." While we were eating together he uttered many pious and gracious words, so that the two merchants as well as we were more interested in what he said than in what we ate. Among other things he complained, with a sigh, of the princes and lords who were then assembled at the Diet of Nuremberg on account of the religious difficulty and the burdens of Germany, but were disposed to do nothing but waste valuable time with costly tournaments, sleigh-riding, debauchery, pomp, and unchastity, when piety and earnest prayer to God were most needed. "But such are our Christian princes!" He also expressed the hope that evangelical truth would bear more fruit in our children and descendants, who were not poisoned by the papacy but nourished by the pure word of God, than in their parents, in whom error was so firmly planted it could not be easily rooted out. . . .

After supper the merchants went out to the stable to look after their horses, while Martin remained with us in the room. We thanked him for the honor he had done us and for his kindness in paying for the meal, letting him see we thought he was Ulrich von Hutten. He declared, however, that he was not, and when the landlord appeared he said to him, "I have become a nobleman tonight, for these Swiss imagine I am Ulrich von Hutten."

The landlord replied, "You are not he, but Martin Luther."

He laughed merrily, exclaiming, "They take me for Hutten and you take me for Luther; I shall soon be Marcolfus."

Then taking up a large mug of beer, according to the custom of the country, he said, "Swiss, let us have one more friendly drink for health's sake."

When I was about to take the mug from him he changed it and ordered wine, remarking, "The beer is new to you; drink the wine." Then he stood up, threw his cloak over his shoulder and bade us good-night, offering his hand and adding, "When you reach Wittenberg give my regards to Dr. Jerome Schurf." We replied we should gladly do so if he would tell us what name to say. He answered, "Say only he who is to come sends greetings." . . .

The Saturday following we called on Dr. Jerome Schurf to present our letters of introduction. When we entered the room we found Martin, looking just as he had at Jena, and with him Philip Melanchthon, Justus Jonas, Nicholas Amsdorf, and Dr. Augustine Schurf, who were telling him what had happened at Wittenberg during his absence. He greeted us with a laugh; and, pointing at one of them, said, "This is the Philip Melanchthon of whom I told you."

Elsewhere in the same work on the Reformation the Swiss describes Luther's personal appearance in the following words:

When I saw Martin in 1522, in his forty-first year, he was moderately fleshy, so upright in carriage that he bent backward rather than forward, with face raised toward heaven, and with deep brown-black eyes, flashing and sparkling like a star, so that you could not easily bear their gaze. . . . By nature he was a friendly and affable man, but not given to fleshly lust or unseemly pleasures,

while his earnestness was so mingled with joy and kindliness that it was a pleasure to live with him.

Arrived in Wittenberg on March 6, 1522, Luther at
once took command, and speedily brought order out
of chaos. Never was the power of the man more
strikingly exhibited than at this critical juncture of
his career. Hitherto he had been a radical iconoclast,
striking right and left at existing principles and practices. Now he gave himself to the much more difficult
task of controlling and moderating the forces he himself had set in motion. In a time of wide-spread
discontent it is comparatively easy to inflame the
smoldering passions of men and lead the populace in a
more or less unreasoning assault upon existing institutions; but to control the tremendous forces thus let
loose, and so to guide them that they do not merely
spend themselves in impotent fury, but lend their
strength to the building of a new and stable structure,
is another matter altogether. And yet we should entirely misunderstand Luther if we imagined that at
this great crisis of his career he turned his back upon
his past and became another man. It is most illuminating to see how calmly and confidently he met the
situation now confronting him. Though the radicals,
as he declared, were doing his cause more harm than
all his papal opponents, he was not dismayed or thrown
off his balance. Nor did he repudiate the principles
hitherto governing him, and seek refuge in other and
safer ways. Moving straight ahead in the path he
had long been traveling, he simply applied to the new
situation the same gospel that had made him an iconoclast, showing how, by its very nature, it conserved as
well as destroyed.

Beginning on the Sunday after his return, he

preached in the city church on eight successive days, handling one question after another frankly, vigorously, and with the greatest common sense. Violence of every kind he strenuously opposed. By the word alone can superstition be overcome and the old system reformed. In one of the sermons he remarked:

Take me as an example. I only preached and wrote God's word and did nothing else. But this accomplished so much that while I slept and while I drank Wittenberg beer with Philip and Amsdorf, the papacy grew weaker and suffered more damage than any prince or emperor ever inflicted. I did nothing; the word did it all. If I had wished to make trouble, I could have plunged Germany into a sea of blood. Yes, I could have started such a game at Worms that the emperor himself would have been unsafe. But what would that have been? A fool's game.

He did not stop with the denunciation of physical violence. Christian liberty, he reminded his followers, as he had clearly shown nearly two years before in his beautiful tract on the freedom of a Christian man, was not an end in itself, but only a means to a higher end —the service of one's fellows in self-forgetful love. Faith, he insisted, is nothing unless followed by love, and not our own rights, but our brother's good, should be always foremost in our thoughts. He acknowledged frankly his dislike for many of the ceremonies and customs of the past. Too often they had no warrant in Scripture, and served only to bind the conscience and obscure the gospel. At the same time he declared the Christian life consists neither in refraining from nor engaging in external religious practices, but in faith and love. Far better to retain indifferent things than to offend weak consciences and imperil the success of the cause by forcibly setting them aside. He had now, as always, a splendid disregard of externals and a magnificent insight into the real essentials. Mere uniformity he cared nothing about. Because the monastic life, or private confession, or fasting, was good for one person was no reason to require it of all. Let those who found such things helpful, as he himself continued to find the confessional helpful, employ them freely; but let them not insist upon others doing the same. He believed when the gospel was everywhere accepted and understood, all things inconsistent therewith would fall of themselves. In the meantime he would have liberty for the old as well as for the new. But in the meantime, too, he would do all he could to instruct Christians in the truly important things, and thus wean them as rapidly as possible from trust in the formal and external.

Before Luther finished his sermons, the lawyer Jerome Schurf wrote the elector:

Dr. Martin's coming and preaching have given both learned and unlearned among us great joy and gladness. For we poor men who had been vexed and led astray have again been shown by him, with God's help, the way of truth. Daily he incontrovertibly exposes the errors into which we were miserably led by the preachers from abroad. It is evident that the Spirit of God is in him and works through him, and I am convinced he has returned to Wittenberg at this time by the special providence of the Almighty.

Under Luther's direction many of the changes in the worship of the city church made during his absence were abandoned, and the old forms for the most part restored. Calm was reëstablished, and the town again speedily resumed its normal aspect. Early in May he could write Spalatin, with great relief, "Here there is nothing but love and friendship."

More important than the return to the old order was the public stand Luther now took against social and economic revolution, and his emphatic denial that his gospel meant the violent overthrow of the existing religious system. The consequence was a great revulsion of feeling toward him on the part of many of the princes of Germany. They saw that he was less radical than they had supposed; that he stood for order, not anarchy; and that he was able to control the seething masses as nobody else could. When at the Diet of Nuremberg, in the autumn of 1522, the attempt was made by the representatives of the devout and pious Pope Adrian VI, successor of Leo X, to induce the German rulers to take steps for the more vigorous enforcement of the Edict of Worms, the majority refused to give their consent. Though the edict had been adopted only a year and a half before, the situation was so changed that they now declined to reaffirm it, and left it to the conscience of each prince to execute it as far as he pleased, while they appealed to a general council for the final settlement of the matter. Thus the whole question, already decided both by pope and diet, was again thrown open, and a quasi and temporary license given to the new movement.

In the meantime its organization was proceeding steadily. Town after town took the management of religious affairs into its own hands and adopted new forms better fitted to the principles of the Reformation. Luther was continually appealed to for counsel, and his help was sought in securing preachers of the right stamp to take the place of those out of sympathy with the new order of things. He was becoming more and more the bishop, or general overseer, of the churches accepting the Reformation, and all sorts of administrative problems were constantly upon his mind. His correspondence during 1522 and the following years had to do increasingly with such matters. He also traveled widely, visiting places in need of advice and bringing his wisdom to bear upon the many difficult questions that were emerging month by month.

The constant temptation, as in Wittenberg, was to go too fast, and he was obliged often to remonstrate with the authorities and urge upon them the considerations governing his own conduct. But as time passed and the influence of his principles spread, he approved both for Wittenberg and elsewhere more radical changes than at first. In 1523 we hear him frequently declaring that the prejudices of the weak had been long enough regarded, and the time had come to do away with many of the more obnoxious forms and customs of the past. Even now he was surprisingly conservative. Many of his followers wished to cast aside everything not sustained by direct warrant of Scripture; but he took the position, and maintained it to the end of his life, that the old was to be left unmolested whenever it did not contradict or obscure the gospel of Christ. He also continued to oppose hasty and violent innovations of every kind. Usually his advice was followed, but occasionally, particularly in places at a distance from Wittenberg, he was unable to control the more radical spirits and had to witness changes he greatly disliked. He did not hesitate in such cases to express himself with the same sharpness as against his papal opponents. Carlstadt, who left Wittenberg in disgust in 1523, and Thomas Münzer, a clergyman of Zwickau and the principal leader of the fanatical prophets of that neighborhood, made him most trouble. They denounced him as a tyrant, declared him recreant to his own principles and untrue to the word of God, and strove in every way to undermine his influence and force a radical reform.

In Orlamünde, a little town not far from Zwickau, he had a humiliating, if somewhat amusing, experience in the autumn of 1524. Carlstadt was for a time pastor there, and gained a large following. Under his influence, images were destroyed, convents forcibly closed, and one after another of the old customs arbitrarily set aside. In the course of a tour of visitation, Luther appeared upon the scene, and in an extended interview with the authorities of the town tried to convince them of the error of their ways. They defended themselves warmly, insisting they were truer to the word of God than he. If to be true to it means to follow it slavishly in all its parts, they were certainly right. But in contrast with their narrow literalism, Luther's moderation and common sense appear to great advantage. He would not allow himself to be carried to fanatical extremes even by his own principle of loyalty to the Bible. In the course of the discussion, a shoemaker justified the destruction of images by a Scriptural argument so picturesque and farfetched that Luther was nearly overcome with laughter and was quite unable to answer. As a matter of fact, he produced no impression upon his interlocutors, and only confirmed them in the opinion that he was inconsistent and half-hearted in the work of reformation. He wrote afterward: "I was glad enough not to be driven out of Orlamünde with stones and mud, for some of them blessed me with the words, 'Get out, in the name of a thousand devils, and break your neck before you leave!'"

Meanwhile there occurred an event which served only to confirm Luther in his attitude toward violence and anarchy. Franz von Sickingen, whose offers of support had meant a great deal to him not long before, and to whom he had dedicated a book on the confessional, written in the early days of his stay at the Wartburg, began war in the summer of 1522 upon an old enemy, the Elector and Archbishop of Treves. The campaign was intended to be only the beginning of a general struggle to curtail the power of the great princes of the realm and restore to the nobles their rapidly waning influence. Its controlling motive was certainly political and economic, but Sickingen claimed to be a champion of the Reformation, interested to promote the true gospel, and announced his purpose to revolutionize ecclesiastical and religious conditions. He undoubtedly hoped thus to enlist the support of Luther's sympathizers, but the hope proved vain. The real significance of the affair was generally understood, and the Archbishop of Treves was supported by the Count Palatine and the young Landgrave Philip of Hesse, both of them already favorably inclined toward Luther and his cause.

Sickingen's campaign was a complete failure. He was obliged to return to his stronghold, the Landstuhl, where he was besieged in the spring of 1523, and where he died of his wounds on the seventh of May, just after the castle was taken by his enemies. His defeat foreshadowed the speedy dissolution of the knights' revolutionary party, and their influence in German affairs was permanently broken.

Ulrich von Hutten, who had done much to encourage the formation of the party, survived his old friend and protector only a few months. He departed before the beginning of Sickingen's last campaign, and in August, 1523, after wandering from place to place, died in poverty at Zurich, befriended by the Swiss reformer

Zwingli, but deserted by all his old friends. Melanchthon spoke bitterly and contemptuously of him after his death. Happily, so far as we are aware, Luther did not follow his example, but we search his writings in vain for an expression of regret at the death of his erstwhile champion and confidant. The cause meant so much to him that he found it difficult to think kindly of any one who hindered or brought disrepute upon it, as Hutten's incendiary writings and final loss of prestige had done.

It was well Sickingen's attempt miscarried. His success would have meant at least a partial return to a state of society already largely outgrown and quite unsuited to the demands of the new age; and had the Reformation become identified with the class interests of the nobles, it would have perished with them in the fall that was bound to come ultimately, if not then.

Naturally, the affair was used by Luther's enemies to discredit his whole movement. Now the rival emperor was fallen, the anti-pope, it was confidently predicted, would soon follow. There was some apparent justification for this attitude. Luther's famous Address to the German Nobility, written in 1520, and his occasional warlike declarations of the same year, which still echoed in the dedication of his book on the confessional, had led many to identify his cause with that of the nobles, and Sickingen's avowed plan to promote the Reformation was taken to mean he had Luther's support, and was fighting the reformer's battles as well as his own.

Melanchthon complained of this as early as January, 1523, denouncing Sickingen's campaign as a dishonorable act of robbery and declaring that Luther was greatly distressed by it. Luther himself had very little to say on the subject. In a letter of December, 1522, to his friend Link, he wrote: "Franz von Sickingen has declared war against the Palatinate. It will be a very bad affair." Beyond this casual remark we have no reference to the matter in his writings; but when a rumor of Sickingen's death reached him, he wrote Spalatin he hoped it was false. Upon its confirmation a day or two later, he added: "The true and miserable history of Franz Sickingen I heard and read yesterday. God is a just but wonderful judge." Half a dozen years later, in a letter to the Landgrave of Hesse he classed the deceased knight with the hated Carlstadt and Münzer as an insurrectionist, including all three in a common condemnation.

Despite the effort of his opponents to hold Luther responsible for Sickingen's abortive attempt, its controlling motive was too apparent and too completely in line with the warlike knight's entire career to furnish an adequate ground for a serious attack upon the reformer, and probably the affair lost him few friends or supporters. On the other hand, it very likely affected his own attitude, serving to confirm his conviction that the preaching of the gospel is incompatible with the use of physical force. He saw more clearly than ever the undesirability and impossibility of promoting the Reformation by the sword. It may be, had Sickingen been victorious, Luther would have seen the hand of God in his victory, as he did in his defeat, and would have been led to tolerate, if not actively to favor, such warlike measures. His somewhat inconsistent utterances seem to show that while feeling the unchristian character of war and violence, he was yet not sure it might not be God's will in the present juncture, as occasionally in the past, to put an end to existing evils by the sword. But if he was really in doubt, Sickingen's fate settled the question for him. Thenceforth he insisted always on the use of peaceful measures only.

CHAPTER XVII

THE PEASANTS' WAR

MUCH more disastrous in its effects upon the Reformation was the Peasants' War. This greatest tragedy of the age had been long preparing. Frequently during recent generations the unhappy condition of the peasant class had led to more or less serious outbreaks, but none of them compared in importance with the tremendous uprising of 1525. Luther was not responsible for it, nor did it begin among his disciples. It was only the repetition on a large scale of many similar attempts, and the interests underlying all of them were not religious, as with him, but economic. At the same time it was due in no small part to him that this particular movement surpassed in magnitude any seen in Germany before or since. His attacks upon many features of the existing order, his criticisms of the growing luxury of the wealthier classes, his denunciations of the rapacity and greed of great commercial magnates and of the tyranny and corruption of rulers both civil and ecclesiastical, all tended to inflame the populace and spread impatience and discontent. His gospel of Christian liberty also had its effect. For the spiritual freedom he taught, multitudes substituted freedom from political oppression, from social injustice, and from economic burdens. Then, too, the extraordinary response he had met with, the confusion all Germany had been thrown into by the Reformation, and the wide-spread weakening of respect for traditional authority resulting therefrom, made this seem a peculiarly favorable time for the peasants to press their claims.

Early in 1525 a series of twelve brief articles was published in southwestern Germany, containing a very moderate statement of the demands of the peasants, as, for instance, the privilege of electing their own pastors, the abolition of villeinage, freedom to hunt and fish and to supply themselves with fuel from the forest, reduction of exorbitant rents, extra payment for extra labor, and restoration to the community of lands unjustly appropriated by private persons. With such demands as these no one could justly find fault. They involved social reform only, not revolution, and looked for the most part simply to the more equitable adjustment of existing conditions.

At first there was apparently no thought of violence. The peasants were a harmless and peaceable folk. But here and there they gathered in large numbers to present their grievances and impress the rulers with the magnitude of the movement. Unfortunately, instead of listening sympathetically to their complaints, some of the princes, fearing the effects of such demonstrations, treated the assembled peasants as insurrectionists and dispersed them with the sword, maltreating and killing them without mercy. Their harshness and cruelty added fuel to the flames, and the inevitable result was a rapid growth of revolutionary sentiment and the spread of a desire for retaliation. The demands of the peasants became more extreme and unreasonable, and their peaceful intentions widely gave way to thoughts of war. Fantastic and impossible notions of a society wherein they should be in complete control took possession of their minds. Communistic ideas of a radical type gained currency, and the desire grew to overthrow the whole social structure and destroy all inequalities in property, employment, and rank. Thomas Münzer and other fanatical religious leaders threw themselves into the movement, and preached a new social order in which there should be no rulers or subjects, no rich or poor, no cities or commerce, no art or science, but all should live in primitive simplicity and equality. What was more, they summoned the peasants and the proletariate of the cities to bring in the new order by the sword. In fiery and impassioned discourse they told the people it was God's will they should everywhere kill and destroy without mercy until all the mighty were laid low and the promised kingdom of God established. Social and religious ideals became inextricably mingled. Counting confidently upon supernatural aid, multitudes without discipline or adequate military preparation threw themselves blindly into a conflict for which, as the event proved, they were wholly unequipped.

During all this time the peasants' attitude toward Luther was very diverse. Münzer and many other radicals hated him, and could not say enough against him; but there were also those who regarded him as the great prophet of the new era of social justice and economic well-being they were trying to usher in. His was a name to conjure with, and they made the most of it. They appealed to his gospel and quoted his writings in support of their programs. They called themselves his followers, and declared it their purpose to put his principles into practice. And whatever was true of the leaders, by the great mass of the peasants themselves it was doubtless honestly believed that Luther was with them, and that they could count on his sympathy and support.

But they utterly mistook their man. For a while he

paid no attention to the more or less spasmodic outbreaks in different parts of the country; but as they began to grow serious, he came out in April, 1525, with a brief tract entitled, "An Exhortation to Peace in Response to the Twelve Articles of the Swabian Peasants." Had he been a demagogue, he would have catered to popular passion and spurred the excited peasants on to war. Had he been a politician, he would have kept still and refrained from taking sides until he saw what the outcome was to be. But he was neither the one nor the other, and he spoke his mind in frankest fashion, sparing neither prince nor peasant. Both sides, he declared, were alike in the wrong, and with his usual vigor and fearlessness he called them both sharply to account, the former for their tyranny and oppression, the latter for their threats of violence. He informed the princes they had God against them, not merely the peasants, and if they did not cease exploiting their subjects, they would suffer the divine vengeance. On the other hand, he exhorted the peasants to present their grievances in an orderly way, without uproar or show of force. Their complaints might be well founded, but violence was not thereby justified. Only the constituted authorities had the right to use the sword, and he who attacked them on any ground whatever was worse than those whom he attacked. The doctrine of the divine right of civil rulers, already stated more than once by Luther, here again found emphatic expression.

It was still worse of the peasants, it seemed to him, to seek justification for their conduct in the gospel of Christ. If they wished to fight for their rights like ordinary men, well and good, but he would not stand by in silence while they used Christ's name in support of their course and brought scandal upon the gospel.

Christianity comports only with passive resistance. If
they really wished to follow Christ, they would drop
the sword and resort to prayer. The gospel has to do
with spiritual, not temporal, affairs. Even to condemn
slavery on Christian grounds is to turn spiritual freedom into physical, and reduce the gospel to a fleshly
thing. Earthly society cannot exist without inequalities; the true Christian finds his Christian liberty and
his opportunity for Christian service in the midst of
them and in spite of them. To this familiar• Pauline
point of view, discouraging every sort of social revolution, unexpected as it might seem in the author of the
radical Address to the German Nobility published five
eventful years earlier, Luther thenceforth always remained true.

But he did not stop with this summary treatment of
the matter, dismissing the whole thing with a mere
exhortation to Christian resignation. Recognizing the
justice of many of the peasants' complaints, he went
on to propose the arbitration of their grievances. The
suggestion was eminently wise, but it showed how little
sympathy he had with social change or reconstruction.
At best, arbitration could do no more than promote
justice in the working of the existing system. It could
not effect its overthrow. Had Luther's advice been
followed, much bloodshed would have been avoided
and the more moderate demands of the peasants might
have had some chance of satisfaction. But it was
wholly disregarded. Whatever was true of the princes,
and some of them actually did show themselves ready
enough to redress the worst grievances, the peasants
were by this time too much inflamed and their leaders
far too radical to listen to such counsel. The depreda-
tions committed by them have without doubt been
grossly exaggerated; but they were bad enough as it

was, and consternation and alarm were spreading rapidly among the middle and upper classes.

In the course of an extended tour through Thuringia, when the excitement was at its height, Luther saw many evidences of the riotous activities of the insurrectionists, and outraged by what he witnessed, he came out early in May with another and still more powerful pamphlet "Against the Murderous and Thieving Mobs of Peasants." In some quarters rulers were in doubt as to their duty. Perplexed by their subjects' appeal to the gospel and to the word of God they were at a loss how to meet the situation. But in Luther's mind there was no question. Consistently with the principle frequently laid down and reiterated in the previous tract, he denounced the mutinous peasants in unsparing terms for their resort to arms. More than three years before, in his protest against uproar and violence, he had said he would support those attacked, however bad they might be, rather than the aggressors, however good their cause. Now he suited his action to his words, and turned upon the peasants with a fury all his own.

The pamphlet opened with the strong words:

In my previous book I did not judge the peasants, for they offered to listen to instruction and yield to the right. But before I could do anything, forgetting their offer, they rushed forward and plunged into the affair with clenched fists. They rob and rage and act like mad dogs. It is easy enough to see now what they had in their false minds. The proposals they made in the twelve articles on the basis of the gospel were evidently nothing but lies.

And a little later:

Our peasants want to share the goods of others and keep their own. Fine Christians they are! I doubt

whether there are any devils left in hell, for they all
seem to have entered into the peasants, and passion has
gone beyond all bounds.

He called upon the rulers, to whom God had intrusted the sword for the punishment of the wicked, to
put down the warring rebels with a stern hand. They
were public enemies, and, like mad dogs, were to be
killed without mercy. He even went so far in the
vehemence of his wrath as to declare that if any ruler,
actuated with the desire of doing God's will in the
matter, died in the attempt to suppress the uprising,
he was a true martyr and entitled to eternal bliss, while
the warring peasant was doomed to hell. To be sure,
not all were to be treated with equal severity. Mercy
was to be shown to those deluded and misled by others,
and if they surrendered, they were to be pardoned and
spared. But the ringleaders and those responsible for
riot and uproar were to be visited with speedy vengeance, and at any cost the rebellion was to be summarily crushed.

The tract seemed over-harsh and cruel even to
many of his friends, and a few weeks later he defended his attitude in an open letter to the Chancellor
of Mansfeld, who had addressed him upon the subject.
The letter is much longer than the tract itself, and dis-
cusses the whole matter in detail, but there is no change
of position at any point, and the language is, if anything, even more severe. "People say," he remarked,
"there you see Luther's spirit. He teaches bloodshed
without mercy. The devil must speak through him.
Well and good. If I were not accustomed to be
judged and condemned, I might be troubled by such
words." And again: "If any one says I am unkind
and unmerciful, I answer, mercy has nothing to do

with the matter. We speak now concerning the word
of God. He will have honor shown the king and
will have rebels destroyed, and yet He is certainly as
merciful as we are." "It is better to cut off a member
without any mercy than to let the whole body perish."

His indignation at the peasants led him to speak of
them in very contemptuous terms, as, for instance:
"What is more ill-mannered than a foolish peasant or
a common man when he has enough and is full and
gets power in his hands?" "The severity and rigor of
the sword are as necessary for the people as eating and
drinking, yes, as life itself." "The ass needs to be
beaten, and the populace needs to be controlled with a
strong hand. God knew this well, and therefore He
gave the rulers not a fox's tail, but a sword."

Luther's treatment of the peasants has brought upon
him severer criticism than any other act of his life,
but the criticism is in part at least misplaced. It must
be recognized, to be sure, and we may reproach him for
it, if we please, that he had very little interest in social
reform. He was so absorbed in religion that he failed
adequately to realize the social and economic evils of
the day, and his calling and associations had been such
as to give him sympathy with the middle rather than
with the lower classes of society, with the bourgeoisie
rather than with the proletariate and peasantry. Had
he appreciated the evil conditions under which the
latter lived, and set himself earnestly at work to improve them, he might have accomplished much. But
it may fairly be doubted whether the era of social
amelioration in which modern reformers are profoundly and justly interested would thereby have been
hastened. Freedom from the traditional religious and
ecclesiastical bondage was a necessary condition of liberty in other spheres. Had it been subordinated to

17

alien ends, or made only one feature of a larger program, it would perhaps have remained unrealized. Not
the peasants alone, but all classes of the population,
must become convinced that religion was possible apart
from Rome before the old absolutism could be permanently broken, and anything less than exclusive
attention to the inculcation of that lesson might well
have resulted in failure.

But this is neither here nor there. The fact remains,
lament it as many may, that Luther was a religious, not
a social, reformer. Despite his temporary venture into
another field in the summer of 1520, he now recognized, as he had for some years, that he was called to
work in the religious field alone. Whether rightly or
wrongly, he had become firmly convinced the Christian
spirit could be trusted to work out all needed social
changes. In the meantime he was interested only to
insure free course for that spirit. To this end he subordinated everything else, and his treatment of the
peasants, when riot and bloodshed had taken the
place of peaceful measures, far from being unworthy
of him and revealing inconsistency and selfish policy
on his part, exhibited in the strongest light his native
independence and strength of character. Order must
be restored, he felt, at any hazard. Not religion alone
was imperiled, but the necessary sanctions of all human
life were threatened with destruction, and every sane
and right-thinking man must hurry to the rescue.

Had he sympathized adequately with the wrongs of
the peasants, it may be thought he could have prevented affairs from reaching such a pass and could
have kept the movement from degenerating into
anarchy. However that may be, and his experience
with the fanatics at Orlamünde and elsewhere gives
little ground for the supposition, at any rate, the situa-

tion being what it was in his part of the world in May, 1525, he did the one thing needed, and he did it with his usual vigor and effectiveness. As always, he was unnecessarily forcible in his language. But to criticize his choice of words in such a crisis is ridiculous. His attitude in the existing situation was essentially sound and does credit both to his wisdom and his courage. At a time when weakness and hesitancy marked the conduct of most of those who should have acted promptly and firmly, unblinded by sentiment and unmoved by personal considerations, he came out boldly and decisively for the one course possible in the circumstances. Though he knew it would cost him his popularity and alienate great masses of those hitherto devoted to him, without hesitating for a moment he spoke the word needed to unite the forces of conservation and bring order out of chaos. He was right when he declared that firm and united action on the part of the authorities at the very beginning of the uprising would have spared much bloodshed. He was right, too, in doing what he could to secure that action at the earliest possible moment.

When the princes took the matter jointly in hand, the rebellion was quickly crushed. Here and there trouble continued for months, but the movement as a whole was suppressed before the end of the summer. It was put down in many places with a heavy hand, as Luther had advised, while the mercy he recommended was unfortunately not always shown to those who capitulated.

A lamentable tragedy it was. The destruction of property both at the hands of the marauding peasants and of the avenging soldiery was very great. Large districts of country were devastated, and thousands lost their lives. As is apt to happen when violence and uproar get control, the general movement toward the amelioration of the lower classes was temporarily retarded. It was not wholly checked, to be sure. In some places great and permanent advances were made. And despite the wide-spread disrepute brought upon the cause by the war, and the strengthening of the ruling classes by their all too easy victory, the uprising was undoubtedly, after all, only a step in the progress of democracy.

It seems a lasting pity that by the failure of its leaders to show sympathy with the peasants in their struggle the Reformation permanently alienated multitudes of them and became almost exclusively identified with the interests of the middle and upper strata of society. But they were not necessarily to blame. The class division was, perhaps, in the circumstances, unavoidable, and if so, the identification of the new religious movement with the peasantry and proletariate would certainly have meant its speedy extinction.

Upon Luther himself the effects were permanent. He was hardened and embittered. He had to endure the chagrin of seeing thousands of his supporters turn away from him, many driven into Catholicism by the apparent demonstration of the destructive effects of his work, many into Anabaptism by what seemed his recreancy to the common cause and his cruel desertion of his own disciples. He ceased to be the popular hero of Germany, and became to multitudes, especially in the south and west, an object of hatred and execration. He never regretted his action. He had done what the crisis demanded, and would have done the same again in like circumstances. But the tragedy sobered him and robbed him of some of his earlier buoyancy and hopefulness. His confidence in the people was permanently shattered, and thenceforth it always seemed

1 5 3 6

Martinus Luther

A LETTER FROM LUTHER TO THOMAS CROMWELL,
HENRY THE EIGHTH'S MINISTER

necessary to hold them firmly in check and control them with a strong hand. The culminating event in a succession of similar experiences covering more than three years, the war led him to realize the dangers of radicalism and to draw more narrowly the bounds within which the Reformation was thenceforth to move. We may be thankful he was able to disentangle his cause from the perilous alliance with radicalism and revolution and to carry it forward despite friends and foes; but the disentanglement cost both him and Protestantism dear, and we may well deplore the situation which made it necessary.

CHAPTER XVIII

THE BREAK WITH HUMANISM

ONE of the tragedies of Luther's career, in its effects scarcely less unfortunate than the peasants' war, was the alienation of the great mass of humanists, many of them at first his warmest admirers and supporters. The liberals of the day, they were opposed, as he too was, to scholasticism and ultramontanism. They were also interested to reform educational ideals and methods, and some of them religion and morals as well. Their cause and his thus seemed for some time identical, and he was generally regarded as a rising champion of the newer learning.

The acknowledged prince of living humanists was Desiderius Erasmus of Rotterdam. Born in 1467 and enjoying already before Luther came into public notice a world-wide reputation as scholar and writer, he exercised during the first quarter of the sixteenth century an influence in the commonwealth of European letters equaled by no other man. He was forced into the monastic life against his will when but a boy, and although later released by a papal dispensation, retained a lifelong aversion to monasticism and a lifelong contempt for the average monk. The superstitions and vices both of monks and priests he castigated in merciless fashion, above all in his famous satire "The Praise of Folly," gaining thereby with many the name of a mere scoffer at sacred things, with others the fame of a reformer.

Inconsistent as much of his mockery and persiflage seems with any serious purpose, he was really profoundly interested in religious reform. In his "Handbook of a Christian Soldier" he set forth in fascinating style the program of an ethical Christianity, simplified by the stripping off of unessential accessories of ritual and dogma, and consisting chiefly in imitating Jesus in unselfish labor for one's fellows. "Back to Christ" was his program, as of so many other reforming spirits of the age, and on its behalf he employed his great learning in editing the texts of the New Testament and the works of some of the early fathers, thus performing a lasting service to biblical and patristic scholarship.

Though ready enough to attack existing evils with caustic wit and biting sarcasm, and though deeply concerned in the purification of the Christian system, he was essentially a scholar and a man of letters, not a warrior. He not only shrank instinctively from violence and tumult, but earnestly deprecated them as tending always to do more harm than good. Evils he believed could be eradicated only by a slow and gradual process. Education, not revolution, was the one effective method of reform. He therefore remained to the end of his days within the Catholic fold, declining to be dragged into open conflict with the ecclesiastical authorities and refusing to countenance rebellion and schism.

When Luther's theses on indulgences came to his notice, he praised the acumen and boldness of the Wittenberg monk, and for some years followed his career with interest. He spoke favorably of him to the Elector Frederick as well as to many others, and did what he could to prevent his condemnation at the Diet of Worms, not so much, to be sure, on Luther's account as from general hostility to the use of force in dealing with matters of faith.

He was not blind to the fact that Luther's spirit and ideals were different from his own. At the very beginning he detected the note of passion in the Saxon reformer's writings and feared he would go too far. He was careful to express his sympathy very guardedly and to disavow all responsibility for the Wittenberger's acts, even declaring repeatedly that he had not read his writings and hence could form no judgment as to the right or wrong of his opinions. Luther's radical work on "The Babylonian Captivity of the Church" seemed a grave blunder to him, and he was particularly irritated to have it laid by many at his own door before its real authorship was generally known. He had carefully avoided attacking the doctrines of the Catholic system and thus incurring the charge of heresy, believing that if the ethical elements of Christianity were put in the forefront the existing dogmas would insensibly lose importance and cease to do harm. To pursue the opposite course he saw was to precipitate war and make quiet and peaceful amelioration impossible. Even now he refrained from openly opposing Luther, but in conversation and letters he let his growing disapproval of his course be clearly known, and after the papal bull appeared in 1520 he wrote an obsequious letter to the pope, disclaiming all sympathy with the condemned heretic.

Luther, too, felt at an early day the difference between Erasmus's spirit and his own. Although sharing the general admiration for the great humanist's learning and ability, he wrote his friend Lang in the spring of 1517:

I am reading our Erasmus and my liking for him is daily decreasing. I am pleased indeed to see how constantly and learnedly he censures monks as well as priests and exposes their inveterate and somnolent ignorance. But I fear he does not sufficiently advance the grace of Christ, concerning which he is much more ignorant than d'Étaples. Human things count more with him than divine.

In March, 1519, when the storm was gathering about his head and he was beginning to feel the need of allies in the war against the common foe, he wrote at Melanchthon's instigation his first letter to Erasmus, expressing his veneration in strong terms and saying nothing of his disagreements with him. Later, as the conflict waxed warm, and the necessity of taking sides grew more imperative, his impatience with the attitude of the great humanist increased, and he too let his dissatisfaction be widely known. Ultimately his hatred and contempt became so bitter that he could hardly speak of him with moderation. It was impossible for him to do justice to the older man. Convinced as he was of the necessity of strong measures, he was quite unable to appreciate Erasmus's attitude, and to the latter's great annoyance laid his conduct wholly to levity and skepticism, or to cowardice and self-interest. In 1533 he referred to him as a "foe of all religions and particularly of Christ; a perfect example and image of Epicurus and Lucian." In this condemnation he set the fashion for his followers, and Erasmus has ever since received scant credit for sincerity and seriousness of purpose. Of a different kind was Luther's somewhat amusing judgment expressed in the following epigram: "Philip has both matter and words, Erasmus words without matter, Luther matter without words, Carlstadt neither matter nor words." Realizing Erasmus's tremendous influence and recognizing his great services to the cause of letters, Luther wished no open controversy with him and exercised an unusual degree of self-restraint in the effort to avoid giving him open occasion of offense. Erasmus was equally averse to a conflict with the Wittenberg reformer. Unsympathetic as he was with Luther's aims and impatient with his methods, to attack him openly meant only to strengthen the hands of a party in the church to which he was no less bitterly opposed. His was the trying situation of every moderate man when the battle is on between two enemies fighting for extreme positions, both alike alien to him.

Had he been a less important personage, he might have remained silent, but all Europe was eager to know where he stood, and at length, forced to it by importunate friends and by the conviction that he must publicly take sides or be included in a common condemnation, he came out in the autumn of 1524, despite a letter of protest from Luther himself, with a work on "The Freedom of the Will" in which the reformer's doctrine of human bondage was subjected to sharp though formally courteous criticism.

In attacking this particular position, Erasmus singled out the one point where Luther differed most widely at the same time with Romanists and humanists. In most of his departures from the traditional faith more or less secret if not avowed sympathy must be felt with him by the modern spirits of the day, but in denying the freedom of the human will and in insisting upon absolute divine control he was not only rejecting the basis for the Catholic belief that the Christian must earn his salvation by meritorious works, but was also flying in the face of the modern tendency to emphasize the natural ability and independence of man. Here at least orthodox and liberals must agree to think him wrong.

Luther recognized Erasmus's book as the most telling of all the attacks made upon him, and long afterward declared it was the only one he had ever read through. He wrote some of his friends of his purpose to reply to it as soon as he had leisure, but his answer was deferred for more than a year, when he finally published a large book on "The Bondage of the Will," the most carefully written and in his own opinion the best of all his works. In replying to the great litterateur he felt the importance of adopting a tone unlike his usual one, and the whole discussion moves on a high plane. The style is careful and the personalities so frequently indulged in are almost wholly lacking. It is an example of dignified polemic such as we might wish had been commoner with him.

But in the subject-matter itself there was no compromise. Nothing could be more extreme than his statement of the theory of determinism. Regarding it as a fundamental doctrine, inextricably bound up with his gospel of salvation by faith alone, he defended it with all the earnestness and vigor he was capable of; while he took the pains to denounce in sweeping terms any dependence upon human reason as impious and heathen. To accept unquestioningly God's revelations of truth, however irrational they may appear, is as much a duty as to submit uncomplainingly to His absolute decrees, however harsh they seem.

Nowhere does the difference between Luther's religious principles and those of the typical humanist appear more clearly than in this book. What we know as the evangelical type of Christian experience, with its renunciation of all self-confidence, is as far as possible from the rationalistic, with its emphasis upon the moral and intellectual ability of man. Luther was a genuine evangelical. And if Erasmus was not a thoroughgoing rationalist, as his book on free will, with its recognition of the constant need of divine grace, abundantly shows, his spirit was akin to that of the rationalists of all ages. Religious and ethical as the great humanist really was, to Luther he appeared no better than a heathen; while to Erasmus Luther's Christianity seemed benighted to the last degree.

The controversy between the two great men was very unfortunate. It completed the break between humanism and the Reformation. Luther's violence had alienated some of his admirers, and his program of ecclesiastical revolution had driven others from his side. It now became apparent to everybody that his principles and ideals were wholly unlike those of the humanists, and it seemed necessary to choose between the two. Many remained faithful to the reformer, counting his cause the more important. But to not a few humanism was still dearer, and they turned their backs on him forever. He lost in 1525 the devotion and confidence of the peasants; the same fateful year confirmed the alienation of the leading intellectuals. Once more the new movement was narrowed and its appeal circumscribed.

In these years the complaint was very frequently heard that the Reformation had put a stop to all intellectual development and sadly retarded learning and culture. Instead of bringing greater freedom and enlightenment, it had promoted narrowness and bigotry, substituting religious controversy for the quiet pursuit of the humanities and for the peaceful growth of a higher civilization.

There was, no doubt, some truth in this complaint, as Luther himself realized. But though his controlling interest was religious, not intellectual, and the aims

ERASMUS

From a carbon print by Braun & Co. of the painting
by Holbein in the Louvre

of the Reformation were other than those of the humanists, he had as keen an appreciation as anybody of the importance of education and did all he could to prevent ignorance and barbarism among his followers. In the spring of 1523 he wrote the humanist Eoban Hess:

Do not be troubled by the notion that letters will be overthrown by our theology and we Germans become more barbarous than ever. Some people fear where there is no fear. Without the knowledge of letters pure theology, I am persuaded, will in the future be unable to flourish, as in the past it has most miserably fallen and lain in ruins whenever literature has declined. Never, I can see, has there been a signal revelation of the word of God unless, as by a John the Baptist, the way was prepared for it by a revival of languages and letters. No youthful crime would I decry more than the failure to study poetry and rhetoric. It is my earnest wish that there may be as many poets and rhetoricians as possible, for by these studies, I perceive, as by no other means men are made apt for undertaking and skilfully pursuing sacred employments.

In his "Address to the German Nobility" he emphasized the need of a reformation of schools and universities and called upon the civil rulers to take it in hand. In 1524 he published an open letter addressed to all the city councils of Germany, urging the immediate erection of public schools and public libraries, setting forth the tremendous importance of popular education, on secular, not merely religious grounds, and laying upon the municipal authorities the responsibility for its maintenance, hitherto largely borne by the church.

Even if we had no souls, and schools and languages were not needed for God's sake and the Bible's, there would still be ground enough for establishing the best possible schools both for boys and girls, for the world needs fine and capable men and women to conduct its affairs, that the men may rule land and people wisely and the women keep house and train their children and servants as they should. Such men are made of boys and such women of girls, and hence it is necessary to educate the boys and girls properly. As I have already said, the common man does nothing to help. He cannot and will not and does not know how. Princes and lords should do it, but they have to go sleigh-riding, drink, and play at masquerades, and are burdened with multiform and important duties of cellar, kitchen, and chamber. And even if some of them were well disposed, they would be afraid to take hold lest they be regarded as fools or heretics. And so, dear magistrates, the thing remains wholly in your hands.

Public schools, he insisted, should be established for instruction especially in the ancient languages—Latin, Greek, and Hebrew—and in history, mathematics, and music.

So far as I am concerned, if I had children, and could manage it, I would make them learn not only languages and history, but music and the whole of mathematics as well. What is it all but mere child's play? And yet the Greeks trained their children in it and thereby raised a wonderfully capable people, skilful in all sorts of things. How sorry I am that I did not read more poetry and history and that they were not taught me! Instead of them, I had to spend my time on devil's filth, the philosophers and sophists, with great labor and damage, so that I had enough to get rid of.

In good humanistic fashion he advised that the texts used in the schools should not be limited to Christian authors. He would have heathen writers studied as well for training in language and literature. For the physical sciences he made no place in school or university curriculum, but in this he was not singular. They had not yet dawned upon the horizon of the advocates either of the older or the newer learning. Nor was he alive to the significance of the awakening scientific interest of the day. The following passage from the "Table Talk," referring to his contemporary Copernicus, who had a disciple in the Wittenberg faculty in the person of the mathematician Rheticus, illustrates Luther's general attitude, which was shared, it may be remarked, by most men of the century, including many of its greatest thinkers:

A new astrologer was mentioned who wished to prove that the earth moves and revolves instead of the heavens, the firmament, the sun and the moon; just as when one sitting in a wagon or ship imagines he is still and the earth and the trees are marching by. So it is nowadays. Who would be wise must not allow himself to be pleased by anything which others do; he must do something original and claim his way of doing it is best of all. The fool wishes to revolutionize the whole science of astronomy. But, as the Holy Scriptures show, Joshua commanded the sun to stand still, not the earth.

In 1530, in a very important pamphlet, entitled "That Children Should be Kept in School," he re-emphasized the necessity of an elementary education for everybody, girls as well as boys, and advocated compulsory school attendance. In this work he also pleaded with people of wealth to found scholarships for the support of indigent students of exceptional promise who were fitted for a more advanced training.

In much of this he was laying foundations upon which our modern educational systems are built in no small part. In spite of his break with humanism and his primary interest in religious reform, he rendered incalculable services to the cause of popular and secular education. The University of Wittenberg remained for many decades a noble monument to his influence as well as to Melanchthon's. It was the first European institution to teach the three ancient languages, Hebrew, Greek, and Latin, and already before his death it was the greatest university of Germany. The little Saxon town, long distinguished as the Athens of the empire, was resorted to by aspiring scholars from all parts of the world. Late in the century the fugitive philosopher Giordano Bruno found there a hospitable welcome, and spent two of the happiest and most active years of his life within its walls.

CHAPTER XIX

NOT far from the banks of the Mulde, just above the town of Grimma, stand the ruins of the wealthy Cistercian convent of Nimbschen. In 1523 one of its inmates was Katharine von Bora, daughter of a nobleman, Hans von Bora, whose modest estates lay only a few miles to the west. She was born on January 29, 1499, probably in the little village of Lippendorf, where her father had a residence. Her mother died and her father married again when Katharine was but a small child, and after spending some time away at school, she was set apart for the religious life, and put into the convent at Nimbschen when only nine or ten years old.

Like many another, this particular convent drew its inmates chiefly from the daughters of the local nobility. At the time of Katharine's entrance, one of her relatives was abbess, and her father's sister was among the nuns. The residents numbered more than forty, and included many young girls like herself in training for the religious life. Though not of her own choosing, she grew into the life naturally, as her companions did, and was quite ready to take the veil when she reached the age of sixteen.

The discipline of the convent was not over-strict, and Katharine and her sister nuns were apparently happy and contented until the influence of Luther's movement began to be felt. The convent, with the neighboring town of Grimma, lay within the borders of electoral Saxony, in a region permeated with the new ideas. As early as 1522, the prior of the Augustinian monastery at Grimma, a relative of two of the Nimbschen nuns, renounced monasticism with a number of his monks. It was perhaps the contagion of their example that led some of the inmates of the near-by convent to wish for freedom, and when their relatives refused to do anything for them, they appealed to Luther for help. Their consciences, enlightened by the gospel, did not permit them, so they claimed, to live longer as nuns, and hence he felt in duty bound to come to their assistance. A Torgau friend, Leonard Koppe, who had business dealings with the convent, was commissioned to arrange the escape. On Easter eve, 1523, a number of nuns, including Magdalen von Staupitz, a sister of Luther's old superior, and Katharine von Bora, left the place secretly, and made their way hurriedly to Wittenberg, where they arrived on Tuesday of Easter week.

A month later a Wittenberg student wrote his old teacher, Beatus Rhenanus: "I have no other news to write except that a few days ago a wagon landed here full and loaded down with vestal virgins, as they call them, who desire as much to marry as to live. May God provide them husbands, that they may not in course of time fall into worse evils!"

As Luther had helped the nuns to escape, he felt responsible for their welfare, and put them up temporarily in the Wittenberg cloister, already emptied of most of its monks. Immediately after their arrival, he wrote Spalatin of his plans for them, expressing the hope that he could find homes for some of them and husbands for others. At the same time he asked

for money to support them until they were properly
disposed of, for he was too poor to help them himself.
Luther's colleague Amsdorf also wrote Spalatin:

Not nine, but twelve nuns escaped. Nine of them have
come to us. They are beautiful and ladylike, and all are
of noble birth and under fifty years of age. The oldest
of them, the sister of my gracious lord and uncle, Dr.
Staupitz, I have selected, my dear brother, as your wife,
that you may boast of your brother-in-law, as I boast
of my uncle. But if you wish a younger one, you may
have your choice among the most beautiful of them. If
you desire to give something to the poor, give it to them,
for they are destitute, and deserted by their friends. I
pity the creatures. They have neither shoes nor clothes.
My dearest brother, I beg, if you can get something for
them from the court, you will supply them with food
and clothing. You must make haste, for they are in
great poverty and anxiety, but very patient. I wonder
indeed how they can be so brave and merry when in such
distress and want.

Within a short time six of the nuns were taken in
charge by relatives or friends, while three of them
remained in Wittenberg, two sisters finding a home
with the Cranachs, and Katharine von Bora with the
family of a prominent lawyer, Philip Reichenbach.

Katharine was a girl of considerable spirit, and
apparently held her head high. When she reached
Wittenberg a former student, Jerome Baumgärtner,
son of a patrician family of Nuremberg, was visiting
Melanchthon. He and Katharine speedily fell in love,
and it was hoped a match could be arranged between
them; but he returned home in June, and perhaps because of the objections of his family to his marriage
with an escaped nun, the affair was broken off. Nearly
a year and a half later Luther still hoped they might

yet marry and wrote Baumgärtner: "If you wish to keep your Käthe von Bora, make haste before she is given to another who is at hand. She has not yet conquered her love for you, and I should certainly rejoice to see you joined to each other." Whether Baumgärtner replied to this letter, we do not know. At any rate, nothing came of it, though Luther, and Katharine, too, for that matter, remained his friends as long as they lived.

The new suitor referred to by Luther was the theologian Casper Glatz, rector of Wittenberg University. Not finding him to her liking, Katharine refused him, and in March, 1525, when the wealthy bachelor Amsdorf, then pastor of the city church in Magdeburg, was visiting Luther, she begged him to urge the latter not to force her into a marriage which was distasteful to her. At the same time she naïvely assured him that while she was unwilling to marry Glatz, she would take either Amsdorf himself or Luther, if she were asked. Amsdorf, feeling no inclination to marry either then or later, passed the information on to Luther, who began to think of Katharine, apparently for the first time, as a possible wife for himself.

He had not been attracted by her at first. She seemed over-proud. And if he had been in a mood to marry at the time, he would have preferred her friend Ave von Schönfeld, as he remarked years afterward. But Katharine's suggestion seemingly had its effect. He began to regard her in a new light, and within a few weeks had made up his mind to marry her himself. She was not beautiful, as her existing portraits abundantly show, but Erasmus once spoke of her, probably on the authority of Wittenberg friends, as wonderfully charming, and she was at any rate a girl of strong character and unusual gifts. She was highly thought

LUTHER'S WIFE, KATHARINE VON BORA,
IN MIDDLE LIFE

From a medallion made in 1540 and now
in the church at Kieritzsch

of in Wittenberg, where she was known among her young companions by the name of Catharine of Siena, and the best people in town were her warm friends. When the exiled King Christian of Denmark was visiting Lucas Cranach in the autumn of 1523, he presented her with a gold ring which she prized as long as she lived. She was certainly no ordinary girl, and her remark to Amsdorf shows her own appreciation of the fact.

Luther himself had for a long time been gradually growing accustomed to the thought of marrying. One after another of his followers had renounced his priestly or monastic vows and taken a wife, and he had been repeatedly urged to do the like. Others were putting his principles into practice, why should he hold back? It was hoped he would marry a wealthy woman of some prominent family, and more than one eligible young lady was warmly recommended to him by his friends. In the summer of 1521 he wrote Spalatin from the Wartburg: "Good God! will our Wittenbergers give wives even to the monks? But they shall not force a wife on me!" In his Church Postils of 1522, after attacking the monastic vow, he remarked: "I hope I have come so far that by God's grace I can remain as I am. At the same time, I am not yet over the mountain, and do not venture to boast of my continence." We hear no further references to the matter until November, 1524, when he wrote Spalatin:

I thank Argula for what she writes me concerning my marrying. I do not wonder at such gossip, for all sorts of reports are circulated about me. Thank her in my name, and tell her I am in God's hands, a creature whose heart he is able to change and change again, to kill and make alive every hour and moment. But so long as I am in my present mood I shall not marry. Not that l do not feel my sex, for my heart is neither wood nor stone; but my inclination is against marriage, for I am in daily expectation of death and of punishment suited to a heretic. I will not on this account set bounds to God's· work in me, nor will I rely upon my own heart. But I hope he will not let me live long.

Although in 1521 he had admonished Spalatin not to marry, and so incur tribulation of the flesh, in April, 1525, he wrote him:

Why do you not proceed to get married? I am urging others with so many arguments that I am myself almost persuaded; for our enemies do not cease to condemn this way of living, and our wiseacres daily laugh at it.

A few days later he wrote again, in a jocular vein:

So far as my marriage is concerned, about which you write, do not be surprised at my not marrying, celebrated lover as I am. Rather wonder that I who write so much about marriage, and have so much to do with women, am not already a woman myself, to say nothing of taking one for a wife. But if you desire me for an example, behold I have given you a most signal one. For I have had three wives at once, and loved them so ardently that I have lost two of them, who have taken other husbands. The third I scarcely hold on my left arm, and am perhaps about to lose her, too. Tardy lover as you are, you dare not be the husband even of one wife. But take care lest it happen that I, with a mind strongly set against marriage, yet anticipate your most imminent espousals, for God is accustomed to do what one least hopes. Joking aside, I say this that I may induce you to do what you have in mind.

On the fourth of May, in a letter to the Mansfeld councilor John Rühel, concerning the riotous conduct of the peasants, he remarked, in passing:

If I can manage it, to spite the devil, I will yet marry my Käthe before I die, if I hear that the peasants go on as they are doing. I hope they will not take from me my courage and my joy.

On the second of June he wrote an open letter to the Archbishop of Mayence, urging him to marry and turn his dominions into a secular principality. The next day he sent a copy of the letter to Rühel with a note in which he said:

If his Electoral Grace should again ask, as I have heard he has, why I also do not take a wife, when I am inciting every one else to do it, tell him I am still afraid I am not clever enough. But if my marriage would be an inducement to his Grace, I should be ready to set him the example, for I have already had it in mind, before departing this life, to enter the married state, which I regard as commanded by God.

Ten days later, on Tuesday, June 13, he and Katharine were married in the cloister, in the presence only of Jonas, dean of the castle church; Bugenhagen, the city pastor; Apel, a colleague of the law faculty; and the town councilor Lucas Cranach and his wife. In a letter written the next day to Spalatin, who was at the time in Torgau, Jonas announced the event, speaking of the mingled emotions with which he had witnessed it, and added: "To-day he gave a small breakfast. A fitting service I suppose will be held in due time, when you also will be present." Two days later Bugenhagen wrote Spalatin: "Malicious talk has brought it to pass that Dr. Martin has unexpectedly become a husband. After a few days we have thought these sacred nuptials should be celebrated before all the world by a public ceremony, to which you also without doubt will be invited."

Accordingly, a fortnight later, on the twenty-seventh of the month, a service was held in the city church, and a wedding-feast was given in the cloister, Luther's father and mother, with a large circle of friends, being present. A few extracts from the invitations sent out for this occasion are worth quoting for the light they throw upon the mood he was in and the motives prompting him to marry.

To Rühel and two other Mansfeld councilors he wrote:

What an outcry, dear sirs, I have caused with my book against the peasants! All is forgotten that God has done for the world through me. Lords, priests, peasants, and everybody else are now against me, and threaten me with death. Well and good, since they are so mad and foolish, I have determined before my death to be found in the state ordained of God, and so far as I can to rid myself entirely of my former popish life, and make them still madder and more foolish, all for a parting gift. For I have a presentiment that God will one day give me His grace. So, at my dear father's desire, I have now married, and have done it in haste that I might not be hindered by these talkers. A week from Tuesday I purpose giving a small party, which I want you as good friends to know about, and I beg you will add your blessing. Because the country is in such a turmoil, I do not venture to urge you to be present. But if you can and will kindly come of your own accord with my dear father and mother, you may imagine it will give me special pleasure. I shall also be delighted in my poverty to see any good friends you may bring with you, only asking you to let me know by this messenger.

To Spalatin:

I have stopped the mouths of those who slandered me and Katharine Bora. If I can manage to give a banquet as a witness to this marriage of mine, you must not only be present, but also lend your aid, if there should be need of provisions. Meanwhile, give us your benediction and your good wishes. I have brought myself into such contempt by my marriage that I hope the angels are laughing and all the demons weeping.

To Amsdorf:

The report is true that I married Katharine suddenly that I might not be compelled to hear the noisy talk customary on such an occasion. I hope I shall still live for a little while, and this last service I did not wish to refuse my father, who asked it of me. At the same time I wished to confirm what I had taught by my deed, for I find so many pusillanimous despite the light of the gospel. Thus God has willed and done. For I am not passionately in love, but I esteem my wife. And hence to celebrate my marriage I shall give a banquet next Tuesday, when my parents will be present. I want especially to have you here; wherefore I now invite you, and beg you will not stay away if you can possibly help it.

To Marshal von Dolzigk:

Doubtless you have heard the news of my venture upon the sea of matrimony. Although it seems strange enough to me, and I can hardly believe it myself, the witnesses are so positive that I am obliged in honor to credit them. I have therefore undertaken, with my father and mother and other good friends, to set a stamp upon the affair and make it certain by a banquet to be given next Tuesday. If convenient, I beg you will kindly support me with venison, and will be present yourself and help seal the affair with joy, and do whatever else the circumstances demand.

To Leonard Koppe:

Suddenly and unexpectedly God has taken me captive in the bonds of holy matrimony, so that I must confirm it with a banquet on Tuesday. That my father and

mother and all my good friends may be the merrier, my
Lord Katharine and I beg you will send us as soon as
possible, at my expense, a keg of the best Torgau beer
you can find. I will pay all the costs. I would have sent
a wagon, but I did not know whether I could find what
I wanted. For it must be seasoned and cool, that it may
taste well. If it is not good, I have determined to punish
you by making you drink it all yourself. In addition,
I hope you and your Audi will not stay away, but will
appear in good spirits. Bring with you Master Gabriel
and his wife, if you can do it without expense to him,
for I well know he is almost as poor as I am.

Luther's marriage raised a great hue and cry. The
union of a renegade monk with an escaped nun, violating as it did their own personal vows, and ecclesiastical
and civil law as well, seemed to many to throw a sinister light upon the whole reform movement. Now,
they declared, the significance of the Reformation was revealed to all the world, and it was clear
what Luther had had in mind from the beginning.
Satirical attacks appeared in great numbers. Slanderous tales were spread about him and his bride. Even
many of his friends were thrown into consternation,
and feared he had dealt a death-blow to the cause.
The lawyer Jerome Schurf, when he heard the rumor
that Luther was contemplating marriage, remarked:
"If this monk takes a wife, the whole world and the
devil himself will laugh, and all the work he has accomplished will come to naught." Others, though wishing to see him married, regretted he had chosen Käthe
rather than some woman of wealth and position. The
time, too, seemed to almost everybody particularly
inopportune. His prince and supporter, the Elector
Frederick, had died only a month before, and all
Saxony was still mourning him, as Luther was, too,

for that matter. Moreover, the peasants' war was not yet ended, and the whole country was in an uproar. In these circumstances many not unnaturally felt as though the great reformer's mind and heart should have been full of other things than marriage.

But Luther, as usual, was unmoved by the criticisms of his friends and the attacks of his foes, and never regretted what he had done. His reasons for the step were many. The varying accounts he gives of them are doubtless all true to the facts. His motives were complicated, as might be expected, and he could not himself have analyzed them fully. He had long believed and taught that marriage was higher than celibacy, and the conviction had been forcing itself upon him that he ought sometime to put his principle into practice, and thus bear public testimony to his own attitude and give his followers the benefit of his example. He had at first no personal inclination to the step. He had had very little to do with women, and was so absorbed in his great work that marriage was the last thing he cared for. But the unhappy experiences of the spring of 1525 led him to believe the end of the world, or, at any rate, his own death, imminent, and he began to think it time to marry, if he was ever to do so. His naturally belligerent temper, excited to an unusual pitch at this time, also urged him on. The more his enemies raged against him, the more he loved to provoke them. Many men in his position—Melanchthon, for instance—would have avoided all unnecessary grounds of offense; but Luther was of a different type. Though he would do nothing his conscience disapproved, he was glad enough when his deeds offended those opposed to him. As he often said, he never felt so confident he was right as when they denounced his conduct.

It is not surprising, the situation being what it was, that Katharine's suggestion to Amsdorf should find him in a receptive mood. To marry a nun would only make his testimony the stronger and the hostility of his opponents the more bitter. As if all this were not enough, he visited his parents in Mansfeld late in April, and was impressed with his father's eager desire that his oldest son, now finally freed from his monastic bonds, should marry, as he had wished him to do long years before. To please him thus became an added motive for the step. And it may be he felt he owed something to Katharine herself, whom he had assisted to escape from the convent, and for whom he had failed as yet to find a husband. Perhaps he was thinking of this when he once remarked that he married his Käthe out of pity.

When he came to an understanding with Käthe we do not know. He probably met with no obstacles from her after he had decided to press his suit, and his courtship, it may fairly be presumed, was brief and matter of fact enough. Neither he nor Käthe was violently in love. Her willingness to accept either him or Amsdorf shows that her own heart was not deeply engaged, and Luther himself no doubt correctly described his feelings toward her in the letter to Amsdorf already quoted. But a protracted engagement was the last thing he desired. Constantly under the eyes of the whole world as he was, with enemies and friends observing his every movement, he naturally wished the matter concluded as speedily as possible. Years later he remarked:

It is very dangerous to put off your wedding, for Satan gladly interferes and makes great trouble through evil talkers, slanderers, and friends of both parties. If I had not married quickly and secretly, and taken few into my

From the painting by Lucas Cranach

LUTHER'S WIFE, KATHARINE VON BORA, IN 1526

confidence, every one would have done what he could to hinder me; for all my best friends cried, "Not this one, but another."

Melanchthon, who was kept in the dark until the wedding was over, was almost beside himself with annoyance. On the sixteenth of June he wrote the following characteristic letter to an intimate friend:

On the thirteenth of June, without informing any of his friends of his intention, Luther unexpectedly married Von Bora. The customary ceremony took place in the evening, Bugenhagen and Lucas the painter and Apel alone being invited to the feast. You will perhaps wonder that in this unhappy time, while good and right-minded men are everywhere sore distressed, he does not sorrow with them, but rather, as it seems, lives voluptuously and tarnishes his reputation, when Germany specially needs his wisdom and strength. I suppose it has happened in this wise. The man is very accommodating, and the nuns fell upon him and plotted against him with all their wiles. Perhaps his much association with them, though he is honorable and high-minded, softened or even inflamed him. In this way he seems to have fallen into this untimely alteration of his mode of living. But the rumor that he misbehaved with her beforehand is an evident lie. Now the deed is done, you ought not to take it ill or find fault with it. I suppose marriage is a natural necessity; and the married life, though humble, is at the same time holy and more pleasing to God than celibacy. Because I see that Luther himself is in somewhat low spirits and disturbed over the change, I try as earnestly and wisely as possible to encourage him, for he has as yet done nothing deserving to be called unworthy or inexcusable. I still have evidences of his piety, and so cannot condemn him. Besides, I should prefer to have him humble rather than exalted and lifted up. The latter is dangerous not only for the clergy, but for all other men as well. For success becomes the occasion of evil thoughts, not only, as the rhetorician says, to the foolish, but also to the wise. Then, too, I hope his marriage will make him more sober, and lead him to give up the buffoonery we have often blamed him for; since, according to the proverb, another life will bring another mode of living. I write thus at length that you may not be troubled overmuch by the incredible affair. For I know you care for Luther's reputation and regret to see it lowered. I exhort you to take the matter calmly, for in the Holy Scriptures marriage is said to be honorable, and to marry is probably a necessity. God has related for us many errors of the old saints, wishing us to prove His word and not to depend on man's reputation or person, but only on His word. He is most godless who on account of the mistake of the teacher despises the teaching.

Luther evidently understood his friend, and had good reason for not taking him into his confidence. But despite Melanchthon's impatience at the event, he was soon reconciled to the new order of things, and became a stanch friend and warm admirer of Frau Käthe.

Luther himself, though not at first deeply in love, grew very fond of his wife, and cherished her warmly to the end of his life. We have only a few of the many letters he wrote her. They contain no particular endearments beyond the greeting "Meine herzliebe Käthe" in one case, and the signature "Dein Liebchen" in others. But they show clearly the good terms on which husband and wife lived and the sympathy and understanding they could count upon from each other. In the summer of 1526 he wrote a friend: "Käthe sends greetings, and thanks you for thinking her worthy of such a kind letter. She is well, by the grace of God, and is in all things more compliant, obedient,

and obliging than I had dared to hope,—thanks be to
God!—so that I would not exchange my poverty for
the wealth of Crœsus." Some years later, referring
to his marriage, he remarked: "It has turned out well,
God be thanked! For I have a pious and true wife,
on whom her husband's heart can rely." To Käthe
herself he once said: "Käthe, you have a pious husband who loves you. You are an empress." And on
other occasions he declared he held her dearer than
the kingdom of France and the dominions of Venice,
and even loved her better than his own life. To be
sure, he did not think her perfect. He recognized her
faults as well as his own. He was hot-tempered, and
she had a quick tongue, and often hard words passed
between them. "If I were to marry again," he once
exclaimed, "I would hew me an obedient wife out of
stone, for I doubt whether any wives are obedient."
But despite temporary ebullitions, he and Käthe lived
for the most part on good terms, and he found her
congenial notwithstanding the great difference in their
temperaments and interests.

The following words throw a flood of light upon
the experiences of his married life:

Ah, dear Lord, marriage is not an affair of nature, but
a gift of God. It is the sweetest and dearest, yes, purest
life. It is far better than celibacy when it turns out
well; but when it turns out ill, it is hell. For though all
women as a rule know the art of taking a man captive
with tears, lies, and persuasions, and are able to distort
everything and employ fair words, nevertheless, when
truth and faith, children and fruits of love are there,
and marriage is regarded as holy and divine, then it is
indeed a blessed state. How eagerly I longed for my
dear ones as I lay deadly ill at Schmalkalden! I thought
I should never again see wife and children here. How

I mourned over the separation! I am convinced that the natural longing and love a husband has for his wife and parents for their children are greatest of all in those who are dying. Now that I am by God's grace well again, I cherish my wife and children so much the more. No one is so spiritual as not to feel such inborn love and longing. For the union and communion of man and wife are a great thing.

Luther's ideas about women were not modern. She was the weaker vessel, he maintained, and was made to be subject to the man. Her true life was in the home. The faithful, obedient, and efficient wife fulfilled the highest ideal of womanhood. The eloquent description of a virtuous woman in the thirty-first chapter of Proverbs he regarded as valid for his own time and all times. Of the so-called emancipation of the sex he knew nothing, and would have been entirely out of sympathy with it, had he heard of it. But he performed an incalculable service in dignifying married life and ascribing to it a sacredness above the career of monk or nun. Instead of a temptation to a less perfect way of living, as woman was too commonly represented by the religious teachers of the Middle Ages, he saw in her one ordained of God to be the companion and helpmate of man, and in their union, not in their separation, he found the ideal life. Religion had been making too much of the abnormal. Luther's greatest service to the modern world lay in his recognition of the normal human relationships as the true sphere for the development of the highest religious, as of the highest moral, character.

CHAPTER XX

HOME LIFE

LUTHER'S marriage took place in the cloister where he had lived ever since he came to Wittenberg. Here he and Käthe made their home for the rest of their lives. It was a roomy building and had accommodated at one time as many as forty monks. While Luther was at the Wartburg, its inmates, under the influence of his teaching, began to renounce monasticism and to return to the world. He himself had no inclination to follow their example. Writing to Link in December, 1521, he said, "Do thou meanwhile continue with Jeremiah in the ministry of Babylon, for I also will remain in this habit and rite unless the world become another."

The exodus went on steadily until in 1523 only Luther himself and the prior Brisger remained in residence. Although criticized and laughed at both by enemies and friends for not putting his own principles into practice, and turning his back upon the monastic life, he continued for a long time to observe the convent rules and to keep up the required devotions. But gradually one after another of the traditional ceremonies and practices fell into abeyance, until finally the building ceased to be a monastery in aught but name. At the same time the traditional monastic hospitality was still maintained, and the place was overrun with escaped monks and others temporarily in need.

In 1523 Luther laid off the monastic dress when in

the convent, but continued to wear it in public, "to strengthen the weak and to spite the pope," as he remarked in a letter to a friend. Finally, in October, 1524, he discarded it altogether, and appeared thenceforth in the ordinary costume of a university professor.

In December of the same year, when he and Brisger proposed to vacate the monastery and let it be devoted to other purposes, the elector virtually made Luther a present of the building, with the court in front and the garden behind, and put a small house belonging to it at the disposal of Brisger. The gift to Luther was legally confirmed seven years later by Frederick's successor, the Elector John. The building in which Luther was married, and where he continued to live for the rest of his life, was thus no longer a cloister, but his own private dwelling.

While the monastery was still flourishing, he depended entirely upon it for his support, as all the other monks did. But with the exodus of most of its inmates, and with the waning respect for monasticism in Wittenberg and its neighborhood, the income of the monastery from begging and from the voluntary gifts of the faithful was greatly reduced, and it was found difficult even to collect the rents and other taxes legally due, as Luther frequently complained in letters to the elector and Spalatin. The situation was finally met by giving him a salary for his university work, and for the rest of his life this remained his only regular source of income. For his services as preacher in the city church he received nothing, and in accordance with a not uncommon custom of the day he refused to take money for his books, though more than one publisher made a fortune out of them. His salary at first amounted to a hundred gulden, intrinsically equal to fifty dollars of our money, but probably the equivalent in purchasing power of six or eight hundred dollars to-day. When he married it was doubled, and some years later another hundred was added, making, with the payments in kind regularly allowed him by the elector, an assured income of about four hundred gulden. This was the same amount received by Melanchthon, and was unusually large for a university professor of the day.

In addition, gifts of all sorts poured in not only from the elector and the town council of Wittenberg, but from admirers in all parts of the world. Occasionally he had to protest that he was given too much, as, for instance, in the following letter to the Elector John, written in 1529:

I have long delayed thanking your Electoral Grace for the clothes and the gown you sent me. I respectfully beg your Electoral Grace not to believe those who say I am in want. I have, unfortunately, especially from your Electoral Grace, more than I can conscientiously bear. It does not become me as a preacher to have a superfluity, nor do I desire it. I feel your Grace's all too mild and gracious favor so much that I am beginning to be afraid. For I should not like to be in this life among those to whom Christ says, "Woe unto you rich; you have your reward." Besides, to speak humanly, I do not want to be burdensome to your Electoral Grace. I know your Grace has to give to so many that nothing remains over; for too much destroys the sack. The brown cloth is too splendid, but, in order to show my gratitude to your Electoral Grace, I will wear the black coat in your honor, although it is too costly for me; and if it were not your Grace's gift, I should never wear such a garment. I beg your Electoral Grace will henceforth wait until I ask, that I may not be prevented by your Grace's anticipation of my wants from begging for others who are much more worthy of such favor.

As this letter suggests, he was continually asking gifts for others, but he did it rarely for himself, and as a rule only when venison or wine was needed for some social festivity. Not infrequently he sent to the town vaults for wine without asking anybody's permission, but the council apparently took it in good part and made no objection. They knew the city owed its growth and prosperity largely to him, and frequently showed their appreciation of the fact. He would not consent to be relieved from taxation, but scarcely a year passed that he was not voted substantial gifts of one kind and another.

Despite it all, the early years of his married life were full of money troubles. He was very free with what he had, giving away his last gulden without hesitation, and when there was no more money, tableware and household ornaments, presented to Käthe or himself by admiring friends, would often go to relieve the wants of the needy. He frequently complained humorously of his own soft-heartedness and gullibility, lamenting that anybody could take him in with a smooth story.

Käthe kept as firm a hand on him as she could, and many a gulden was saved which would otherwise have found its way into the pocket of some friend or stranger. On the occasion of Agricola's marriage, he wrote him he was sending as a wedding-present a vase received sometime before from another friend; but in a postscript he had to inform him that Käthe had hidden it away, so it could not be found.

Curiously enough, a wedding-gift of twenty-five gulden was sent him by Archbishop Albert of Mayence. Luther himself declined to receive it—it was his boast that he never took presents of money—but the more thrifty Käthe accepted it without his knowledge, and

PRESENT APPEARANCE OF THE MARTIN LUTHER HOUSE IN WITTENBERG, WHICH WAS A PART OF THE OLD AUGUSTINIAN MONASTERY

when he learned of it, he did not know whether to be more annoyed or amused.

Now and then he got into trouble through indorsing notes for his friends when he had no money of his own to lend. In order that he might not altogether impoverish himself, Lucas Cranach and other capitalists of the town finally refused to honor his signature, and this way of helping the needy was thus closed to him.

He was rather deeply in debt when he married, and it took some time for Käthe, by judicious management, to straighten out his tangled affairs. In 1527 his own imprudence, he wrote Brisger, made it necessary for him to plunge still deeper into debt and to pawn some silver goblets. A little later he could announce that all his debts were paid, but he not infrequently had to lament the burden of new ones. "I justly remain in the catalogue of the poor," he once remarked, "for I keep too large an establishment." Gradually, despite his free-handedness, a certain measure of worldly prosperity was attained through Käthe's energy and economy, and they were able to make considerable improvements in the Wittenberg house, and to buy an orchard, a hop-garden, and some other pieces of land in the neighborhood, where Käthe raised cattle and did farming on a small scale. Finally Luther purchased from her brother a farm at Zulsdorf, a part of the small family inheritance, not far from her birthplace. In the management of this she took particular delight. One of her husband's letters to her opens with the playful greeting, "To the rich wife at Zulsdorf, Frau Doctor Luther, in the body at home at Wittenberg, but in spirit busy at Zulsdorf."

Even then petty economies were still necessary, and ready money was often entirely lacking. As late as

1540 he had to go for weeks without his nightly glass of beer because there was none left in the house and no money to buy more with. In 1542, when he made his will, he carefully reckoned up his possessions, and wrote out detailed accounts covering a number of years. We still have some of the original pages, decorated with amusing rhymes, ruefully lamenting his extravagance and making sport of his lack of business capacity. At his death he left a respectable property, perhaps amounting, all told, to eight thousand gulden; but most of it was unproductive, and Käthe found considerable difficulty in making both ends meet. She once complained that he might have been a rich man had he wished; but wealth was the last thing he cared for, and with his disposition he could hardly have compassed it had he tried.

Käthe was a vigorous and efficient housewife. The monastery had been sadly neglected before she became its mistress. Luther had lived very carelessly, often leaving his bed unmade, as he once remarked, for a year at a time, and tumbling into it at night too tired from his strenuous labors to notice the difference. His marriage brought order into the place, and transformed the bare and cheerless monastery into a real home. In 1536, after a visit to Wittenberg, Wolfgang Capito of Strasburg wrote him: "My greetings to your wife, Lady Katharine, best of women! When I have returned home I will send her something to remember me by. I love her with all my heart. She was born to look after your health, that you may the longer serve the church which has come into existence through you."

Luther's own personal habits changed little. He remained negligent about his dress, as he had always been, and his study continued a wilderness of disorder.

Desks, tables, chairs, and every available spot were covered with books, letters, and manuscripts, and he often lost things altogether in the confusion of the place. Even before his marriage he kept a dog, which frequently played havoc with his papers. He was also careless about his food. Before Käthe came upon the scene he ate very irregularly, often forgetting his meals altogether. His bodily needs, indeed, meant little to him. As he once wrote Melanchthon, when he could not get meat and wine, he contented himself with bread and water. On the other hand, he was often as imprudent in his eating as in his fasting. Käthe set a bountiful table, and whatever the condition of his health, and despite her protests, he was apt to eat anything that seized his fancy, bad as it might be for him. In 1539 he remarked: "I don't bother about the doctors. They give me a year to live, and I will not make my life miserable, but will eat and drink, in God's name, whatever tastes good." His irregular habits and strenuous labors combined with the ascetic practices of his early years to undermine his health. He was a sufferer from severe kidney and liver trouble during most of his life, and had to endure a great deal from headaches, which often completely incapacitated him for work.

A masterful person Käthe was, with a mind and will of her own. The cloister she made her particular domain, and ruled it with a strong hand. Strength and energy, indeed, were her prominent characteristics. Among her neighbors she bore the reputation of being a capable but somewhat over-thrifty housewife, and while generally respected, she was not generally liked. To many she seemed proud and domineering. As the wife of the great reformer, it was not unnatural she should hold her head high and expect her will to count in the little university city. Luther once compared her to Moses and himself to Aaron, and he often spoke of her jestingly as "My Lord Käthe." In October, 1535, he wrote his friend Jonas: "My Lord Käthe greets you. She rides about, cultivates the fields, raises and buys cattle, brews beer, and the like. At the same time she has begun to read the Bible, and I have promised her fifty florins if she finishes before Easter. She is very earnest about it, and has already reached the fifth book of Moses." Her reason for taking up the reading of the Bible at this particular time, it may be remarked, was the recent appearance of Luther's German version in its first complete edition.

With all his playful raillery, her husband valued her highly for just those practical qualities he lacked himself, and he was very glad to turn the management of family affairs wholly over to her. Though we hear of her chiefly as a housewife, she was not simply that. While her tastes were not intellectual or literary, she had a fair education, and knew enough Latin to follow and bear her share in the table conversation, commonly carried on in a curious mixture of German and Latin intelligible only to one acquainted with both. A pious woman she was, too, and deeply interested in Luther's great reforming work. As his references to theological and ecclesiastical affairs in some of his letters to her show, he took her into his confidence and talked matters over freely with her. Evidently she understood and appreciated what was going on, and at times made her influence felt even in important affairs, as when she induced him, so he says, against his will, to engage in open controversy with the great Erasmus.

Their home was the center of a very active social life. Not only his colleagues and neighbors were frequently with them, but guests from abroad were numerous; for Wittenberg was more and more the Mecca of Christians from all parts of Europe, and Luther's hospitality to all comers was generous and abundant.

Among the regular members of his large household, besides a number of nephews and nieces and other poor relatives, were many university students. Following a custom common among the Wittenberg professors, Käthe began immediately after her marriage to take student boarders, and kept up the practice to the end of her life. It is to some of them we owe the interesting records of Luther's table-talk, through which we catch many fascinating glimpses of his home life. Beginning in a small way, early in the thirties, certain of them finally got into the habit of writing down, under his very eyes and while he was talking, the substance of his conversation. At times his dining-room must have presented the aspect of a class-room, with the auditors diligently transcribing the lecturer's words of wisdom. It might seem as if the effect would have been to take all spontaneity and naturalness out of his talk, but this was by no means the case. Even the most carefully edited collections are full of informal and unstudied expressions of opinion on every conceivable subject, grave and gay, serious and trivial, while some of the original records more recently recovered show that he talked as freely and unconsciously as if no faithful scribes were waiting upon his words. Often the talk, as we have it, sounds commonplace enough, but again it flashes with brilliancy and reveals rare wisdom and insight.

The records of course have to be used with caution, for we cannot always be sure he was rightly understood or correctly reported, but frequently we run upon characteristic sayings which could have come from no

one else, and which enrich and add to the vividness of
our portrait of the man.

His conversation was apt to be much freer than
would be at all admissible to-day. In that respect he
was a child of his age, for high and low alike were less
careful in speech then than now. To be sure, he was
often coarser than even the loose standards of the day
approved. His humor was broad rather than subtle
and delicate, and to men of the type of Erasmus and
Melanchthon it often seemed only buffoonery. To the
end of his life he retained many of the characteristics
of a peasant, and he wielded in talk, as in controversy,
an ax rather than a Damascus blade. But with all his
lack of refinement, he was essentially a wholesome and
clean-minded man. Despite the many unquotable
things he said and wrote to illustrate a point or enforce
an argument or give sting to his polemic, there is surprisingly little vulgarity or obscenity for its own sake
either in his table-talk or in his writings.

Pure he was in life, too. Attacks of course were
made upon his moral character by his enemies, and all
sorts of unsavory stories were told about him. But
for none of them can a shred of evidence be found,
though he lived for twenty-five years in a blaze of publicity, observed of all the world and spied upon by
countless critics. The most his bitter enemies, the radicals, who lived near by and knew him well, could urge
against him when they tried to blacken his character
was his liking for society, his fondness for playing the
lute, his luxurious living, and, strange to say, his fine
dressing, for on state occasions, it seems, he was fond
of wearing starched cuffs and a gold chain.

The radicals were the Puritans of the day, and their
standards were very rigorous. Luther himself was
certainly not a Puritan. He believed in innocent plea-

sure of all sorts, and had no desire to make of Wittenberg what Calvin later made of Geneva. He encouraged gymnastic sports because they strengthened the
body and decreased over-drinking and similar vices.
He played at bowls himself, and was something of an
expert at chess according to his friend Mathesius. In
1534, in accepting an invitation to visit Prince Joachim
of Anhalt with some other friends, he wrote: "Your
Grace must look out for Master Francis at chess. He
thinks he can play very well, but I will wager a beautiful rose he cannot play as well as he pretends. He
knows how to assign their places to the knights, to
seize the castles, and to hoodwink the peasants
(pawns), but the lady is his master in the game, perhaps elsewhere as well." He particularly liked to see
young people enjoy themselves, and heartily approved
of dancing and private theatricals for them. Music he
was very fond of and passed many a happy evening
singing and playing with his friends. He was also not
indifferent to pictures, and had a Madonna in his
chamber, to the great scandal of the Protestant rigor-
ists.

His chief relaxation he always found in social intercourse. Particularly when depressed, as he often was,
he sought comfort and relief in the society of his
friends, and was continually prescribing the same
remedy for like depression in others. He once remarked: "When Eve went walking by herself in Paradise the devil tempted and led her astray"; and on
another occasion he declared he would rather associate with his swineherd and the swine than stay
alone. Light conversation, jesting, and story-telling
he thought especially good for low spirits, and often
indulged in them, he said, just on that account. He
also advised hearty eating and drinking for many a

one, though not for everybody. To one of his young table companions, Jerome Weller, who was subject to frequent attacks of the blues, he wrote: "Whenever the devil vexes you with such thoughts immediately seek the society of men, or drink more freely, or joke, or talk nonsense, or do some other hilarious thing. Why do you think I drink so much, converse with such freedom, and eat so often, if not to make sport of the devil and vex him when he is trying to vex and make sport of me?"

When in the mood he could be a fascinating comrade, and many were the merry hours spent at table with colleagues and friends. Speaking once of his faith in the gospel and of his confidence in his divine call, he added: "But when I consider my own weakness, how I eat and drink, and at times am merry and a good table companion, I begin to be in doubt." On another occasion, when entertaining some of his colleagues at dinner, he called the company's attention to a large wine-glass encircled with three rings. The first, he said, represented the Ten Commandments, the second the Creed, and the third the Lord's Prayer. Having emptied it at a single draft, he filled it again and passed it to Agricola, something of a fanatic on the subject of faith, who was able to get no further than the Ten Commandments, to Luther's great amusement.

Beer and wine he partook of freely, as was the custom of his countrymen, and his table conversation may often have been less restrained in consequence; but his enemies exaggerated when they accused him of being a hard drinker. While he never criticized the moderate use of wine and beer, he always severely denounced over-indulgence in them, not sparing even his own elector, John Frederick, who, with all his

Painted by Lucas Cranach

BUGENHAGEN, 1537

piety, was prone to frequent intoxication. According
to Melanchthon, Luther was always abstemious both
in food and drink, and often, when absorbed in work,
fasted completely for days at a time. An immoderate
drinker, at any rate, he certainly was not. Had he
been, he could not possibly have kept up year after
year, day in and day out, to the very end of his life,
his tremendous and unremitting labors. Almost super-
human they seem, as we look back upon them. Only
a man of extraordinary self-control and constant con-
centration of purpose could have accomplished what
he did.

Despite his public labors, which continued unabated,
Luther showed himself no little of a family man. He
did considerable gardening, and took a great interest
in getting rare plants from distant parts of the country.
Not long after his marriage he wrote Spalatin: "I have
planted a garden and dug a well, and both have turned
out successfully. Come, and you shall be crowned
with lilies and roses." He provided himself with a
carpenter's bench and a turning-lathe, securing through
his friend Link in Nuremberg the best tools to be had,
and he proved not unskilful in making useful articles
for the house. He continued to mend his own clothes,
not, as he declared, for the sake of economy, but because the tailors were so poor. On one occasion, Käthe
had to complain, he cut up one of the children's garments to patch his own trousers with.

Instead of working night and day, as before his marriage, he now permitted himself more leisure of an
evening, and confined his study and writing chiefly to
the daytime. It was his custom, so he remarked in
1537, to go to bed regularly at nine o'clock, an extraordinary contrast to the late hours kept in earlier
years. When the children came, he loved to spend

such time as he could spare with them, and they were devotedly attached to him. From Torgau he once wrote to Käthe: "Although it is market season here, I can find nothing in this city for the children. Have something on hand if I should fail to bring anything home for them."

In 1530, while at Coburg during the meeting of the Diet of Augsburg, he wrote his four-year-old son the following charming letter:

To my dear son, Hans Luther: Grace and peace in Christ, my darling little son. I am very glad to hear that you are studying well and praying diligently. Go on doing so, my little son, and when I come home I will bring you a beautiful present.

I know a lovely, pretty garden, where there are many children. They wear golden coats, and pick up fine apples, pears, cherries, and plums under the trees. They sing and jump and are very merry. They also have beautiful little horses with bridles of gold and saddles of silver. I asked the man who owned the garden who the children were. He answered, "These are the children who gladly pray and study and are good." Then I said, "Dear man, I also have a son named Hans Luther. Would n't he like to come into the garden and eat such beautiful apples and pears and ride such fine horses and play with these children!" Then the man said, "If he prays and studies gladly, and is good, he too shall come into the garden, and Lippus and Jost with him. And when they are all here they shall have whistles and drums and lutes, and all sorts of things to make music with, and they shall dance and shoot with little crossbows." And he showed me a beautiful meadow in the garden fixed for dancing. Gold whistles were hung there, and drums and silver crossbows. But it was still early and the children had not yet eaten, so I could n't wait for the dance, and I said to the man: "Dear sir, I will go as fast as I can and write it all to

my dear son Hans, that he may study and pray well and
be good and so come into this garden. But he has an
Aunt Lena whom he will have to bring with him." Then
the man said, "Very well, go and write it to him."

Therefore, dear little son Hans, study and pray
bravely, and tell Lippus and Jost to do so too, and you
shall all come into the garden with each other. The dear
God take care of you. Greet Aunty Lena and give her
a kiss for me.

Your loving father,
MARTIN LUTHER.

April 22, 1530.

His marriage was blessed with six children, Hans,
who was named after Luther's father; Elizabeth;
Magdalen, after Käthe's aunt, who made her home
with her niece; Martin; Paul, named for Luther's
favorite apostle; and Margaret, for his mother. Hans,
Martin, Paul, and Margaret survived their parents.
In spite of his father's dislike for the legal profession
and oft-expressed hope that none of his sons would
enter it, Hans studied law and spent his life in a minor
government position. Paul, the ablest of the three
boys, studied medicine and had a successful and honorable career as court physician to the Electors of
Saxony. Only Martin took up theology, and his
health was so poor that he was unable to engage in
active work and died at thirty-four. The reformer's
hope of leaving a son who would be a great theologian
and continue the campaign against the pope was thus
doomed to disappointment. His daughter Margaret
married a Wittenberg student of noble birth, and both
she and her brother Paul have descendants still living.

Luther's oldest daughter, Elizabeth, died in infancy.
Immediately afterward, in a letter to a friend, he
wrote: "My little Elizabeth, my wee daughter, is dead.

It is wonderful how sorrowful she has left me. My soul is almost like a woman's, so moved am I with misery. I could never have believed that the hearts of parents are so tender toward their children. Pray the Lord for me!"

The great grief of his life was the death, in 1542, of his favorite child, Magdalen, when thirteen years of age. She was a sweet and gentle character, and her parents' hearts were wrapped up in her. As she lay dying, a friend tells us, Luther threw himself on the floor beside her bed, weeping bitterly and praying for her restoration; but she passed away in his arms, while Käthe stood apart, overcome with emotion. For all his Christian faith and the consolations of the gospel he had brought to many others in similar affliction, he realized now, as he never had before, the clamorous insistence of human grief. "It is strange," he exclaimed, "to know she is certainly well and at peace, and yet to be so sorrowful." Her parents never ceased mourning her. Not long before his death, Luther wrote a friend: "It is extraordinary how the loss of my Magdalen continues to oppress me. I cannot forget her."

Despite these afflictions, Luther's married life, taking it as a whole, was genuinely happy. Few of the world's greatest men have been privileged to enjoy for many years the solace and comfort of home and family as he did. It seems at first almost incongruous. The modern world's foremost prophet living the life of a family man and interesting himself in the petty affairs of a German professor's home! But it helped to keep him human, and it should help us to realize his humanness.

CHAPTER XXI

THE FORMATION OF A NEW CHURCH

IN renouncing allegiance to the pope and following the lead of Luther, the church in Saxony and elsewhere became in reality a new institution, going its own way and living its own life. But from Luther's point of view it was simply the old church with certain unessential and disturbing accessories stripped off. This fact explains the leisurely and almost casual way in which the new movement was organized and new churches were formed.

When Luther was condemned as a heretic, his activities both as professor and preacher should have ceased at once. But the papal bull counted for so little in Wittenberg that he could go on teaching and preaching as if nothing had happened. The imperial ban was taken more seriously by the elector, who induced Luther to go into retirement for a season; but in the spring of 1522, despite Frederick's protest, the reformer was back again in Wittenberg, carrying on his work in university and church just as before. The elector might have closed the doors of the university to him, and the town council might have refused to let him preach in the city church, but they preferred, in tacit defiance of pope and emperor, to keep their hands off, and allow him to go on unmolested.

The circumstances being what they were, the establishment of a new church seemed quite unnecessary. From the beginning it was reformation, not revolution, Luther wished—the old church brought into conformity with the word of God, not a new church independent of the old. At first he hoped that the ecclesiastical rulers, both pope and bishops, would coöperate with him in accomplishing the needed reforms. When they refused, and he found their authority blocking the way, he became convinced that they were not a necessary part of the church. Even without them it remained intact. As he continued to preach and administer the sacraments in Wittenberg, he was still, he believed, within the church of his fathers, and to effect changes in its doctrine, discipline, and worship in defiance of pope and bishops was not to found a new church, but only to purify the old. No declaration of independence, no explicit renunciation of existing authorities, no formal constitution was needed, but simply quiet and gradual alterations as the new principles seemed to demand them and the new situation to justify them.

Had Luther been forced out of the existing organization, he might have felt compelled to gather his followers into a new society, and they might have formed an independent sect, as some of the Protestants later did in England and elsewhere. But the necessity was not upon him, for, in spite of papal bull and imperial ban, he was left in reality unmolested in the church he was in and was even allowed to reform it as he saw fit. To be sure, the ecclesiastical rulers withheld their consent; but without the elector's support they were powerless, and their fulminations went for naught. Though the reformer was in active rebellion against them, and his conduct in open violation of law, the Saxon government was on his side. His rebellion was therefore crowned with success, and the local ecclesiastical institution, with all its belongings, was wrenched from the pope's control.

After 1522 much of Luther's time was spent in the laborious task of organizing the new movement in Saxony and elsewhere. The work was often of a prosaic character. The dramatic interest attaching to the earlier years was largely lacking, and the heroism of the warrior and the inspiration of the prophet had little opportunity to show themselves. And yet the achievements of this period in the reformer's life must not be thought lightly of.

It is commonly said that he was not a constructive genius, and his prowess as a fighter is praised at the expense of his skill as a builder. But to belittle the latter is to mistake appearance for reality. Indifferent he was to the details of organization and willing to let many things take their course, but he had the one great gift, rare enough then as always, of distinguishing the important from the unimportant and knowing what to insist upon despite all opposition and criticism. Often his clearsightedness and iron firmness alone prevented shipwreck.

In his great days of conflict with the papacy he seemed a radical theorist, eager to carry his principles to their logical conclusions and to force their universal application, whatever the consequences might be. But when it came to the organization of the new movement he frequently showed an extraordinary amount of practical sense and a surprising willingness to accept what was attainable and to postpone, or waive altogether, cherished measures that proved impracticable. At the same time he stood like a rock for certain things he deemed indispensable, preferring, as he frequently said, to lose all he had gained and start over again from the beginning rather than to build on insecure foundations.

We may disagree with many of the positions he took; we may count unimportant in our day and generation not a few of the matters he thought essential, and may deplore his failure to put some of his most advanced principles into more consistent practice; but, the situation being what it was, it would be difficult to conceive how any other course than that he followed could have conserved the new movement and enabled it to maintain itself permanently despite foes without and dissensions within.

For some time no new ecclesiastical government was formally substituted for the old. In the city church of Wittenberg such changes as were made under Luther's direction had the approval of the town council, and no other permission was asked. The Bishop of Brandenburg, within whose jurisdiction Wittenberg lay, was entirely ignored, but he was not unfriendly to Luther and made no serious protest. In many other towns similar independence was shown, the municipal authorities taking things into their own hands and reforming as they saw fit. Sometimes the elector also lent his aid, as, for instance, in 1522, when, at Luther's solicitation, he supported the town council of Altenburg in appointing an evangelical pastor in accordance with the wishes of the people but against the protest of the authorities of the church. "It is the business of the Altenburg council," Luther wrote the elector, "and of your Electoral Grace as well, to keep false preachers out, and to permit, or if necessary, compel the installation of a proper preacher, seals, letters, custom, law to the contrary notwithstanding." This did not mean the formal recognition of state control. It meant only that, when ecclesiastical rulers refused to take up the work of reformation, civil rulers must come to the rescue. Not official duty, but Christian love, required them to do what they could to provide for the religious welfare of their subjects.

Except on rare occasions, the Elector Frederick kept his hands off and took no active part in the work of reformation; but with the accession of his brother John, in May, 1525, the situation was changed. He was devoted heart and soul to Luther's cause and was glad to let it be known. Abandoning Frederick's policy of non-interference and ostensible neutrality, he took an active and open share in pushing the work in Saxony. One of the principal difficulties the new movement had to face was the lack of adequate financial support. In many cases those in control of ecclesiastical livings were out of sympathy with the Reformation and refused to employ the funds for the support of evangelical preachers. In other cases the abolition of indulgences, private masses, and the like, greatly reduced the income of the churches, and too little was left to maintain a regular incumbent. In the summer of 1525, Luther advised the new elector not to respect the right of patronage when it operated to the disadvantage of the Reformation, and in the autumn he urged him to use his authority to prevent the complete impoverishment of the churches and to turn existing funds to the support of the gospel. Thus he wrote on the thirty-first of October:

As the university is now in good order and the subject of worship has been taken in hand, there are two other matters demanding the attention of your Grace as civil ruler. The first is the wretched condition of the parishes. No one gives, no one pays. Offerings have ceased, and regular incomes are lacking altogether or are too meager. The common man respects neither preacher nor pastor,

so that unless the parishes and pulpits are taken in hand
by your Grace, and proper support provided, in a short
time there will be no homes for the clergy left, and no
schools or pupils. Thus God's word and service will fall
to the ground. Therefore may your Grace permit God
to make still further use of you, and may you be his true
instrument, to your Grace's comfort and satisfaction of
conscience. For to this God certainly calls you through
us and through the existing need. Your Grace will find
a way of doing it. There are cloisters, foundations, endowments, and funds enough, if your Grace will appropriate them to this purpose. God will also add his blessing, and will give the business success.

A year later he wrote the elector again:

Since all of us, particularly rulers, are commanded
above everything else to educate the young, who are daily
born and are growing up among us, and to keep them in
order and in the fear of God, schools and preachers and
pastors are necessary. If the parents won't see to it, let
them go to the devil. If the young remain uncared for
and uneducated, the fault is the government's. Moreover, the land becomes full of wild and loose persons, so
that not only God's command, but our common need,
obliges us to find some way to meet the situation. Since
papal and clerical law and order are now at an end in
your Grace's realm, and all cloisters and foundations have
fallen into the hands of your Grace as chief ruler, you
have also the duty and responsibility of looking after these
affairs. For there is no one else who can or should
do it. . . .

Where a city or village has sufficient means, your Grace
has the right to require them to support schools, pulpits,
and churches. If they will not do it for their own good,
it is the duty of your Grace, who are the chief guardian
of the young and of all in need, to compel them by force
to do it, just as they are compelled to contribute money

and labor for the building of bridges and roads and for other needed improvements.

About the same time, at the suggestion of others, Luther urged upon the elector the appointment of a commission to visit the churches throughout the country and to report on their condition and needs. The visitation began early in 1526, and, after being carried on for a time in a somewhat desultory fashion, was finally carefully organized and became a most important agency in the reformation of Saxony. The visitors did not confine themselves to the financial status of the churches, but took up the whole matter of life, worship, and doctrine. They did much to improve religious conditions and to give strength and homogeneity to the new movement. As they were named by the elector and reported to him, the control of the church by the civil government received an added impetus.

In his preface to a book of instructions prepared by Melanchthon for the use of the visitors, Luther wrote:

Now that the gospel, by the rich and unspeakable grace of God, has mercifully been restored to us, and shines so clearly that we can see how deranged, distracted, and torn Christendom is, we should have liked to erect again the genuine office of bishop and visitor, which is greatly needed. But as none of us was called, or had a clear commission thereto, and St. Peter will have nothing done among Christians unless it be certain it is God's work, there was no one to undertake it rather than another. And so, wishing to do only what we were sure of, we kept to the law of love, which is laid upon all Christians alike, and humbly and earnestly begged the serene, high-born, Prince John, Duke of Saxony, etc., our most gracious lord, ordained of God to be our country's prince and our earthly ruler, that out of Christian love—for by

civil law he is not bound thereto—and for the sake of
God, the good of the gospel, and the benefit and salvation
of the poor Christians in his dominions, he would graciously summon and appoint certain qualified persons to
this office, which by God's good pleasure his Grace has
kindly done.

The visitation of the churches of his diocese had
always been one of the most important, though widely
neglected, functions of the bishop, and the new commissioners, under the elector's authorization, were
therefore assuming episcopal duties and prerogatives.
As Luther remarked, when referring to the matter in
a letter to Amsdorf, "We are visitors; that is, bishops."

The visitors found things in a very deplorable state.
For a long time the religious interests of the people
had been sadly neglected, and the Reformation had
not done much to mend the situation. Rather it had
brought wide-spread demoralization, and had broken
down respect for the old sanctions, without as yet
supplying new ones to take their place. Luther himself was loud in his complaints of what he found.
Thus he wrote Spalatin, in 1529:

Everywhere the condition of the churches is most
miserable. The peasants learn nothing, know nothing,
and do nothing except abuse their liberty. They do not
pray at all, nor do they go to confession or communion.
They act as if they were wholly free from religion. As
they neglected their own papal usages, they now despise
ours. Dreadful it is to contemplate the administration of
the Roman bishops.

His experiences as a visitor only increased his distrust of the common people already sown in his heart
by the peasants' war. He became more than ever

convinced that they were not fit for self-government and needed to be controlled with a strong hand in religious as well as in civil affairs. To the end of his life he retained his belief in the universal priesthood of believers, so beautifully expressed in his book on Christian liberty, and the church he defined as a community of true Christians already saved, completely free, and needing no rulers and no laws. But though he had this ideal always in mind, he was too practical, and too much concerned for the welfare of the mass of men, to become absorbed in the formation of such a select community of saints. He would be glad to have a company of genuine Christians meet for mutual edification and inspiration, but he would not have them separate themselves from the larger church, and, forming an independent sect, live in selfish communion with kindred souls. The church existed for the sake of the world, not for the sake of its own members. Its great mission was to proclaim the gospel to unbelievers and half-believers. The last thing he wished was to substitute for the existing church, to which all sorts of people flocked, whatever their spiritual state, a small and private conventicle accessible only to the elect. On the contrary, he would gather all he could into the churches day by day, and so reach as many as possible with the Christian message.

He did draw a distinction between the indifferent masses and genuine Christians. To the Lord's Supper he would admit only the latter, thus making it a means of testifying publicly to their Christian faith. But baptism, he insisted, should continue as heretofore to be administered to every child in the community, that all might share in the promise of forgiveness, and none grow up alien to the church. Thus, whatever his theory of a true spiritual company of saints, for all practical purposes the church continued, as it had been, a public institution, constituting an integral part of the life of the community.

Luther's notion of the church as established to proclaim the gospel made it necessary, so he thought, to see that it actually did proclaim the true, and not a false, gospel. To permit its ministers to go on opposing the word of God and leading the people astray was to destroy the church altogether by making it a curse instead of a blessing to the community. Accordingly, as early as 1522 we find him insisting that only evangelical preachers should be allowed to minister in the churches, and those opposing the gospel should be removed from their positions. "For it is not unjust," he declared in a letter of that year to Count John Henry of Schwarzburg, "but the highest justice, to drive the wolf out of the sheepfold, and not to mind if he be disemboweled in the process. A preacher is paid to do good, not harm. If he does harm, he thereby forfeits his stipend."

In 1526, in a letter to the Elector John, he went so far as to say that only one kind of preaching should be tolerated in any town. When preachers disagree, discord is sown among the people, and it is the duty of the civil ruler to prevent all uproar and tumult.

In the matter of religious rites and ceremonies he was more liberal. Here he was quite willing the widest variety should reign even in a single community. In 1524, a clerical friend urged the convening of a synod to agree upon a common form of worship for all the churches in sympathy with the new movement; but Luther opposed the plan as tending to produce mechanical conformity and infringe liberty in unessential matters. A little over a year later, in response to numerous requests, he published his

"Deutsche Messe," or "German Order of Worship,"
not as a law to govern the services, but as an indication
of what was done in the Wittenberg church. "First
of all," he said, "I beg those who examine this order
of worship, and desire to follow it, not to make out of
it a binding rule or constrain any one's conscience,
but in accordance with Christian liberty to use it as
they please when, where, and as long as it proves
adapted to their needs."

The book, he went on to say, was not intended for
those already Christians,—they had their own spiritual worship and needed none of his help,—but for
those who wished to become Christians and particularly for the young and immature. "For their sakes
you must read, sing, pray, write, and versify. If it
would do any good, I should be glad to have all the
bells ring and organs play and everything make a
noise that could." And a little farther on: "Let us
not be too proud and despise such child's play. When
Christ wished to attract men, he had to become a man;
and if we would attract children, we must become
children with them."

He recommended the use of German in the services, but, curiously enough, with the interest of a
pedagogue rather than a pastor, he wished to retain
some Latin as a help to pupils in the schools. For the
same reason, he said, he would be glad to introduce
Greek and Hebrew, if they were as generally studied
as Latin!

More important for the future of the evangelical
cause than any of his labors over details of organization and worship were some of the products of his
pen, upon which German Protestantism has nourished
itself from that day to this. His Bible translation has
been already spoken of. In 1529 appeared his large

and small catechisms, the latter containing a most beautiful summary of Christian faith and duty, wholly devoid of polemics of every kind and so simple and concise as to be easily understood and memorized by every child. It has formed the basis of the religious education of German youth ever since. Though preceded by other catechisms from the pen of this and that colleague or disciple, it speedily displaced them all, not simply because of its authorship but because of its superlative merit, and has alone maintained itself in general use. The versatility of the reformer in adapting himself with such success to the needs of the young and immature is no less than extraordinary. Such a little book as this it is that reveals most clearly the genius of the man.

Some of his many hymns have also had permanent influence. He was greatly interested in the production of good German songs for use in the services of the church, and he enlisted the aid of everybody he could to enrich evangelical hymnody. It was characteristic of him that he liked strong and rugged rather than smooth and musical verse, and was fond of unsymmetrical rhythms and stanzas closing with an unrhymed line. He frequently lamented his own lack of poetic gifts. As a matter of fact, most of his hymns are prosaic and commonplace enough, but some of them show inspiration of a high order, and "Ein' feste Burg," the noblest of them all, with its splendid music from an unknown hand, has sung itself into the lives and hearts of multitudes of Protestants of his own and other lands.

In spite of the reformer's desire not to enforce uniformity of worship and not to make the order he employed a law for other churches, the example of Wittenberg was generally followed throughout Saxony, and the evangelical services in all parts of the country were much alike. In general they were similar to the Catholic services they had displaced. In his "Deutsche Messe" Luther declared nothing ought to be changed unless it violated the word of God or was harmful in itself. Gowns, candles, altars, the elevation of the host, festivals, fast-days, and many other things, he would allow to remain unmolested. Not that they were all ideal, but the people were accustomed to them, and it did no harm to retain them. In 1528 he wrote a friend:

I condemn no ceremonies but those opposed to the gospel. All others I retain intact in our church. For the font stands, and baptism is administered with the same rites as heretofore, though the language used is the vernacular. I even leave the images undisturbed, except those destroyed by the rioters before my return. We also celebrate mass in the customary vestments and forms, only adding certain German songs, and substituting the vernacular in the words of consecration. I do not by any means want the Latin mass done away, nor would I have permitted the use of German had I not been compelled to. In short, I hate nobody worse than him who upsets free and harmless ceremonies and turns liberty into necessity.

As late as 1541 he could inform Chancellor Brück:

Our services, God be praised! are so conducted as regards unessential things that a layman from Italy or Spain, not understanding German, would be compelled to say, on seeing our mass, choir, organs, bells, and the like, that ours is a true papal church, not at all or very little different from what he has in his own country.

Writing in 1539 to a Berlin clergyman who was troubled by the many Catholic ceremonies retained in the worship of the newly established evangelical church of Brandenburg, he said:

In God's name make your processions with a silver or gold cross and with cowl and mantle of velvet, satin, or linen. And if your lord, the elector, does not find one hood or cassock enough, put on three, as Aaron the high priest wore three richly adorned garments from which the priestly robes under the papacy got their name. And if his electoral Grace does not find one circuit or procession enough, with its ringing and singing, make seven, as Joshua marched about Jericho with the children of Israel, shouting and blowing trumpets. And if your lord, the margrave, would enjoy it, let his electoral Grace leap and dance in front of the procession with harps, kettle-drums, cymbals, and bells, as David did before the ark when it was brought into the city of Jerusalem.

At the same time, though tolerant of the greater part of the old worship, Luther condemned certain features of it as wholly inconsistent with the gospel. Chief among these was the traditional form of celebrating the mass, which represented it as a sacrifice and good work. He early revised the service in such a way as to remove this objection, congratulating himself that it was in Latin, and the change would therefore not greatly disturb the common people. The withholding of the cup from the laity he also disliked, as many others did, because out of harmony with Christ's words of institution. But he regarded this as less of a scandal, and for some time was willing to tolerate it in many places for the sake of weak consciences.

In 1525 he went so far as to insist that Catholic worship—meaning particularly the sacrifice of the mass, which was its very heart—should be prohibited altogether in Saxony. The government, he asserted repeatedly, is charged with the responsibility of punishing and putting a stop to open blasphemy and profanity of all kinds. Within the category of such crimes he classed engaging in Roman Catholic worship, as well as teaching doctrines contrary to "a public article of the creed clearly grounded in the Bible and everywhere believed."

Even this was not enough. The prohibition of Catholic worship and of the preaching of false doctrine he wished to have supplemented by the requirement of compulsory attendance upon the established services. In 1529 he wrote:

Since the decalogue and the catechism teach also civic and domestic duties, and these need to be frequently inculcated, such persons, whether they believe the gospel or not, should be required to attend the services, that they may learn how to behave themselves in public and private and may not do others harm by their contempt of civic and domestic instruction. For if they wish to live in society, they should hear and learn its laws, even though unwillingly, not only on their own account, but for the sake of their children and servants.

Little enough place for freedom would seem to be left where such ideas prevailed, but as long as he lived Luther avowed himself in favor of full liberty of conscience. "Thoughts are tax-free," he exclaimed in the words of an old proverb. "Heresy is a spiritual thing. It cannot be slain with the sword, burned with fire, or drowned with water. Over the soul God can and will let no one rule except Himself alone," he declared in his work on civil rulers published in 1523. Again and again, while insisting most earnestly upon the necessity of prohibiting false teaching and Catholic worship, he asserted with equal emphasis complete freedom of faith. Writing to the Elector John early in 1526, he said:

They are not obliged to believe; only open scandal is forbidden them. . . . In their chambers they may worship whom they wish and as many gods as they please, but publicly they shall not so blaspheme the true God and lead people astray.

And to a friend he wrote in 1529:

Although no one is to be compelled to believe, no one, on the other hand, is to be permitted to blaspheme the doctrine, but he must give his reasons and listen to argument. If his grounds stand the test, well and good. If not, he must keep his mouth shut and believe in private what he pleases. So it is done in Nuremberg and here in Wittenberg. For, when it is possible, opposing doctrines are not to be tolerated under one government, that trouble may be avoided.

Clearly Luther's was not the Catholic principle. Unbelief and heresy were not crimes deserving punishment. Only the public teaching of them was to be forbidden. Consistently therewith, he always refused to approve the traditional death penalty for heresy. Those who persisted in inculcating false doctrines and openly carrying on Catholic worship should be excluded from the country, but no other punishment should be inflicted upon them. There were Catholic lands where they could find things to their liking. Thither they ought to betake themselves, and not to be allowed to disturb the public peace. In the same way he repeatedly exhorted his followers in Catholic countries to refrain from disobeying and defying the authorities. If their consciences did not permit them to do as they were bid by their rulers, they should quietly withdraw, and seek a home in evangelical territory. Luther's attitude toward non-conformity in doctrine and worship was thus very unlike the traditional Catholic attitude. To exile non-conformists for the sake of public peace and order, mistaken though the policy may be, is an altogether different matter from imprisoning or executing them for the crime of sacrilege or treason. With all his intolerance, Luther prepared the way, in some degree at least, for the toleration of modern days. And, in any case, it may fairly be doubted whether any larger measure of freedom would have been possible in that period of strife; whether the infant movement, the forces arrayed against it being what they were, could have maintained itself without the strong measures of self-protection he advocated.

In 1526 an imperial diet met at Spires, on the upper Rhine. Though largely in the minority, the evangelical princes and the representatives of certain free cities let their sympathy with the Reformation be clearly known and insisted that the Edict of Worms could not be carried out. Pope Clement VII, who had succeeded the luckless Adrian in 1523, was in league with King Francis against the emperor, and Charles was too much occupied to pay any serious attention to German affairs. As a result, the diet agreed upon a compromise, postponing the final settlement of the religious question, and providing that in the meantime, so far as concerned the Edict of Worms, each ruler should conduct himself in such a way as to be able to defend his course before God and the emperor. Though not an official authorization of the Reformation, this action strengthened the hands of the Elector of Saxony and other evangelical princes. It was widely interpreted as laying upon

21

them the responsibility of continuing the work already begun and organizing the church within their respective territories as they saw fit. Therein the Protestant state churches of Germany were already foreshadowed.

For a time it looked as if the Reformation would sweep the entire country and a national German church be the result of Luther's labors; but the hostility of the emperor and of many princes of the realm made this impossible. Instead of one national church taking the place of the historic Catholic institution, there came into existence a number of separate and independent bodies, bound together by devotion to a great leader, by the acceptance of the same standards, and by common hostility to Rome, but each subject to the local state government and controlled thereby. Of independency, or separation of church and state, there was none. With the generally prevalent belief that only one form of religion should anywhere be tolerated, and with Roman Catholicism intrenched in most of the states of Germany, a new church could gain a permanent foothold only where made a state affair and backed by the civil power. The princes in sympathy with the Reformation could therefore do nothing else than follow the example of Saxony and organize an evangelical state church each for himself.

The spread of the Reformation as an organized movement depended upon them. Where they refused to accept it, while evangelical sentiment might exist, evangelical churches were impossible. When they were won over, a state church was constructed as a matter of course, and Catholicism was put under the ban. The people had little to say in the matter either way. The great mass of them, indeed, had small interest in it. The pope's prestige had long been low in

Germany; but to break with him, it had been generally believed, was to put oneself outside the Christian church and imperil one's eternal salvation. The net result of Luther's work was the establishment of a non-papal church, still in possession of the means of grace, and so like the old as to appeal to the same emotions and inspire the same confidence. Few were so devoted to the papacy that they felt compelled to turn their backs upon the church they had been brought up in when it ceased to avow allegiance to Rome. Few were so devoted to the principles of Luther that they could not find their religious needs satisfied in a church still under papal control. Lutheran sentiment might prevail more widely here, Catholic sentiment more widely there; but in every case the ruler determined whether his state should stand by the old or throw in its fortunes with the new. *Cujus regio, ejus religio* (Whose the rule, his the religion) became the universal formula.

Many and various were the motives leading one and another ruler to embrace the Reformation. There were those like the electors of Saxony, Frederick the Wise, John the Constant, and John Frederick the Magnanimous, who were honestly convinced of the truth of Luther's gospel, and ready, if necessary, to sacrifice personal and political advantage to the maintenance of his cause; but there were others who were moved by considerations of a different kind. Regard for the wishes of their people, impatience with ecclesiastical encroachments and clerical corruption, hostility to pope or emperor, desire for political independence, the wish to be on the winning side, the hope of possible advantages in any change, greed of gain looking with covetous eyes upon the property of the church—all these had their place.

As time passed, the evangelical states multiplied rapidly. At Luther's death the greater part of northern Germany was officially Protestant, while most of southern Germany remained Catholic. Despite the varying fortunes of the two confessions in the religious wars which followed, and the liberty ultimately won everywhere, the prevailing complexion of North and South is still much as it was then. Nothing else was to be expected. More and more, as time passed, patriotism and local pride tended to promote loyalty to the established religion and contempt for the rival faith.

CHAPTER XXII

LUTHER AND ZWINGLI

HAND in hand with the organization of the Lutheran movement went its segregation from other and parallel movements. The radicals were repudiated in the early twenties, the break with humanism soon followed, and later came the split between the German and Swiss Protestants, for which Luther was wholly responsible. His intolerance appeared most clearly not in his attitude toward Catholic doctrine and worship, but in his dealings with other evangelicals who disagreed with him or walked in different paths. As time passed, he grew more impatient of dissent and more insistent upon complete agreement. This was not a mere consequence of advancing years, for he showed it in his dealings with Carlstadt and the radicals as early as 1522, when he was still under forty. It was in part temperamental, the natural accompaniment of his strong convictions and masterful will, in part the result of his growing interest in the consolidation of the new movement. A free-lance he had been for years; now he was becoming an organization man, and he felt the need of harmony and coöperation within the ranks of the evangelicals. Characteristically it seldom occurred to him to promote peace by waiving any of his own principles or prejudices. Peace was to be had, as a rule, only by all his followers and associates accepting his opinions and living by his ideals. His general attitude in the matter appears clearly enough from the following passage of the "Table Talk":

They have plagued us in their books and writings with the word "charity": "You Wittenbergers have no charity!" When we ask what charity is, they say, "That we should be harmonious in doctrine and abandon these quarrels over religion." Yes, do you hear? There are two tables, the first and the second. Charity belongs to the second table; there it is above all works. But it is said, "Fear God and hear His word." About this they care nothing. Christ says, "He that has loved mother and father more than me is not worthy of me." Charity you ought to have toward relatives and servants. Love, love, and be kind to mother and father. But "he that has loved them more than me"! When the "me" comes charity ceases. And so I am glad to be called obstinate, proud, pig-headed, uncharitable, and what they please, so long as I am not a participant with them. From that may God preserve me!

The most notable example of Luther's intolerance was his attitude toward the famous Swiss reformer Ulrich Zwingli. Beginning his reforming work independently, Zwingli soon felt the influence of the Wittenberg monk, and accepted a considerable part of his religious teaching. In practical matters more of a radical than Luther, he broke more completely with Catholic rites and ceremonies, among other things rejecting the notion of the real presence in the Eucharist and making the Supper only a memorial feast. To Luther this seemed the worst of heresies, and a warm controversy broke out, which continued for many years. Personal considerations doubtless had much to do with his attitude. The growth of the Swiss reformer's influence in southwestern Germany,

ULRICH ZWINGLI

Painted by Hans Asper

resulting in the alienation of many of Luther's followers, could hardly fail to prove irritating, and that
Zwingli's doctrine was identical with Carlstadt's did
not particularly commend it to him. In December,
1524, he wrote Amsdorf:

Carlstadt's venom crawls far. Zwingli at Zurich, Leo
Jude, and many others have accepted his opinion, constantly asserting that the bread of the sacrament is in no
wise different from that sold in the market.

And a few weeks later he wrote another friend:

Carlstadt, wholly given over to the demons, rages
against us in many little books, full of the poison of
death and hell. He denies that the sacrament is the body
and blood of Christ. I am now replying to him, though
with his secret machinations he has tricked many of the
populace in many places. . . . In His own good time
God will find Carlstadt, who, I think, has sinned the sin
unto death.

But there were deeper reasons for the disagreement.
The belief in the real presence supplied too potent a
guaranty of the gospel of God's forgiving love in
Christ to be willingly abandoned by Luther, and his
conviction that it was explicitly taught in the New
Testament gave him warrant for insisting upon it as
a necessary article of faith. As a matter of fact, the
disagreement over the sacrament was only a symptom
of a general difference of spirit and interest. Zwingli
was a humanist, and his horizon was broader than
Luther's and his emphasis on Christianity less exclusive. Though for the most part in formal agreement
with the Wittenberg reformer, he was not so con-
trollingly religious, and his evangelicalism was of a
less extreme type. He had large political plans, and

hoped to secure a permanent place for Protestantism in Europe by a coalition of the German Protestant states with Switzerland and France against the emperor and the pope. More a man of the world than Luther, he cared as much for changing the map of Europe as for saving the souls of men.

At a second diet of Spires held in 1529, when pope and emperor were once more at peace, drastic measures were adopted to check the farther spread of the Reformation. As a consequence, five evangelical princes, including the Elector of Saxony and the Landgrave of Hesse, together with the representatives of fourteen free cities, signed a formal protest, from which the name "Protestant" comes. In this protest they criticized the diet for reversing by a majority vote the unanimous action of 1526, and declared themselves unable to submit to its decision; for in matters affecting the honor of God and the salvation of the soul their consciences, they claimed, required them to obey God rather than man.

In order to consolidate the anti-papal forces and prevent their division into permanently hostile camps just at the time they were threatened by the common foe, Philip of Hesse, the political genius among the evangelical princes, conceived the idea of arranging a meeting between Luther and Zwingli, where they could discuss their differences and possibly come to some agreement. He had long been favorably disposed toward the Swiss reformer, and believed if Luther understood him better he would be willing to waive the matters in controversy for the sake of the general cause. He therefore invited both of them, with other representatives of the two parties, to a conference at Marburg, his principal seat of residence. Luther was opposed to the conference and expected no good from it, as he frankly informed the landgrave in the following characteristic letter:

To the serene, high-born Prince and Lord, Philip, Landgrave of Hesse, Count of Katzenellenbogen, Nidda, and Ziegenhain, my gracious Lord: Grace and peace from Christ, serene, high-born Prince, gracious Lord. I have received with pleasure your Grace's letter, written, I doubt not, with a gracious and Christian mind toward me, in which you fix Michael's day for my coming to Marburg to talk with the opposite party in friendly and private fashion. I have also read the letter of my most gracious Lord, Duke John, Elector, in which his Grace is earnestly concerned to answer your Grace favorably for the good of the cause, that God may show His favor, and the division among us over the sacrament may be done away. I believe with all my heart that your Grace has the very best intentions, and I am therefore ready to perform for your Grace the service you ask, even though it will come to nothing, as I fear, and will perhaps prove dangerous for us. For I also desire peace, about which others have so much to say with tongue and pen, while their conduct is such as to give no hope of it.

All the more I will take this opportunity of saying frankly to your Grace what I think. It looks to me as if the other side were seeking through your Grace's zeal to gain something which will result in no good, namely, to be able to boast afterward of having done everything they could, even to influencing so great a prince, and load us with reproach on your Grace's account, as if we had no liking for peace or truth. God grant I may not be a true prophet! I have had experience of such tricks for twelve years and have often been badly burned.

For if it be not a stratagem, and they are really in earnest, they ought not to adopt such a spectacular course and make use of great and mighty princes who have other things to do. All this was not needed, for we are not so exalted, nor so wild and barbarous, that they could not long ago have shown us in writing their boasted love of peace and truth. Accordingly, if your Grace is willing to do it, I should be glad, since your Grace wishes to take a hand in the affair, to have inquiry made of the other side whether they are disposed to yield their opinion, that the evil may not at length become worse. For your Grace can easily see that all conference will be in vain if both sides come with the determination to give up nothing. All I have seen hitherto leads me to think they will stand by their position even after they have rightly understood our reasons, as I know well I cannot yield when I have heard theirs, for I am certain they are wrong. If, then, we separate still unreconciled, not only will your Grace's expense and trouble and our time and labor be wasted, but they will also continue their boasting as heretofore, and thus compel us to answer them again. So it were better to leave things as they are. For, in a word, I can expect nothing good from the devil, however fine an appearance he puts on.

So far as concerns your Grace's fear that bloodshed may follow such disunity, your Grace knows well that if it come by God's will, we shall be guiltless of it. It is not a new thing for sectaries to cause bloodshed. They have shown it in Francis von Sickingen, and in Carlstadt and Münzer, while we, by God's grace, were afterward found wholly blameless. May Christ our Lord trample Satan under His feet and ours. Amen.

Your Grace's obedient
MARTIN LUTHER.

June 23, 1529.

As the Landgrave, however, in spite of this letter, persisted in his plan, Luther finally yielded to his importunity and promised to be present. Writing in July to a friend named Brismann, he remarked:

The Landgrave of Hesse has invited us to Marburg on St. Michael's day, in the hope of promoting harmony be-

MARBURG CASTLE FROM THE SOUTH

tween us and the sacramentarians. Philip and I, after
long refusing and vainly holding back, were at length
compelled by his insistence to promise we would come.
I don't yet know whether the project will be carried out.
We have no hope of a good result, but suspect the whole
thing is a trap to give them the glory of victory.

The colloquy was actually held from the first to the
fourth of October in Philip's castle at Marburg, which
still crowns the hill above the town. There were
many theologians of both parties present, Luther and
Melanchthon being the chief representatives of Wittenberg; Zwingli and Œcolampadius, of Switzerland.

As might have been expected, in view of Luther's
attitude, the meeting failed altogether to bring about
the desired result. Taking his stand upon the literal
interpretation of the words "This is my body," he
refused to budge, though plied with all sorts of arguments. His contempt for human reason, avowed in
his early attacks upon Aristotle and repeated over and
over again since, was never more strikingly exhibited.
Rational considerations, drawn from the nature of a
physical body, counted for naught, and were peremptorily brushed aside as heathenish. Nothing could
better have shown the diversity of interest between the
two men than this colloquy. Luther was right in declaring Zwingli's spirit different from his. For
Zwingli, with his more advanced views and broader
outlook, it was easy to tolerate his antagonist and
coöperate with him; for Luther it was impossible. It
must be recognized, too, that while the former, like the
Landgrave Philip, hoped for a great political league
against emperor and pope, Luther, opposed on principle to armed resistance, was altogether averse to it.
The motive driving the others to seek peace and harmony was therefore not his.

In reading the reports of the Marburg colloquy, we are inevitably reminded of the great Leipsic debate of eleven years before. As Eck then insisted upon blind and unquestioning submission to the authority of the church, Luther now insisted on the same kind of submission to the authority of the Bible. The servant should not question the will of his master; he should simply shut his eyes and obey. No wonder Œcolampadius complained that he was a second Eck. The rôle of conservative was now his instead of Eck's, and though the authority to which he appealed was different, his attitude toward it was the same.

Although the conference at Marburg failed to accomplish what Philip hoped for, it was not wholly without benefit. Luther discovered, to his surprise, that Zwingli was less heretical than he had supposed. At the request of those present he drew up a confession of faith consisting of fifteen articles, and while its wording was not altogether satisfactory to the Swiss theologians, they were able to agree to the whole of it with the exception of a portion of the article on the sacrament. Luther was entirely wrong in taking their assent as an indication of a change of faith, and he was unjust in concluding that their convictions meant little to them. Their action showed only an honest desire for peace and a commendable willingness to overlook mere verbal differences.

On his way home Luther wrote Agricola:

We were magnificently received by the Prince of Hesse and splendidly entertained. There were present Œcolampadius, Zwingli, Bucer, and Hedio, with three excellent men, Jacob Sturm of Strasburg, Ulrich Funk of Zurich, and another from Basel. They begged most humbly for peace. The discussion lasted for two days. I replied to both Œcolampadius and Zwingli, insisting upon the

words "This is my body." All their objections I refuted.
The day before we had a friendly discussion in private, I
with Œcolampadius, Philip with Zwingli. In the meantime there arrived Andrew Osiander, John Brenz, and
Stephen of Augsburg. To sum it all up, the men are
unskilful and inexperienced in debate. Although they
perceived their arguments proved nothing, they were unwilling to yield in the one matter of Christ's bodily presence, more, as I think, from fear and shame than from
wickedness. In everything else they backed down, as
you will see from the published report. At the end they
asked us at least to recognize them as brethren, and this
the prince earnestly urged; but it was quite impossible.
Nevertheless, we gave them the hand of peace and charity, agreeing that bitter words and writings should be
stopped, and each should teach his own opinion without
invective, but not without argument and defense. So
we parted.

This agreement unfortunately did not put an end to
the controversy. The old asperities soon reappeared
in the writings of both Luther and Zwingli. Though
the latter was less bigoted than the former and readier
to unite forces with him, there was little to choose
between the two men in the matter of temper and style
of polemic. Arrived home, Zwingli spoke very contemptuously of his antagonist's arguments and loudly
claimed he had completely vanquished him, to the
older reformer's great disgust. Writing the following
June to Jacob Probst of Bremen, Luther said:

In boasting that I was vanquished at Marburg the
sacramentarians act as is their wont. For they are not
only liars, but falsehood, deceit, and hypocrisy itself, as
Carlstadt and Zwingli show both in deeds and words.
They revoked at Marburg, as you can see from the articles drawn up there, the things hitherto taught in their

pestilential books concerning baptism, the use of the sacraments, and the preaching of the word. We revoked nothing. But when they were conquered also in the matter of the Lord's Supper they were unwilling to renounce their position, even though they could see it was untenable, for they feared their people, to whom they could not have returned if they had recanted.

In the autumn of 1531, while performing a chaplain's duties, Zwingli was killed in a battle between Zurich and the Swiss Catholic cantons. Commenting soon afterward upon the sad and untimely event, Luther wrote his friend Link, with no sign of relenting:

We see the judgment of God a second time—first in the case of Münzer, and now of Zwingli. I was a prophet when I said, God will not long endure these mad and furious blasphemies with which they overflow, laughing at our God made bread, and calling us carnivora, savages, drinkers of blood, and other horrible names.

In 1536, through the efforts of the Strasburg theologian, Martin Bucer, peace was finally concluded between the Lutherans of Saxony and the Protestants of southwestern Germany, whose sympathies had hitherto been decidedly Zwinglian. The death of the Swiss reformer had made union with Wittenberg seem imperative to Bucer and his associates, and at the same time by removing the fear of Swiss ascendancy had rendered it easier for Luther to waive his objections to it. After a week's conference at Wittenberg, during which the theologians of southwestern Germany made many concessions and succeeded in convincing Luther of their belief in the real presence, despite their different way of expressing their faith, the Wittenberg concord was signed by both parties on the twenty-ninth of May. Though efforts were later made to include the Protestants of Switzerland in the same agreement, they were without result. The Swiss remained loyal to Zwingli, while Luther persisted in thinking them heretical. The old asperities continued, and one of Luther's latest books was an exposition of his doctrine of the Eucharist, full of the bitterest denunciations of the sacramentarians, as Zwingli's followers were commonly called.

The whole controversy was most unfortunate. Though we can easily understand Luther's attitude, it is difficult to excuse it. As in too many other cases, difference of opinion gave rise to personal hatred and vindictiveness, which the great reformer was unhappily unable, as many a one has been unable in similar circumstances, to distinguish from zeal for God's glory and devotion to His cause.

CHAPTER XXIII

AT COBURG

IN 1530, another imperial diet met at Augsburg, and the Emperor Charles appeared in Germany for the first time since the diet of Worms. As he let it be known that he would insist upon a final settlement of the religious question, the Protestant princes came prepared for the worst. Being still under the imperial ban, Luther could not appear at Augsburg, nor was it felt desirable he should, for conciliation, not controversy, was the need of the hour. Accordingly, while Melanchthon and other theologians accompanied the elector to the diet, he was left behind at Coburg, on the Saxon frontier, about a hundred and thirty miles from Augsburg. Writing to the humanist Eoban Hess of Nuremberg, whom his friends were expecting to see on their way to Augsburg, he said:

I send you, my Eoban, four epistles at once. Living and speaking epistles they are, yes, and most eloquent— Justus, Philip, Spalatin, and Agricola. I should gladly have been the fifth, but there was one who said, "Shut up; you have a bad voice."

Upon arriving at the imposing castle of Coburg, where he was to reside, as the event proved, for nearly six months, he wrote Melanchthon:

We have at length come to our Sinai, dearest Philip, but out of this Sinai we will make a Zion, and will build three tabernacles, one for the psalter, one for the proph-

ets, and one for Æsop. But this by the way. The place
is very agreeable, and most convenient for study, except
that your absence darkens it. . . . There is nothing lacking suitable to a life of solitude. The great building
crowning the summit is wholly mine, and I have keys to
all the rooms. They say more than thirty men eat here,
among them twelve night-watchmen, and two scouts in
each tower.

A few days later he wrote the inmates of his house
at Wittenberg the following charming letter, revealing
a side of his nature not often seen:

To my dear table-companions, Peter and Jerome Weller, and Henry Schneidewin, and others at Wittenberg,
severally and jointly: Grace and peace in Christ Jesus,
dear sirs and friends. I have received the letter you all
wrote and have learned how everything is going. That
you may hear in turn how we are doing, I would have you
know that we, namely, I, Master Veit, and Cyriac, did
not go to the diet at Augsburg, but have come to another
diet instead.

There is a grove just under our window like a small
forest. There the jackdaws and crows are holding a
diet. They ride in and out, and keep up a racket day and
night without ceasing, as if they were all crazy-drunk.
Young and old chatter together in such a fashion that I
wonder voice and breath hold out. I should like to know
whether there are any such knights and warriors still left
with you. It seems as if they must have gathered here
from all the world.

I have not yet seen their emperor; but the nobility and
bigwigs constantly flit and gad about before our eyes, not
very expensively clothed, but simply, in one color, all
alike black, and all alike gray-eyed. They all sing the
same song, but there is an agreeable contrast between
young and old, great and small. They care nothing for
grand palaces and halls, for their hall is vaulted with the

22

beautiful, broad sky, its floor is paved with lovely green branches, and its walls are as wide as the world. They do not ask for horses or armor; they have feathered chariots to escape the hunters. They are high and mighty lords, but I don't yet know what they are deciding. So far as I have been able to learn from an interpreter, they plan a great war against wheat, barley, oats, malt, and all sorts of grain, and many a one will show himself a hero and do valiant deeds.

So we sit here in the diet, listening and looking on with great pleasure, as the princes and lords with the other estates of the realm so merrily sing and feast. It gives us special delight to see in how knightly a fashion they strut about, polish their bills, and fall upon the defenses that they may conquer and acquit themselves honorably against corn and malt. We wish them fortune and health, that they may all be impaled on a spit together.

Methinks they are none other than the sophists and papists with their preaching and writing. All of them I must have in a crowd before me that I may hear their lovely voices and sermons, and see how useful a tribe they are, destroying everything on earth, and for a change chattering to kill time.

To-day we heard the first nightingale, for she was afraid to trust our April. We have had lovely weather and no rain except a little yesterday. It is perhaps otherwise with you. God bless you! Take good care of the house.

From the Diet of the Malt-Robbers, April 28, 1530.

MARTIN LUTHER, *Doctor.*

Worthy to be placed beside this is the following humorous protest against the conduct of his old and faithful servant Wolf, written some four years later:

To our gracious lord, Dr. Martin Luther, preacher at Wittenberg: We, thrushes, blackbirds, chaffinches, linnets, goldfinches, together with other pious and honor-

From a photograph by the Photoglob, Zurich

THE FORTRESS OF COBURG

able birds who are to journey this autumn over Wittenberg, beg to advise your Reverence that we have been
credibly informed that one named Wolfgang Sieberger,
your servant, having determined upon an act of great
and cruel boldness out of anger and hatred for us, has
paid a high price for some old worn-out nets, that he
may rig up a snare and take away not only from our
friends the finches, but also from all of us, the liberty
given us by God to fly in the air and gather grains of corn
on the ground. He also seeks our bodies and lives, although we have done nothing to harm him and have not
earned such a serious and sudden attack from him. Since
all this, as you can well imagine, is very hard for us,
poor free birds, who have no barns, nor houses, nor anything in them, we humbly and civilly beg you to induce
your servant to abandon his designs, or, if that be impossible, persuade him to strew corn on the traps the
evening before and not get up and visit them before eight
in the morning. We will then make our journey over
Wittenberg. If he will not do it, but insists so cruelly on
seeking our lives, we will pray God that he may be re-
paid by finding in his trap, when morning comes, frogs,
locusts, and snails instead of us, and at night be overrun
with mice, fleas, lice, and bedbugs, and so forget us and
not take away our freedom of flight. Why does he not
employ such wiles against the sparrows, swallows, mag-
pies, daws, ravens, mice, and rats, which do you so much
mischief, steal, rob, and carry off corn, oats, malt, and
barley? We do none of these things, but seek only little
crumbs and scattered grains of corn. We place our
cause before the bar of reason. Is it not unjust for him
to plan such harsh measures against us? However, we
hope in God that as so many of our brothers and friends
have preserved their lives in spite of him, we too may
escape his torn and dirty nets which we saw yesterday.
Given under our customary seal and quill, in our residence beneath the sky, among the trees.

Behold the fowls of the air: for they sow not, neither

do they reap, nor gather into barns; yet your heavenly
Father feedeth them. Are ye not much better than they?

While he was at Coburg his father, who had been
ill for some months, passed away, to Luther's great
grief. Writing Melanchthon on the fifth of June, he
said:

To-day Hans Reinicke writes me that my dear parent,
Hans Luther, senior, departed this life the Sunday before
Whitsuntide, at one o'clock. His death has thrown me
into sorrow as I recall not only our natural relationship
but also the great love I bore him, for from him my
Creator gave me whatever I have. Although it is a
solace to me to know that he fell asleep softly, strong in
the faith of Christ, nevertheless misery and the memory
of his most delightful companionship have stricken my
heart so that I have scarcely ever so despised death. But
"the righteous is taken away from the evils to come and
enters into rest." How often we die before we really die!
I succeed now to the heritage of his name, being almost
the oldest Luther of my race. To me also is now due not
only the opportunity but the right of following him
through death into the kingdom of Christ, which He, on
whose account we are more miserable than all men and a
reproach to the whole world, will graciously give to us
all. I will not write more now, for I am sad. Worthy
and pious it is for me, a son, to mourn such a parent, by
whom, through God's mercy, I was begotten, and by
whose labors I was brought up and made what I am. I
rejoice that he lived in these times and saw the light of
truth. God be blessed forever in all His works and coun-
sels. Amen.

A year later his mother followed his father to the
grave. Luther was unable to go to Mansfeld, but he
comforted her in her last illness with a long letter, the
only one we have addressed to his mother. It is unexpectedly formal and conventional in tone, suggesting a

somewhat surprising lack of intimacy between the two; but it closes with a genuinely human touch: "All your children, as well as my Käthe, are praying for you. Some weep; some eat and say, 'Grandmother is very sick.' God's grace be with us all!'"

Arrived in Augsburg, Melanchthon, at the elector's request, began work at once upon a defense of the Protestant cause to be presented to the emperor and diet. The result was the famous Augsburg Confession, the first of the great Protestant symbols. The purpose was to make as favorable an impression as possible, and the confession was therefore framed in such a way as to magnify the agreements and minimize the differences between Protestants and Catholics. The evangelical faith found definite expression in it, but the emphasis was laid upon the common Catholic doctrines accepted by both parties, and in the matter of forms and customs repeated attention was called to the conservative character of the changes made.

When the document was sent to Luther for his inspection, he wrote the elector: "I have read Master Philip's apology. It pleases me very well, and I have no improvements or changes to make. Nor would it do for me to make any, for I cannot walk so softly and lightly."

On the twenty-fifth of June the confession was read before the diet. The Catholics were greatly surprised at its moderation, and began to hope the Protestants would yield altogether. Making the most of their conciliatory temper, they tried to secure all manner of concessions from them. Loving peace above everything, and greatly alarmed at the hostile attitude of the emperor, Melanchthon gave up one thing after another, until he was accused by many of his associates of weakly betraying the whole cause. He felt the responsibility of his position very keenly, and was almost beside himself with worry. Luther, in his far-away castle, though suffering much from ill health as at the Wartburg nine years before, grew firmer and more confident the greater the fear and anxiety of his friends at the diet. He encouraged, comforted, exhorted, and admonished them as only he could. We still have a hundred and twenty-five of his Coburg letters, among them some of the finest he ever wrote. The following passages will serve to show his attitude and state of mind.

To Melanchthon he wrote on the twenty-seventh of June:

I vehemently hate the miserable anxieties with which you write you are consumed. That they reign in your heart is due not to the magnitude of the affair, but to the magnitude of our unbelief. For this same affair was greater in the time of John Hus and of many others than in our time. And though it were great, its Author and Controller is also great, for it is not our cause. Why, then, do you thus torment yourself perpetually and without respite? If the cause be false, let us revoke it. But if it be true, why do we make Him a liar who gives us such promises and commands us to be of a quiet and restful heart?

On the twenty-ninth he wrote him again:

I am pondering this affair day and night, reflecting upon it, turning it over and over, arguing, reviewing the whole Bible, and the certitude of our doctrine constantly grows upon me. I am more and more confirmed in it, so that, if God will, I will allow no more of it to be taken from me, let come what may.

And the next day:

In private conflicts I am weaker, you more bold. On the other hand, in such public affairs you are as I am in

private, while I am as you are in private, if that should
be called private which goes on between me and Satan.
You despise your own life, but fear for the general cause,
while I am in good enough spirits over the latter, for I
know certainly it is just and true, is Christ's and God's,
and so need not grow pale over its sins, as I, little saint,
when by myself am compelled to grow pale and tremble.
Therefore I am almost a care-free spectator, and take no
account of these threatening and ferocious papists. If
we fall, Christ, the ruler of the world, will fall with us.
And if he falls, I would rather fall with Christ than stand
with Cæsar.

Early in August he wrote Chancellor Brück:

Recently I have seen two miracles. As I looked out of
the window, I saw the stars in heaven and God's whole
beautiful sky, and nowhere were any pillars in sight, supporting it. But the heavens fell not, and the sky still
stands. There are people who look for the pillars and
want to grasp and feel them. Since they cannot, they
fidget and tremble, as if the heavens would certainly fall,
for no other reason but because they neither touch nor
see the pillars. Could they lay hold of them, the heavens
would stand firm.

Again I saw big, thick clouds floating overhead, so
heavy they were like a great sea. And I saw no foundation whereon they rested, and no vessel containing
them. Yet they did not fall on us, but greeted us with a
sour countenance and flew away. When they were gone,
the rainbow appeared, at once the floor supporting them
and the roof protecting us. A weak, thin, slight floor
and roof it was, almost hidden by the clouds, more like
a ray of light shining through painted glass than a mighty
floor, so that you could hardly help being afraid for the
foundation as well as for the great mass of water. Nevertheless, this frail phantom carried the burden and sheltered us. There are those, again, who notice the weight

and size of the water and clouds more than this thin, slender, and light phantom, and are afraid. They would like to feel the rainbow's strength. Because they cannot, they fear the clouds will cause an everlasting flood.

This, I venture to write your Honor in jest, and yet not in jest, for I have been specially pleased to hear that your Honor, above all the others, has good courage and a confident heart in this our trial. I had hoped at least political peace could be preserved, but God's thoughts are far above our thoughts. It is right, too, since, as St. Paul says, He hears and does better than we ask or think. For we know not how to pray. If He were to hear our prayer that the emperor should grant us peace, perhaps this would be worse, not better, than we think, and the emperor, not God, would have the glory. But now He will himself give us peace, that the glory may be His alone, to whom it belongs. . . .

They are not half through with what they have begun, these men of blood. Nor are they all at home again, or where they would like to be. Our rainbow is weak, their clouds are mighty; but in the end it will be seen whose are the thunders.

Three weeks later he wrote Melanchthon again:

You write that Eck has been compelled by you to confess we are justified by faith. Would that you had compelled him not to lie! Eck, forsooth, may confess that righteousness is of faith, but meanwhile he defends all the abominations of the papacy; he kills, he persecutes, he condemns those professing this doctrine, nor does he yet repent, but goes right on. The same is done by all our enemies. With them, if it please Christ, seek conditions of peace, and labor in vain, until they find a chance to destroy us. . . .

So far as concerns what you write about the restoration of obedience to the bishops in the matter of jurisdiction and ceremonies, take care you do not give more than you have, lest we be compelled hereafter to wage a more difficult and dangerous war for the defense of the gospel. I know you always except the gospel in these compacts, but I fear they will accuse us in the future of perfidy and inconstancy if we do not keep to what they wish. For they will interpret our concessions largely, more largely, most largely; their own narrowly, more narrowly, most narrowly.

In short, the negotiations looking to harmony in doctrine wholly displease me. For harmony is clearly quite impossible unless the pope be willing to abolish his papacy. It was enough to give a reason for our faith and ask for peace. How can we hope to convert them to the truth? We have come to hear whether they approve our teaching or not, leaving them free to remain as they are. And we ask whether they will approve or disapprove. If they disapprove, what good does it do to seek concord with enemies? If they approve, what is the use of trying to keep the old abuses? But since our doctrines are certainly condemned by them, for they do not repent, but insist on retaining their own, why do we not see the deceit and falsehood in all they are attempting? You cannot say that their efforts are prompted by the Holy Spirit when there is no penitence, faith, or piety in them. May the Lord, who has begun His work in you, perfect it. To Him I commend you with all my heart.

Finally, on the twentieth of September, he wrote his friend Justus Jonas:

I am almost bursting with wrath and indignation. I beg you will abruptly break off negotiations with them and return home. They have the confession, they have the gospel. If they will, let them accept it. If they will not, let them go where they belong. If war comes as a consequence, come it will; we have prayed and done enough.

The concessions made by Melanchthon proved, after all, of no avail. The Catholic leaders would yield nothing, and most of the Protestants refused to indorse Melanchthon's course. Some of them, indeed, were so incensed at him that Luther had to come to his rescue and defend him against their wrath. On the third of August a confutation of the Augsburg Confession was read before the diet, and declared by the emperor to represent his own faith. He insisted upon its acceptance by all the princes, for he would allow no schism, so he announced, in Germany.

On the twenty-second of September, with the approval of the Catholic majority, he laid before the Protestants the decision of the diet, declaring their confession unsatisfactory and giving them until the fifteenth of April to repent and submit.

On the first of October Luther wrote Lazarus Spengler of Nuremberg:

The Augsburg decision, my dear sir and friend, of which you have written Master Veit, was told me verbally and in writing by my gracious lord Duke Ernest of Lüneburg. That, I take it, is called worldly wisdom. There it can be seen that our Christ, though condemned by them, is yet so mighty that he can rain not only water but also fools. What else was to be expected, when they rage against God's manifest wisdom, than that they would blaspheme God and mock us, as the second psalm says? But it will not end there. They must also experience the next little verse, "He will speak to them in His wrath." They will have it so; let it be as they wish. We are guiltless and have done enough. Their blood be upon their own heads.

A couple of days later he wrote the Elector John:

Grace and peace in Christ, most serene, high-born Prince, most gracious Lord! I rejoice with all my heart that your Grace, by the grace of God, has come out of the hell at Augsburg. Though the disfavor of men looks sour not only to God, but to the devil as well, we yet hope God's grace, already ours, will be still more richly with us. They are in God's hands as well as we, that is certain, and they will neither do nor accomplish anything unless He wills it. They cannot hurt a hair of our heads, or of any one's, unless God compels it. I have commended the cause to my Lord God. He began it; that I know. He will also continue it; that I believe. It is not in man's power to start or create such a doctrine. Since it is God's, and all depends on His power and skill, not ours, I will watch to see who they are that wish to oppose and defy God Himself. Let things go as they please, in God's name. It is written in the fifty-fifth psalm, "Bloodthirsty and deceitful men shall not live out half their days." They must be allowed to begin and to threaten, but to finish and bring to a successful issue, that they cannot. Christ our Lord strengthen your Grace in a firm and joyful mind! Amen!

CHAPTER XXIV

RELIGION AND POLITICS

IN the winter following the adjournment of the Diet of Augsburg, certain Protestant princes and the representatives of a number of free cities met in the city of Schmalkalden to form a defensive league for mutual protection against the emperor and the Catholic princes, who, it was feared, would attempt to compel submission with the sword. Hitherto Luther had consistently opposed armed resistance to the emperor, not because he disapproved of war as such, for as a German patriot he warmly advocated war against the Turks, but because he believed in submission to lawful rulers in all circumstances and whatever their character. But after the Diet of Augsburg the elector's lawyers succeeded in convincing him, as they had already convinced their prince, that in certain contingencies resistance was legal. He consequently withdrew his objections, and threw upon them the responsibility of determining what those contingencies were. The arguments of the Landgrave of Hesse, laid before Luther in a letter of October 21, may also have had something to do with his change of attitude. In February, 1531, writing to his friend Lazarus Spengler, he justified the change as follows:

Master Veit has informed me you are troubled by the report that I have recanted my former advice not to resist the emperor. I am not aware of any recantation. It is true they disputed sharply with us at Torgau, and since some of them wished to do what they thought best without consulting us, we were obliged to let it go at that. But when we finally insisted that the principle, "Force may be met by force," was not enough, they declared that imperial law permitted violent resistance to the authorities in cases of notorious injustice. Whether this was so or not we said we did not know; but if the emperor had thus bound himself, we would leave him to his fate, and they might see to it. For since our doctrine says, "Render unto Cæsar the things that are Cæsar's," and Cæsar has decreed that he may be resisted in cases of notorious injustice, we ought not to alter or criticize his law. The affair then reduced itself to this syllogism: whatever Cæsar, or the law of Cæsar, decrees, must be obeyed; but the law decrees that he must be resisted in such a case; therefore he must be resisted. Now, we have always taught the major premise, that the authorities must be obeyed in civil affairs; but we do not assert the minor premise, nor do we know anything about it. Wherefore we drew no conclusion, but referred the whole matter to the jurists.

Evidently the pressure of events was too much for Luther. It was not to be expected that the Protestant states, aware of their strength and with so aggressive a prince as Philip of Hesse among their leaders, would permanently follow the policy of passive resistance hitherto advocated by the reformer. He therefore made the best of the situation, and allowed himself to be convinced by somewhat flimsy arguments. The appeal to the law was only a pretext. The Protestants would doubtless have protected themselves against armed attack quite without regard to the legality of their action. Luther showed common sense, if not consistency, in accepting the technical plea of the lawyers and making the best of a situation he was powerless to mend.

Later he went still further, as appears, for instance, from the following memorandum of 1539, signed by himself and other theologians:

Doubtless every father is bound to protect wife and child as far as he can against violent death, and there is no difference between a private murderer and the emperor, when the latter goes beyond his office and makes use of unjust force, particularly force notoriously unjust; for by natural law open violence does away with all duty between subject and ruler. The present case is of this sort, since the emperor wishes to compel his subjects to blasphemy and idolatry. Thus Constantine overthrew his ally and brother-in-law Licinius, who refused to give up his tyranny, although Licinius was practising tyranny only in his own dominions. All this, as I have said, is without doubt right and Christian, and we are bound to confess it in danger and death. But it is all to be understood as referring to defense. How can a man use his body and his miserable life in a better and more praiseworthy way than in such service of God, for the rescue of divine honor, and the protection of poor Christendom, as David, Hezekiah, and other holy kings and princes did? Such affairs are worth venturing body and life for.

The other question is whether the defender is bound to wait until his enemy actually begins the attack. Our answer to this is, When the ban is pronounced against one or more allies the enemy has already declared war and the defender has the right to anticipate attack, as both natural and written law prescribe, according to the rule referred to above. For the gospel does not forbid, but confirms, the ruler's office and natural law.

The complete change of attitude is very interesting, showing to what a degree the necessities of the developing political situation had influenced the originally simple-minded and unworldly monk.

From a photograph by Wilhelm Ernst & Son, Berlin

LUTHER'S ROOM IN THE COBURG

The spring of 1531 found the emperor in no position to enforce the decision of the Diet of Augsburg and compel the Protestants to recant and submit. Banded together as they were, the evangelical states presented too strong a front to be attacked with impunity, while among the Catholic rulers there was too much jealousy of the growing power of the house of Hapsburg to enable the emperor to count upon their united support. Meanwhile the need of internal harmony became ever more imperative. On the east, Germany was menaced with a Turkish invasion, from which the territory of the emperor's brother Ferdinand of Austria must suffer most. On the west, Charles's old enemy Francis was continually threatening war, and an alliance between him and the Schmalkald league seemed not improbable. In these circumstances a conflict with the Protestant princes of Germany was the last thing the emperor desired. In the summer of 1532, to Luther's great satisfaction and to the decided advantage of the evangelical cause, there was concluded the religious peace of Nuremberg, suspending all hostilities and leaving the adherents of the new faith unmolested until a general council should decide the questions in dispute between them and their opponents. When some of the Protestant rulers hesitated to accept anything less than permanent and unconditional peace, and demanded other concessions which the emperor was unwilling to grant, Luther assumed the unaccustomed rôle of moderator, writing to the Elector John:

His imperial Majesty has done enough, and the guilt and shame will be ours if we refuse the offer of peace. God greets us graciously; if we do not thank Him, we shall sin grievously, and enjoy no good fortune.

And to the Crown-prince John Frederick:

I am afraid if we let such an opportunity for peace go by, so good a one will never come again. As the proverb says, "Opportunity has a head full of hair in front, but bald behind." This the papists discovered when they would not yield at Augsburg.

The emperor hoped a council could soon be secured, but year after year went by without its meeting, and the *status quo* continued virtually undisturbed until after Luther's death.

During this period Protestantism spread very rapidly. With the passing away of the older princes, many of them Luther's bitter enemies, there came upon the scene a new generation imbued with Protestant ideas, and the reformer had the joy of seeing one after another state join the ranks of the evangelicals. Most satisfactory of all was the winning of ducal Saxony, where until almost the end of Luther's life there ruled to his great annoyance old Duke George the Bearded, one of the most determined and influential opponents of the Reformation. The death of his two sons threw the succession to his brother Henry, already an avowed evangelical, and despite George's last desperate effort to prevent the Protestantizing of his realm by making the emperor's brother Ferdinand his heir, Henry came to the throne in 1539, and the country, already honeycombed with Lutheran doctrine, at once officially embraced the Reformation. On the twenty-second of May Luther entered Leipsic in company with his elector, and had the satisfaction of occupying the pulpit of the principal church, where he had been refused permission to preach twenty years before, at the time of his great debate with Eck.

Other states followed in rapid succession the example of ducal Saxony. For a time it looked as if all Germany would soon be won to the new faith and ecclesiastical unity be reëstablished by the complete disappearance of Catholicism.

In 1534, Pope Clement VII was succeeded by Paul III, and the project of holding a council, consistently opposed by Clement, for fear his authority and revenues would be curtailed, was taken up in earnest by the new pope. Recognizing the existence of many abuses within the church, he hoped to stem the growing tide of revolt in Germany, France, England, and elsewhere, and also to put a stop to doctrinal heresy, by yielding to the emperor's importunity and taking seriously in hand the work of reform on Catholic principles and along Catholic lines.

In 1535 he sent a legate, Pietro Paolo Vergerio, to Germany to inform the princes of his plan of holding a council somewhere outside of Germany, and, if possible, to secure their promise to attend. Vergerio could not restrain his curiosity to see the great heresiarch, and early in November took occasion to stop over in Wittenberg and secure an interview with him. Writing to his friend Justus Jonas, a few days afterward, Luther remarked:

The legate of the Roman pontiff suddenly appeared in this very town. Now he is with the margrave. The man seems to fly, not ride. But would that you had been present! When I declined an invitation to supper in the evening after the bath, he invited me and Bugenhagen to breakfast. We went and ate with him in the castle, but what was said it is not lawful for a man to utter. I played the Luther during the whole meal, and as the Englishman Anthony was also invited, I acted as his representative, with the most aggravating words, as he has written you. When I see you I will tell you about it.

In preparation for the interview, which occurred on a Sunday morning, Luther put on his best clothes and had his hair dressed with unusual care, informing the surprised barber that he wished to look as young as possible that Vergerio might think: "The devil! if Luther has made so much trouble while still young, what will he do when he gets old?" To the barber's protest that he would offend the legate, he replied: "That is just what I want to do. They have offended us enough, and you must deal thus with serpents and foxes."

His effort to appear young was a success, for according to Vergerio though he was over fifty, he looked only forty. But his costume made a decidedly bizarre impression on the Italian, who wrote a friend:

Because it was Sunday, the crazy man wore his best clothes, consisting of a gown of dark camel's-hair, with sleeves trimmed with satin, and a rather short coat of serge bordered with fox-skin. He had a number of rings on his fingers, a heavy gold chain around his neck, and a cap on his head such as priests wear.

The personal appearance of the heretic Vergerio described as follows:

He has a rather coarse face, but he tries to give it as soft and sensitive an expression as possible. His speech is moderately rapid and not much roughened by German. His Latin is so poor that it seems clear he cannot be the author of the books which go by his name, and which have a certain pure flavor of Latinity and eloquence. He confessed himself his unfamiliarity with Latin, but claimed he knew well how to talk in his mother tongue. His eyes are wide open, and the more I looked at them the more I felt they were like the eyes of a possessed person I once saw, fiery and restless, betraying the delirium and fury within.

POPE PAUL III

From a carbon print by Braun, Clement & Cie.
of the portrait by Titian

From the legate's report of the interview we can see that Luther's account of his conduct in his letter to Jonas was not overdrawn. He treated the Italian ecclesiastic with scant courtesy, and said all he could to shock him. At the same time, to Vergerio's surprise he promised to attend the council, wherever it might be held and whatever the danger involved.

In February, 1537, a council in the meantime having been actually called to meet at Mantua, representatives of the Schmalkald league gathered at Schmalkalden to consider what attitude to take in the matter. The question was not an easy one. At an earlier day the evangelicals had frequently demanded a general council, where their positions could be frankly and freely discussed, but the pope had consistently opposed the plan. Now that the council had finally been summoned, they could with ill grace decline to accept an invitation to attend. Though Luther would have been the last one to submit his teachings to its judgment and yield obedience to its decision, believing the pope to be no more in favor of such an assembly than his predecessors, and convinced, rightly as the event proved, that it would be again indefinitely postponed, he favored accepting the invitation, that the Protestants might not be held responsible for its failure to meet.

On the other hand, the Elector John Frederick, who had succeeded his father in 1532 and was an even more zealous disciple of Luther and supporter of the new faith, was quite unwilling to follow such a course. He even wished to hold an opposition council where Protestant principles might find public and authoritative expression before all the world. True to his general policy, Luther disapproved this aggressive plan as savoring of wanton and unnecessary schism, and it was finally, though reluctantly, abandoned by the elector.

That the reformer's attitude was not at all a sign of growing friendliness toward Rome is shown by a document which he drew up at this time in anticipation of the meeting at Schmalkalden. It was prepared at the elector's request and contained a statement of the matters needing to be maintained at any cost against the Catholics. Written in Luther's usual style, it was in striking contrast with the Augsburg Confession. The differences between the two communions were set forth in sharp and uncompromising fashion, and no effort whatever was made to conciliate opponents. The elector hoped to have it adopted at Schmalkalden, but as it contained characteristic statements about the Lord's Supper calculated to alienate the sacramentarians and destroy the harmony recently established between the two wings of German Protestantism, Melanchthon, in Luther's absence, succeeded in having it shelved altogether, and it was not even discussed at the conference. Luther's associates were so careful of his feelings, or perhaps so afraid of his wrath, that they apparently never told him of its fate. At any rate, he published it the next year as the official platform of the Schmalkald league, and sometime later it attained the dignity of a doctrinal symbol of the Lutheran church.

Though Luther attended the conference at Schmalkalden, in company with Melanchthon and other theologians, he was kept from active participation in it by a serious attack of illness which almost cost him his life, and the discussion went on without him. In his absence, realizing that they could hope for nothing from a council held on Italian soil, under the control of the pope, and unwilling in any case, at the advanced stage the new movement had reached, to submit it to arbitration, the princes finally voted to decline the in-

ELECTOR JOHN FREDERICK, 1531
From a carbon print by Braun, Clement & Cie.
of the portrait by Cranach

vitation and go their own independent way. The act
was full of significance, clearly showing that they no
longer regarded their churches as a part of the Roman
communion or in fellowship with it.

Meanwhile, finding his long-cherished plan for heal-
ing the religious schism in Germany completely shattered, the emperor undertook to treat with the Protestants on his own account and to discover some basis of
union independent of the pope. In 1540 successive
conferences were held at Hagenau and at Worms, and
finally, in the spring of 1541, at Ratisbon, where an
imperial diet was in session, attended by the emperor
in person.

The attitude of the two parties had completely
changed since the Diet of Augsburg. There the evangelicals were seeking toleration and were willing to
yield much for the sake of peace. Now the overtures
came from the emperor, while the leading Protestants,
including even Melanchthon, were disposed to hold
back and doubt the possibility of an agreement. Nevertheless after a number of interviews between Catholic
and Protestant theologians, Melanchthon and Bucer
being the chief spokesmen of the latter, a preliminary
agreement was reached upon a number of points, and
it seemed to many as if a satisfactory basis of union
might at length be found.

Luther's attitude toward the negotiations is abundantly shown in the following passages from his letters. To the Elector Joachim of Brandenburg, who
had sent him the draft of a document which it was
hoped could be made the basis of an agreement, he
wrote on the twenty-first of February:

I have read the document carefully, and in response to
your Grace's request for my opinion, I beg to say that,
whoever the authors are, they mean very well, but their

propositions are quite impracticable, and cannot be accepted by pope, cardinals, and bishops. For who can compel these ecclesiastics, since the pope claims to be free and above all laws, whether old or new?

In truth, gracious sir, it is vain to attempt such expedients and compromises. We can never escape the pope and his train until God is allowed to finish doing what He will with him. For everybody knows they will give up nothing, but will stand where they are and keep everything they have.

To Chancellor Brück he wrote on the fourth of April:

If harmony be desired in religion, the beginning must be made with fundamentals such as doctrine and sacrament. When an agreement is reached in these, other and indifferent matters will take care of themselves, as has happened in our churches. God will then be in the concord, and quiet and peace will last. But if essentials are passed by and unimportant things discussed, God is forgotten, and if peace is concluded it is without Him and worse than none. It is just as Christ said: "A new patch on an old garment only makes the rent worse, and the new wine bursts the old wine-skins." Either make the whole thing new, or let the rent remain, as we have done. Otherwise all is vain. I fear the landgrave allows himself to be led and would like to carry us all with him. But, in my opinion, he has already dragged us far enough in his business. He shall drag me no farther. Rather I will take the whole cause again on my own shoulders and stand alone as in the beginning. We know it is God's affair. He began it, He has himself managed it hitherto, and He will bring it to completion. Who will not follow Him may remain behind. The emperor, the Turks, and all the devils shall win nothing here, let come what may. I am disgusted to see them treat this affair as if it were a worldly, imperial, Turkish, princely matter, wherein hu-

man reason is to decide everything.   It is rather an affair
wherein God and the devil together with their angels are
themselves working.   Who believes it not will accomplish
nothing good.

The same day he wrote Melanchthon:

I see they think this cause is a sort of human comedy,
when it is really a tragedy between God and Satan, where
Satan's interests flourish, while God's decline.   But a
catastrophe will come, as always since the beginning of
time, and the omnipotent Author of this tragedy will
Himself liberate us.   I write in anger and indignation at
their wantonness in an affair like this.

In June he wrote his friend Link:

I have heard no news concerning the concord between
Christ and Belial at Ratisbon.   I predicted that the concord would be of this sort, for the anger of God has
come upon the papacy and the hour of its judgment is at
hand.

And about the same time he wrote Melanchthon
again:

I hope you will soon return, for it is in vain you have
been there and negotiated with those lost souls.

As a matter of fact, as Luther clearly foresaw would
be the case, all the negotiations finally proved futile.
Nothing else was to be expected.   Even had an agreement been reached upon most of the doctrines and
practises in dispute, it must have broken down because
of the irreconcilable difference touching the authority
of the Roman church.   However willing the conferees
might be to subscribe to ambiguous statements leaving

room for all sorts of differences of opinion, there could be no compromise at this point. An infallible church, as the pope himself declared, could be content with nothing less than complete submission. The emperor hoped the differences could be glossed over, in the interest of peace and political unity, but he failed to realize the radical character of the division, and all his efforts came to naught.

CHAPTER XXV

THE BIGAMY OF THE LANDGRAVE PHILIP

JUST when the Schmalkald league was at the height of its power an incident occurred which brought great discredit upon the Reformation and entailed very disastrous consequences—the second marriage of the Landgrave Philip of Hesse. Early in 1540, while his wife Christine, daughter of the recently deceased Duke George of Saxony, was still living, he secretly married, with Christine's consent, Margaret von der Sale, one of his sister's ladies-in-waiting. By the law of the empire bigamy was a crime, and when the act became known, he was in an embarrassing position, and felt obliged to protect himself by making concessions to the emperor, which seriously hampered his activities and permanently weakened the Schmalkald league. The way was thus paved for the untoward defeat of 1546, from which Protestantism never fully recovered.

Of chief interest to us is Luther's connection with the unfortunate affair. Finding Margaret's mother unwilling to give her consent to the irregular marriage until the approval of the elector of Saxony and of some of the leading Protestant theologians had been secured, Philip laid his case before Luther and Melanchthon. Concealing his main reason for desiring their assent, he informed them that his conscience, as seems really to have been the case, had long been seriously troubled by the flagrant immorality in which he had been living for many years, and which he found it quite impossible to avoid except by taking another wife, for his present wife was not only repulsive to him, but was also in poor health and unable to follow him about on his inevitable journeys. After considerable hesitation the reformers finally gave their consent on condition the affair be kept strictly secret.

Nearly twenty years before in his work on the "Babylonian Captivity of the Church" Luther had declared bigamy better than divorce. In 1531, when his approval was sought by King Henry VIII of England for his divorce from Catharine of Aragon, he emphatically declined to give it, because of the injustice to wife and child. At the same time he suggested the possibility of bigamy, already thought of by Pope Clement VII as a conceivable substitute for the projected divorce.

Some of the radical Anabaptists undertook to introduce polygamy, appealing to the patriarchal order of society in justification of their position. Even among Luther's followers and associates there was no little uncertainty about the matter, as was not altogether surprising when the old order of things was undergoing revision at so many points, including the marriage of monks, priests, and near relatives. But Luther himself was unalterably opposed to any such revolution. Monogamy he considered, under ordinary circumstances, alone tolerable in a Christian community, and held that no Christian ruler has any moral right to legalize polygamy. At the same time, finding no explicit prohibition in the Bible, he believed exceptions might be allowed in certain extreme cases such as are now generally recognized in Protestant countries as justifying divorce.

Writing Chancellor Brück about the matter in 1524, he said:

I confess I am not able to forbid anybody to take more than one wife if he wishes to do so, nor do the sacred Scriptures forbid him. But I do not want this custom introduced among Christians, for it behooves them to give up things which are permitted, that scandal may be avoided and honorable living promoted, as Paul everywhere demands.

And in 1526, when asked for an opinion upon the subject by the Landgrave Philip, he replied:

It is my earnest warning and counsel that Christians especially shall have no more than one wife, not only because it is a scandal, which a Christian should avoid most diligently, but also because there is no word of God here to show that God approves it in Christians. Heathen and Turks may do as they please. Some of the patriarchs had many wives, but they acted under necessity, like Abraham and Jacob; and afterward many kings did the same, inheriting the wives of their friends according to the Mosaic law. It is not enough for the Christian to appeal to the conduct of the fathers. As they had, he too must have a divine word for what he does to make him certain. For where no necessity existed, the patriarchs had only one wife, like Isaac, Joseph, Moses, and many others. Therefore I cannot advise it. On the contrary, I must oppose it, especially in Christians, unless there be need, as for instance if the wife be a leper, or be taken away from the husband in some other way.

When Philip appealed to him in 1540 he was moved by the landgrave's representations of his moral condition and distress of conscience to think this a case in which an exception might fairly be made. More severe in his condemnation of sexual irregularity than the common opinion of his day, to continue in sin seemed worse than to take a second wife, and he advised the prince accordingly. He was quite aware that he could not suspend the law of the realm in Philip's favor, and make a legal marriage of an illicit relation by any dispensation he might give. Assuming the rôle of a father confessor, already familiar to him for nearly thirty years, he simply undertook to relieve the landgrave's burdened conscience by pronouncing his secret union with another woman justifiable in the sight of God. In the sight of others, he insisted, the union could be nothing but concubinage, and for Philip publicly to treat a concubine as a wife, and to claim he was legally married to her, would be a wanton defiance of the law of the realm. Rather than consent to such a course he would withdraw his dispensation and openly acknowledge he had played the fool in giving what he had no right to give. All through he was moved not by personal considerations, but by a mistaken regard, at first for the spiritual welfare of the landgrave, and afterward for the public good.

It was of course of the very essence of such a relation that it be kept secret, and when Philip was disposed to let it be publicly known, in order to save the reputation of his new bride, Luther objected strenuously, exhorting him to deny it flatly, if taxed with it, and declaring he would not hesitate to do the same.

The proposed denial of the marriage, which seems to throw so sinister a light upon the whole affair, Luther justified somewhat sophistically by an appeal to the traditional maxim of the inviolability of the confessional, requiring the priest, if necessary, to tell an untruth rather than divulge its secrets. He justified it also by the more fundamental principle that the su-

LANDGRAVE PHILIP OF HESSE IN 1534

From a woodcut of Hans Brosamer after an engraving
by Lucas Cranach

preme ethical motive is regard for our neighbor's good, and it is better to lie than to do him harm. To this principle, taught by not a few ethical teachers of our own as well as other ages, he gave frequent expression.

After rumors of the marriage had got abroad, Melanchthon was almost beside himself with mortification, and a serious illness into which he fell on his way to Hagenau, in the summer of 1540, was attributed by him and his friends to remorse over his part in the unsavory affair. Luther took it more coolly, as was to be expected. When the news of Melanchthon's illness reached him he remarked:

Philip is almost consumed with grief, and has fallen into a tertian fever. Why does the good man so torment himself over this affair? He cannot mend it by his solicitude. I wish I were with him. I know the softness of his genius. He sorrows too deeply over this scandal. I have a thick skin for things of this kind; I am a peasant and a hard Saxon. I believe I am called to go to him. . . . It is fine when we have something to do; then we have ideas. At other times we only guzzle and gorge. How our papists will exult! But let them exult to their own destruction. Our cause is good and our life guiltless, for we are of those who act seriously. If the Macedonian has sinned, it is a sin and a scandal. We have given him over and over again the best and most holy answers. Our innocence they will see, but they have not wished to see it.

Writing to Melanchthon on the eighteenth of June he said:

I beseech you through Christ be of an easy and quiet mind. Let them do whatever they want to and let them bear their own burdens and not accuse us alone; for knowing us to be candid and sincere they cannot convict us of any crime except a too facile pity and humanity.

Believing he had acted in good faith, even though foolishly, Luther cared little for the loss of reputation involved. He did deeply regret the harm done the cause, as many utterances show, but even this he comforted himself by throwing off upon the Lord, as was his wont.

If any one asks, "Does the affair please you?" I answer, "No, if I were able to change it; but since I cannot, I bear it with a tranquil mind." I commend it to the dear God. He will preserve His church as it now stands that it may remain in unity of faith and doctrine and in wholesome confession of the word. If it only does not become worse! I would not so please the devil and all the papists as to bother myself about the matter. God will make it all right. To Him we commend the whole cause.

The unfortunate experience did not lead Luther to abandon the principles which had governed his treatment of the landgrave's case, nor did he ever admit he had done wrong in advising Philip as he had. At the same time, in replying to a book in defense of polygamy, published in 1541 by a subservient Hessian clergyman who wrote under the pseudonym of Neobulus, he used language which showed he was sensitive upon the subject and felt special need of reiterating his belief in the illegality of polygamy. "Whoever," he exclaimed, "following this scoundrel and his book, takes more than one wife, and wishes to give it the sanction of law, may the devil bless him with a bath in the abyss of hell! Amen. This, God be praised, I know well how to maintain even if it were to snow nothing but Neobuli and devils a whole year long. No one shall make me a law out of it. That I will not permit."

Regarded from any point of view, the landgrave's

From a photograph by the Berlin Photographic Co. of the painting by Lucas Cranach

MARTIN LUTHER IN 1533

bigamy was a disgraceful affair, and Luther's consent the gravest blunder of his career. He acted conscientiously, but with a lamentable want of moral discernment and a singular lack of penetration and foresight. To approve a relationship so derogatory to the women involved, and so subversive of the most sacred safeguards of society, showed too little fineness of moral feeling and sureness of moral conviction; while to be so easily duped by the dissolute prince was no more creditable to his perspicacity than thinking such an affair could be kept secret to his sagacity.

It was a case where personal liking and undue regard for the success of the cause warped his judgment and blinded his usually keen sight. Though he disapproved many of Philip's acts, the brilliant and aggressive personality of the prince always attracted him, and made him more compliant than it was his habit to be; while the landgrave's threat to appeal to the pope for the needed dispensation, if the reformers refused their consent, alarmed him for the credit of Protestantism and the fortunes of the Schmalkald league.

If Luther's attitude after the affair was over was thoroughly characteristic, his yielding to the landgrave's request in the beginning was quite unlike him. Fully to explain it, account must be taken of his training as a priest and of his long experience as a pastoral guide. Holding bigamy not to be wrong in itself, else God had not permitted it to Abraham, his concern for the conscientious scruples of the landgrave and for the salvation of his soul could blind him to other evils of far greater consequence. It was not the only time his professional training and career narrowed his vision and hindered his usefulness as a reformer.

CHAPTER XXVI

THE END AND AFTER

THE evening of Luther's life set in early. Though only forty-six years of age when the Diet of Augsburg met in 1530, he thought of himself after that time as an old man, and until his death, in 1546, lived in almost constant expectation of the end. The heroic period of his life, when with prophetic inspiration he was proclaiming a new gospel, and with the enthusiasm of an apostle was daily braving death for his faith, was long past. Successful in breaking the control of the pope over a large part of Germany, his victory, in freeing him from danger, deprived him of the excitement incident thereto, and left him no employment adequate to his powers.

His health, too, was very poor, and he suffered much from all sorts of ailments. Possessed of a naturally vigorous constitution, his tremendous labors and careless way of living brought on grave troubles at an early day, from which he was never afterward wholly free. Indigestion was almost a lifelong burden. Serious kidney affections again and again caused him acute suffering. Gout, rheumatism, sciatica, asthma, and catarrh were frequent plagues. For many years he was afflicted with well-nigh uninterrupted headaches, and a good night's sleep was a rare luxury. After 1530 his letters contain many references to weakness of the heart, severe attacks of vertigo, and continual buzzing in the ears. During the last ten years of his life his physicians were in constant expectation of a stroke of apoplexy. Most of the time he was living, so everybody recognized, at the limit of his strength, liable to break at any moment.

More and more, as time passed, he withdrew from active participation in the laborious work of organizing and visiting the new churches, and left that task to others. Conferences of various sorts were continually held, but it came to be an understood thing that some other Wittenberg divine should attend in his place, and only in cases of grave importance was his presence expected. Upon his colleague Melanchthon the chief responsibility fell for this kind of work. That he found it no light matter is shown by his pathetic remark, on setting out for Hagenau in the summer of 1540, "We have lived in synods, and in them we shall die."

In February, 1537, at the Schmalkald conference, Luther was seized in the midst of the negotiations with a severe attack of his old enemy the stone, and for some days his life was despaired of. Loath to expire under the eyes of the papal legate present at Schmalkalden, he begged to be sent home to die; but on the way his sufferings were relieved, and though recovery was slow, before the end of the spring he was once more in comparatively good health. The whole year, however, was marked by more than usual weakness, and his literary output was smaller than at any time since 1516.

He did not make light of his maladies and sufferings. On the contrary, he expected to die whenever he felt particularly miserable, except now and then when he was sure his life would be preserved to finish some special piece of work, or, it might be, to spite the

24

papists. Seeing in every pain and discomfort the
direct assaults of Satan, he got a religious satisfaction
out of them not shared by everybody. But with all
his belief in their supernatural origin he faithfully
took the many vile and powerful remedies all too
freely prescribed to him, and when asked if it were not
ungodly to do so, as Carlstadt claimed, he replied: "Do
you eat when you are hungry? If you do, you may
also use medicine, which is God's creature as truly as
food and drink and whatever else we need for sustaining life."

In constant expectation of death, as he was for
many years, he was in no fear of it. When the university on a number of occasions moved temporarily
to some other place, on account of the plague with
which Wittenberg was frequently visited, he always
remained behind, despite the protests of colleagues and
friends, and ministered to the people more actively
than ever. In 1527 he did manful labor in the midst
of the worst epidemic experienced during that generation, and in the summer of 1535, when the rumor got
abroad that the pest was raging in Wittenberg, he
wrote the elector in the following humorous vein:

Your Grace's chancellor, Dr. Brück, has told me of
your Grace's kind invitation, if the plague should become bad here. I thank your Grace sincerely for your
thoughtful proposal, and will let you know if things get
serious. But the bailiff Hans Metzsch is my trusty wea-
thercock. He has a regular vulture's scent for the pestilence, and would smell it if it were five cubits under
ground. While he remains in town I cannot believe the
pest is here. It is true one or two houses have had illness, but the air is not yet poisoned, for there have been
no deaths and no new cases since Tuesday. However, as
the dog-days are at hand and the young fellows are

MARTIN LUTHER

Painted in the year he died by Lucas Cranach

frightened, I have given them a holiday to quiet their fears until we see what is to happen. I notice they are pleased enough over such alarms, for some of them catch boils from their school bags, some the colic from their books, some the scurvy from their pens, and some the gout from their papers. Others have found their ink moldy, or have devoured their mothers' letters and caught homesickness from them. There may be more of this kind of weakness than I can say. No doubt there is danger, if parents and magistrates don't come to the rescue with every possible remedy, of a high rate of mortality from such diseases, until we shall have no preachers, pastors, or teachers, but only hogs and dogs, which is what the papists are industriously working for.

About the same time he wrote a Torgau friend:

I wish my letter might at least reach Torgau, for your city is so terribly afraid of us Wittenbergers. Your fear, indeed, is well justified, for yesterday a whole child died here, so that there was not left a live hair on its body, and four children were born. I fancy the devil is holding carnival with such vain alarms, or a kermess is going on in hell, that he should be so greedy of ghosts.

Reading his letters to intimate friends, we get the impression that he must have been wholly incapacitated during most of his later life; but the products of his toil still exist to prove us mistaken. He found it increasingly difficult to work in the morning, and his regular hours of labor grew shorter and shorter. Yet he continued to accomplish an amount of work that would have taxed the powers of most men in perfect health. When not actually on his back he was commonly lecturing twice a day and preaching three or four times a week, and in 1537 Chancellor Brück, who heard him frequently, reported to the elector that he had never preached with such power and effectiveness. He also kept up his writing and publishing, pouring forth from the hundreds of presses which Wittenberg now boasted, as against the one when he began his work, polemic and other pamphlets and books, if not in the same profusion as formerly, still in very respectable numbers.

In 1545, the year before his death, he was almost as active with his pen as ever, making new literary plans, and writing against his old enemies the papists as eagerly and vigorously as in earlier days. There is little sign of flagging powers in these later writings. The same Luther still speaks in them, with all the raciness and humor, biting satire and coarse vituperation, of his best days.

The daily burden of correspondence was also enormous, having grown steadily with the years. There are extant more than three thousand letters from his pen, half of them dating after 1530, and how small a proportion they are of those he actually wrote is shown, for instance, by his reference to ten letters written one evening in 1544, only two of which have been preserved. All sorts of questions, important and unimportant, were laid before him by Protestants in every part of the world. If a parish anywhere in northern Germany was without a minister, or a clergyman without a position, he was immediately appealed to for assistance. His aid was likewise sought even in cases unrelated to religion. He was asked to intercede for persons who had suffered injustice from the civil authorities, or thought they had; to patch up quarrels between great folk and small; to recommend needy people to the elector, or it might be to some other prince; to write letters of comfort to mourners he had never even seen. Most troublesome of all were

the innumerable marriage cases which he had to deal
with. They cost him an infinite amount of annoyance
and worry, and hundreds of memoranda and letters.

Despite the multiplicity of his occupations, his closing years were far from happy. As time passed, he
became more censorious, impatient, and bitter. He
seems to have been troubled less frequently than in
earlier life with doubts as to his own spiritual condition and divine mission, but he grew correspondingly
despondent over the results of his labors and the un-
worthiness of his followers. Instead of finding the
world transformed into a paradise by his gospel, he
saw things continuing much as before, and his heart
grew sick with disappointment. The first flush of
enthusiasm passed, and the joy of battle gone, he had
time to observe the results of his work, and they were
by no means to his liking. He never doubted the truth
of the gospel he preached, but he despaired more and
more of the possibility of making the world better,
falling back, as Jesus had done before him, upon the
approaching end of the world, when the Son of man
would appear in glory and smite his enemies with the
rod of his wrath.

Conditions even in Wittenberg itself were little to
his liking. In this center of gospel light he felt there
should be a devotion and purity seen nowhere else.
Instead, as the town grew in size and importance, and
manners lost somewhat of their earlier simplicity, it
seemed to his exaggerated sensibilities that everything
was going rapidly to the bad.

In the summer of 1545, his health being particularly
poor, he left Wittenberg for a few weeks, seeking
change and rest. As often happens when away from
home, conditions began to look blacker to him than
ever. All sorts of tales were told him by officious busy-

bodies. As a result he fell into a state of disgust, to which the following letter to his wife, written from Leipsic late in July, bears abundant testimony:

Grace and peace, Dear Käthe. Hans will tell you all about our trip, though I am not yet certain whether he will remain with me. If he does, Dr. Caspar Cruciger and Ferdinand will tell you. Ernest von Schönfeld entertained us finely at Lobnitz, and Henry Scherle still more finely at Leipsic. I should be very glad if I could arrange not to return to Wittenberg. My heart has grown cold, so that I no longer like to be there. I wish you would sell garden and land, house and farm. The large house I should like to give back to my gracious lord, and you would do best to settle at Zulsdorf while I am still alive and able to help you improve the place, with the salary which I hope my gracious lord will continue to me for at least the closing year of my life. After my death the four elements will hardly endure you at Wittenberg. So it were better to do while I am alive what would have to be done afterward anyway. Perhaps Wittenberg, as is fitting with its present régime, will catch not St. Vitus's or St. John's dance, but the beggars' or Beelzebub's dance. For matrons and maidens have begun to expose their persons in a shameless way, while there is no one to punish and hinder them, and God's word is mocked. Away from this Sodom! I have heard more in the country than I knew about in Wittenberg. I have consequently tired of the town, and will not return, God helping me. Day after to-morrow I go to Merseburg, for Prince George has urgently invited me. So I will travel about and eat the bread of beggars before I will martyr and plague my poor old remaining days with the disorderly doings at Wittenberg, to the sacrifice of my hard and costly labors. If you wish, tell Dr. Bugenhagen and Master Philip of my determination, and ask the former to say farewell to Wittenberg in my name, for I cannot longer endure the anger and displeasure. Herewith I commend you to God. Amen.

From the painting by Titian

CHARLES V, KING OF SPAIN AND EMPEROR OF GERMANY

It was not the first time Luther had thought of leaving Wittenberg. Only a year before, annoyed by disagreements in the university, he had with difficulty been dissuaded from turning his back upon the place forever. The renewal of the plan threw Melanchthon and other friends into a fit of consternation. A delegation was immediately sent after him with urgent messages from the university and from the elector as well. The angry man was finally pacified, and before the end of August returned home to take up his accustomed duties. We have no evidence that such despondency troubled him again, but late in November he closed his last course of university lectures with the words: "This completes the dear book of Genesis. Our Lord God grant that others may do it better after me. I can do no more; I am weak. Pray for me that He will give me a good and blessed end!"

A few weeks later he wrote a friend: "Old, decrepit, lazy, worn out, cold, and now one-eyed, I write, my Jacob, I who hoped that there might at length be granted to me, already dead, a well-earned rest. As if I had never accomplished, written, said, or done anything, I am overwhelmed with writing, speaking, undertaking, and completing things. But Christ is all in all, powerful and efficient, blessed forever. Amen."

In December, in company with Melanchthon, he visited Mansfeld, his boyhood home, in response to an invitation from the Mansfeld counts, who desired the good offices of the Wittenberg theologians in settling a dispute of long standing. Before the end of the year he was obliged to return without accomplishing his mission; but late in January, despite his poor health and the inclemency of the weather, he made the journey again, this time to the neighboring city of Eisleben. Melanchthon being too ill to leave home,

Luther was accompanied by his friend Justus Jonas and by his three sons, who went with him to visit their relatives in Mansfeld. From Halle he wrote his wife on the twenty-fifth of January:

At eight o'clock to-day we arrived at Halle, but did not go on to Eisleben, for there met us a great Anabaptist, with waves and ice-floes, which covered the whole land and threatened us with rebaptism. We could not turn back because of the Mulde, and so had to lie still at Halle between the waters. Not that we thirsted after them. On the contrary, we took good Torgau beer and good Rhine wine instead, refreshing and comforting ourselves with them while we waited to see whether the Saale would again break out in wrath. As the drivers and attendants as well as we were timid, we did not care to trust ourselves to the waters and tempt God. For the devil has a grudge against us and dwells in the water and is better avoided than provoked. Nor is it necessary to give the pope and his scum a fool's pleasure. I did not suppose the Saale could boil in such a fashion and rush pell-mell over stone walls and everything. No more now; but pray for us and keep pious. I believe, had you been here, you would have advised us to do just what we have done, and so we should have followed your counsel yet once again.

Upon reaching Eisleben, he wrote Melanchthon:

On the way here I was seized with vertigo and with the illness you are accustomed to call a tremor of the heart. Walking beyond my strength, I fell into a sweat and afterward, as I was sitting in the wagon in my damp shirt, the cold seized upon the muscle of my left arm. The consequence was compression of the heart and suffocation in breathing, which is the fault of my age. Now I am well enough, but how long I shall remain so I don't know, for old age is not to be trusted.

The same day he wrote Käthe:

Grace and peace in Christ, and my poor old love, impotent as I know it is, dear Käthe. I was seized with weakness just before reaching Eisleben by my own fault. But if you had been there, you would have laid it to the Jews or their God, for we had to pass through a near-by village where many Jews lived. Perhaps they blew hard on me. Here in Eisleben, too, there are more than fifty of them now resident. True it is, as I was near the village, such a cold wind blew from behind upon my head, through my cap, that my skull was almost turned to ice. This perhaps contributed to my vertigo. But now, God be thanked! I am in good condition, only the beautiful women so tempt me that I neither shrink from nor fear any unchastity.

In Eisleben he lodged in the house of an old friend, the town clerk, where he was shown every attention and carefully watched over as an ill and infirm man. Jonas and others slept in the same room with him, and he was never without some one close at hand. He had frequent attacks of weakness, obliging him to resort to powerful stimulants, as often in Wittenberg, but he slept well at night, and on the whole was fairly comfortable.

The business which had called him to Eisleben proved very annoying and cost a great deal of time and labor. On the sixth of February he wrote Melanchthon:

Here we sit, lazy and busy at once, my Philip—lazy, for we accomplish nothing; busy, because we suffer infinitely, being exercised by the iniquity of Satan. Among so many ways we strike upon one which offers hope. This again Satan obstructs. Then we enter upon another, thinking the whole thing finished. Once more Satan sets up an obstacle. A third has been attempted which seems most

sure and quite unable to fail. But the event will prove
the fact. I beg you to ask Dr. Pontanus to request the
prince to call me home for some important reason, that
in this way I may be able to force them to reach an agreement. For I feel they will not suffer me to depart while
affairs are still unsettled. I will give them yet a week.
After that I want to be threatened by letters from the
prince. To-day is almost the tenth since we began upon
the dispute about the new city. I believe it could be built
with much less trouble. Distrust is so great on both sides
that every syllable is suspected of containing poison. You
might think it a war or a mania of words. This we have
to thank the lawyers for. They have taught and still
teach the world so many equivocations, contradictions,
and calumnies, that their speech is more confused than
the whole of Babel; for there no one was able to understand any one else; here no one wants to. O sycophants,
O sophists, O pests of the human race!

Three days later he wrote Käthe again:

Grace and peace in Christ, most holy Frau Doctor. We
thank you most heartily for your great anxiety which
keeps you from sleeping. For since you began worrying
about us a fire in our lodging, just before my door, almost
devoured us. And yesterday, without doubt because of
your care, a stone fell straight upon my crown and was
crushed as if in a mouse-trap. Plaster and lime were
dripping overhead in my chamber for two days, till I
summoned some men, who moved the stone with a couple
of fingers and it fell down, as long as a pillow and two
handbreadths wide. This was intended to repay your
holy care, but the dear holy angels prevented. I fear,
unless you stop being anxious, the earth will finally swallow us and all the elements persecute us. Have you so
learned the catechism and the creed? Pray, and let God
do the watching; for it is said, "Cast thy care upon the
Lord, who careth for thee."

THE HOUSE IN LUTHER'S NATIVE TOWN, EISLEBEN,
IN WHICH HE DIED

He preached upon a number of occasions while in
Eisleben, for the last time in his life on the fourteenth
of February, Saint Valentine's Sunday. Because of
weakness he was obliged to cut the sermon short and
stop before he wished to.

The same day he wrote the last letter we have from
his pen, as follows:

Grace and peace in the Lord, dear Käthe. We hope to
come home this week, God willing. He has shown great
grace here, for the counts, through their councilors, have
settled almost everything, with the exception of two or
three points, among them that the two brothers Count
Gebhard and Count Albert shall again be brothers. To-
day I am to undertake this, inviting them to dine with
me, that they may talk together, for hitherto they have
had nothing to say to each other and have written very
bitterly in their letters. The young lords and ladies,
on the other hand, are merry, go sleigh-riding together
with fools' bells, play at masquerading, and are in good
spirits, even Count Gebhard's son. Thus we must believe
that God hears prayer.

I am sending you the trout given me by the Countess
Albert. She rejoices with all her heart over the reconciliation. Your little sons are still in Mansfeld. James
Luther will take good care of them. We eat and drink
here like lords, and are cared for all too well, so that we
are in danger of forgetting you at Wittenberg. I am not
troubled by the stone, but Dr. Jonas's leg has become very
bad, and has broken out on the shinbone. God will grant
His help. You may tell all this to Master Philip, Dr.
Bugenhagen, and Dr. Cruciger.

The rumor has reached here that Dr. Martin has been
carried off, as is reported at Leipsic and Magdeburg.
This is the invention of those busybodies, your countrymen. Some say the emperor is thirty miles from here,
at Soest in Westphalia; some that the Frenchman is rais-

ing troops and the landgrave, too. But let them say and sing what they please. We will await what God will do. Herewith I commend you to God. Eisleben, Valentine's Sunday, 1546.

M. Luther, Doctor.

The annoying business of the counts of Mansfeld having been completed, he planned to start home on Thursday, the eighteenth of February; but the day before he was not feeling well, and though he was as merry and talkative as usual at his meals, he had a spasm of the chest in the afternoon, and had to be rubbed with hot cloths, and again in the evening when he was going to bed. At one o'clock he awoke in severe pain and called out: "O Lord God how I suffer! Dear Dr. Jonas, I believe I am going to remain here in Eisleben, where I was born and baptized." Physicians were immediately summoned, and the counts of Mansfeld with other friends hastily appeared upon the scene. Every known means was employed to relieve and restore him, but after uttering a brief prayer, he fell into a stupor from which he was with difficulty aroused by Jonas's question, "Reverend Father, do you stand firm by Christ and the doctrine you have preached?" After replying, "Yes," in a faint voice, he became again unconscious, and passed quietly away between two and three o'clock in the morning, in the sixty-third year of his age.

One of the attending physicians pronounced the immediate cause of death a stroke of apoplexy. This, according to the somewhat untrustworthy report of the town apothecary, was confirmed the next day by an examination of the body. The other physician, thinking it impossible, as he said, that so saintly a man should die of a stroke, gave heart disease as the cause.

His judgment was accepted by Melanchthon, and, despite the physician's curious reasoning, seems to be justified by the recorded symptoms.

The counts of Mansfeld wished to have the reformer buried in Eisleben, where he was born; but the Elector of Saxony insisted on having the body sent back to Wittenberg, the scene of his labors. By way of Halle and Bitterfeld, escorted by two Mansfeld counts and a great cavalcade of horsemen, and greeted en route by mourning thousands, the body reached Wittenberg on Monday, the twenty-second of February, where the largest crowd ever seen in the little city gathered to welcome the dead hero home.

He was buried in the castle church, where his electors Frederick the Wise and John the Constant already lay, and where his co-worker Melanchthon was placed beside him fourteen years later.

His great work had long been done, and though he died before reaching the full span of human days, he left his task complete. Longer life would have added nothing to his fame and little to the fruits of his labor. Dying when he did, he was spared the horrors of the Schmalkald war, which broke out only a few months after his death, and for a time threatened the very existence of Protestantism. Foreseeing the impending troubles, he longed to be taken away before they came. But with all the despondency of his later years over the existing situation and the immediate future of Protestantism, his faith in the ultimate victory of Christ's cause never wavered, nor his assurance that Christ's cause was his.

To estimate the work of such a man as Martin Luther is not easy. To a degree true of few great men he was a child of his age and its mouthpiece. And yet out of his own native genius and personal experience he gave the age what it lacked, and for lack of which it would have failed to realize its destiny. The sixteenth century would have been altogether different had he not lived. Of none of his contemporaries can the same be said. Many were the forces making for change quite independent of him, and what he accomplished seems at first sight so inevitable that it must have come even without him. But there were insuperable obstacles, and there was no one save himself able to remove them.

The great thing he did was to break the dominance of the Roman Catholic Church in western Europe. He was not a modern in his interests and sympathies. Far less enlightened than Erasmus, to many a present-day man of liberal culture he is far less congenial. Conservative and intolerant, he introduced a régime of religious bigotry, for a long time as narrow and as blighting to intellectual growth as Roman Catholicism at its worst. Our ideals of liberty were not his. Nevertheless, with all his medievalism, the modern world owes more to him than to any other. There were many then, and there have been many since, enamoured of the fair dream of modern culture and democracy developing under the ægis of the one holy Catholic Church—many who see in Erasmus and his fellow-humanists the true reformers of the sixteenth century, and consider their program of peaceful and gradual transformation vastly better than that of the violent monk of Wittenberg, with its aftermath of bigotry, division, and war. But the break which they deplore was the one thing most needed. The authority of the Catholic Church had to be destroyed before true liberty could come. And to destroy it was no easy matter. Even such a polemic as Luther was, the most

THE GRAVES OF LUTHER AND MELANCHTHON IN THE
CASTLE CHURCH AT WITTENBERG

Luther's grave is marked by the raised tomb on the pavement in the foreground at the right near
the pulpit, while Melanchthon's grave is similar on the left side of the pavement.

gifted and effective history has seen, would have failed utterly had he not offered the world something as satisfying to take the place of the institution he attacked.

The world was not prepared to do without religion and the church. Skepticism and unbelief, common enough in every age, could not be the resort of the mass of men. The existing church might be honeycombed with evils a thousand times worse than those from which it suffered in Luther's days, but so long as it met men's religious needs and promised them salvation, it must retain its hold upon them, and they must put up with its defects. What Luther did—and this it is gives him his supreme title to greatness—was to convince a large part of Europe that religious consolation and the soul's salvation were to be found elsewhere.

The rise of Protestantism meant not merely the modification of this or that doctrine, ceremony, and custom, but a revolution, where a revolution is hardest of all to achieve—in the sphere of religion. It meant trusting oneself to new guides and staking one's eternal destiny on untried supports. Only a prophet could lead the way in such a revolution—a prophet aglow with religious enthusiasm, strong in faith, eloquent in speech, endowed with a transcendent gift of leadership. His very conservatism was an indispensable element in Luther's success. Keeping much of the old, he was able to satisfy the inherited needs of his followers and retain their confidence unshaken, while he broke with the infallible, saving papal church. Others, like Melanchthon, were willing, or even eager, to remain within the Catholic fold, if evangelical doctrine and certain evangelical practices could be preserved. But Luther, the one real prophet of the Reformation, knew better. He was fighting to maintain the thing that chiefly mattered—assurance of peace and salvation apart from pope and papal church. This assurance alone made the coming of the modern age possible.

Whether he put something better in place of the old, or something worse, is neither here nor there. That he put anything in its place which satisfied multitudes of devout and serious men, and has continued for centuries to satisfy them, is the one important thing.

Ecclesiastical unity was the curse of western Europe. Fortunately the Reformation did not mean the mere displacement of the old church by a new one equally Catholic. It meant the rise of many churches, and thus the gradual dissipation of the belief in any one institution alone in possession of life and salvation. In the conflict of the sects, Protestant with Catholic, and Protestant with Protestant, freedom had a chance to grow and spread.

Even had Protestantism meant only the creation of another infallible institution to rival the old and limit its influence, it would have been a blessing; but happily it denied infallibility to any church, and thus gave the modern world its great charter of liberty. To be sure, infallibility was still claimed for the Bible, but belonging as it did to an age long past and a civilization long outgrown, it had to be continually read anew in the light of the present, and with its ever-shifting reinterpretation it served less and less to shackle the minds of men and impede the march of intellectual progress. Fearing the excesses of the Anabaptists and other radicals, Luther might become as intolerant as any papist, insisting on the recognition of the Augsburg Confession and similar documents as authoritative statements of Bible truth. But in the very nature of the case this could be only temporary. The great principle imbedded in the very heart of Protestantism was

bound to reassert itself, and break the bonds forged
for it even by the reformers.

Luther's service to the modern world was not exhausted in the religious and intellectual liberty he did
so much to make possible. In breaking with the Roman church, he broke also with the traditional principle of ecclesiastical control over civil affairs. The
state is wholly independent of the church, he taught,
and its sphere is altogether different. Many other
Protestants, while recognizing this, and denying the
right of the church to rule the state, insisted upon
making the Bible the supreme law book in civil as well
as in religious affairs. But this, too, Luther denounced
as mischievous. The Bible, like the church, has to do
with religion, not politics. The state is to be governed
according to natural reason. Statesmen, not theologians, are to be its guides.

The political implications of such a position as this
are almost incalculable. With democracy, it is true,
Luther had little sympathy. In his distrust of the
masses he did more to promote than to limit the power
of princes. But in restoring to the state its own
rightful prerogatives, and releasing it from the unwholesome dominance of ecclesiasticism and religious
fanaticism, he took a step without which the political
freedom of the present day would be quite incon-
ceivable. It is not that his teaching in this matter was
original or singular, but that he stamped it upon Protestantism and started the new faith upon its career,
claiming political authority even less than religious
infallibility.

In another and even more important way Luther
served the modern world. He gave Protestantism a
new conception of the relation of religion and life.
Instead of finding its highest manifestation apart from

25

the ordinary relationships and occupations of this
world, it is in them, according to Luther, that religion
best expresses itself. Denying the possibility of gaining special merit by any particular practices and employments, and asserting the equal sacredness of all
callings, he changed the whole tone of society. With
the peculiar sanctity of the religious life went the dominance of the priest and of priestly ideals, and a new
lay culture took the place of the clerical culture of the
Middle Ages, to the immense advantage of society at
large. Mendicancy, about which monasticism had
thrown a noxious halo, ceased to be respectable, and a
vast amount of unemployed energy was turned into useful channels, to the great economic benefit of Protestant lands. The supreme Christian duty was declared
to be labor for the good of one's fellows, instead of
concern for the salvation of one's own soul, and a justification was thus given to social service the worth of
which Christendom is only now beginning to realize.

Other-worldliness, beautiful as its fruit might be in
saintly character and spiritual devotion, lay like a
blight upon medieval society, making the wisest men
too blind to the secrets of the universe and too indifferent to its hidden capabilities, and making the best men
too careless of the welfare of the masses—health,
cleanliness, comfort, education, life, and liberty.
When Luther asserted the religious value of even the
most secular employments, and declared that piety
finds its highest exercise not in serving God, who does
not need our service, but our neighbor, who does, he
contributed mightily to the progress of modern civilization and well-being. This earth and human life
upon it gained an independent interest and value not
attaching to them since ancient times, and the scientific, industrial, and social development of modern

days, resuming the interrupted advance of the classical world, was given its guaranty.

The revolution in this sphere, it is true, was the direct result of older and wider forces, and Luther was obscurant enough in his attitude toward the awakening science of his day; but in denying the identity of religion with asceticism and other worldliness, he removed the greatest barrier in the way of the modern spirit, and made its growing prevalence possible.

As the great prophets are not only they who speak for God, but who discern the currents of their age and anticipate the world's development, so Luther, wedded to the old, as he was in many ways, was also a prophet of the future, foretelling liberation from ecclesiastical domination and from the bondage of religious fear, a new interest in the present world and its employments, and a new concern for human welfare. Backward enough he was both in applying his own principles and in appreciating their implications, but it is the function of the prophet to announce and to forward more than he himself understands or even desires. From every point of view Luther was a prophet. It is the one name which best describes him.

But, after all, the overmastering impression upon any one who has followed day by day the course of Luther's life is not the extent of his influence and the reach of his prophetic vision, but the greatness of his personality. Full of faults he was, faults of temper and of taste,—passionate, domineering, obstinate, prejudiced, violent, vituperative, and coarse,—but he was a man through and through,—a man of heroic mold, courageous, strong, masterful, frank, sincere, and generous, as far from petty jealousy and cowardly duplicity as from priggishness and cant. Deadly in earnest, and yet with the rare and saving grace of humor, which guarded him from the danger of taking trivial things too seriously, relieved the strain both for himself and his followers in times of greatest stress, and gave him entrance to the hearts of men the wide world over. Born to rule, though he never held official position, and owed nothing to his station, though he died as he had lived, a mere preacher and professor of theology in a small and out-of-the-way town, he dominated more than half the western world, and the whole of it is changed because he lived.

He was built on no ordinary scale, this redoubtable German. He was of titanic stature, and our common standards fail adequately to measure him. But his life lies open to all the world, as do few other lives in history. To know it as we may is well worth an effort.

What modern need owes to
Luther —

  1 - Religious freedom

  2. Emphasis on Separation of Church & State

  3. Religion has to do with the
affairs of daily life

     Prophet of better days

Full of faults he was — jewels of temper
haste —   Domineering obstinate, violent
Dead in earnest with humor
He was a man through & through

INDEX

Nov 10, 1483

Peasant stock, proud of it. Mother a woman of conflict
emotions, feared gnomes, fairies + devils. Said "If the world smiles not on
us + me the fault is ours. Martin not pampered, at school + home
discipline harsh + sympathy scant. Rule was that of the Rod. In later
years Martin said "The apple should be beside the rod". At 13 he was
sent away to school + advanced rapidly. His father saw in him the
latent ability. Hans was no usual miner, Martin no usual son.

In Magdeburg his beautiful eyes and fine voice won him
friendship with The Cotta Family + here had his first taste
of refinement + culture. This had a life long influence upon Martin
At 19 he entered Univ. of Erfurt and won his bachelors degree in one yr.
It was the days of the new Humanism awakened + learning was
sought after vigorously. He was no recluse, was fond of joking +
jesting + laughing — loved music. M.A. 1504 - 2½ years after
B.A. 2nd in class of 17 members. Started to study law + was doing well, — one day
overtaken by a thunder storm, in mortal fear of death he fell + ground + promised
patron saint of Miners to become a monk. Much to dismay + more of friends
friends in just a few days he was in Augustinian monastery at age of 21. His conversion
this experience was long coming and once in the monastery he found every
thing congenial to his mood. The surprise was not in the experience
but in the lateness of it. This is true with some distinguished religious leaders.
his deep concern for a spiritual made him sometimes depressed. the Convent
leaders, when opportunity presented itself, made him a teacher of theology in the
newly founded University of Wittenburg.